Silversmiths of North Carolina 1696-1860

No piece of silver yet found in the state is more representative of the work-manship of early North Carolina craftsmen and the character of their customers than the John C. Stedman beaker now in the collection of the North Carolina Museum of History, a gift of the North Carolina Museum of History Associates. Elegantly simple, the beaker was made from a rolled sheet of silver, molded around a tapered form, and held together by a soldered seam. It has a rimmed, circular base, a rimmed upper edge, and is chastely engraved on the front *J.D.A.* (John Devereux Ashe) in script within a shield cartouche and *Mary Jen & Dick* on the back. The maker's mark on the bottom is JCS in a rectangle; a previous owner's personal identification mark was also put on the bottom in recent years. Dating ca. 1833, the beaker is 93 mm. in height and 75 mm. in diameter at the top and 59 mm. in diameter at the base.

Silversmiths of North Carolina 1696-1860

By

GEORGE BARTON CUTTEN

Revised by

MARY REYNOLDS PEACOCK

Raleigh
North Carolina Department of Cultural Resources
Division of Archives and History
Second Revised Edition, 1984

DEPARTMENT OF CULTURAL RESOURCES

Sara W. Hodgkins
Secretary

DIVISION OF ARCHIVES AND HISTORY

William S. Price, Jr.
Director

Suellen Hoy
Assistant Director

NORTH CAROLINA HISTORICAL COMMISSION

To
Lucian Allen Peacock
1906-1984

Contents

Illustrations

Foreword

In 1948 the State Department of Archives and History published a small book entitled *The Silversmiths of North Carolina* by Dr. George Barton Cutten. Dr. Cutten's interest in silver began as a hobby in the 1930s. By the time Dr. Cutten retired from the presidency of Colgate University in 1942, he had collected many fine examples of old silver and published several articles and a book on the subject. Before his death in 1962, he also wrote books on the silversmiths of Virginia and Georgia. (His wife, Mrs. Minnie W. Brown Cutten, was a very capable partner in his research and writing.) In 1956 Dr. Cutten sold representative pieces of early American silver to the state of North Carolina. These pieces are now held by the North Carolina Museum of History in Raleigh.

In 1973 Mary Reynolds Peacock, an editor with the Historical Publications Section, revised Dr. Cutten's 1948 study and added a great deal of new material. The 1973 revised edition of *Silversmiths of North Carolina, 1696-1850* proved extremely popular and quickly went out of print. In the ten years since its issuance, Mrs. Peacock, who retired in 1981, has collected even more information on North Carolina silversmiths and helped identify many pieces of silver. Under the auspices of the North Carolina Museum of History Associates, she has spoken across the state, helped add to the museum's collection of silver, and created increasing demand for a new edition of the silversmiths book.

This new edition of *Silversmiths of North Carolina* incorporates the research and information Mrs. Peacock has accumulated over the past decade. As in the 1973 edition, sources of additional information have been incorporated in the text to avoid the drastic renumbering of footnotes. Even so, the number of footnotes has grown from 763 to 912, indicating Mrs. Peacock's thorough, ongoing research on the subject. In addition, the scope of the research has been extended to include the decade from 1850 to 1860, a period not covered in previous editions of the work.

The reissuance of this book will doubtless spur discovery of other silversmiths and the silver they crafted. Persons who know of other silversmiths are encouraged to write the Division of Archives and History so that future editions of this volume can be updated.

Jeffrey J. Crow
Historical Publications Administrator

August 1, 1984

Acknowledgments

Only through the assistance of many people has it been possible to prepare the second revision of Dr. George Barton Cutten's *The Silversmiths of North Carolina*. There have been those who shared valuable information gleaned from their own research; those who have given to the North Carolina Museum of History silver items made by early craftsmen; those who have arranged for silver from private collections to be photographed for use in the revision; those who have arranged for lectures on North Carolina craftsmen to be attended by people throughout the state—and even a few lectures outside the state; those who have attended the lectures and then searched for treasures hitherto unrecognized; those who assisted in photographing, proofreading, and typing; and those who have offered advice and encouragement throughout the years.

Ms. Betty Tyson, registrar of collections for the North Carolina Museum of History, has been an indispensable partner in the search for silver, never too busy to help locate, identify, and acquire, when possible, silver for the museum. Emyl Jenkins has been cheerfully available for consultation and has been ever alert in the search for silver. While Charles Clark photographed most of the silver for the 1973 revision (some of which is used again in the second revision), it was Walton Haywood who has spent innumerable hours doing this work for the 1984 book. With infinite care and patience he has photographed silver brought in at unexpected, and not always convenient, times. John Ellington, Eve Williamson, and the Museum of History Associates have afforded many wonderful opportunities for contacts with groups throughout the state, and the financial assistance of the Associates has made possible the purchase of invaluable silver for the museum's permanent collection—one of the best of its kind in the nation. Rosemary Estes and the staff at the Museum of Early Southern Decorative Arts, Old Salem, have unselfishly shared ideas and research throughout the project. Members of the various sections of the Division of Archives and History have expressed their interest in many ways and have alertly watched for information about silver-smiths as they conducted their own research in other areas. George Stevenson has made available his own impeccably thorough research, and his enthusiastic support has been a source of inspiration. Robert M. Topkins has meticulously edited the manuscript, adding bits of data from his own files, and Henri Dawkins has assisted with the final typing. I would be very remiss not to express my gratitude to my late husband, who encouraged me and understood the compulsion to pursue every lead pertaining to North Carolina silver. It was he who frequently served as driver, technician, and collaborator on the many jaunts to almost anywhere, in any kind of weather, to speak to anyone interested in this project—and it is to him this book is dedicated.

There are others who have been of inestimable help in ferreting out North Carolina silver and information about the craftsmen. It is with sincere appreciation that I list these, all of whom have demonstrated in some concrete way their appreciation of the silversmiths of North Carolina:

Mrs. Alice Abel
Mrs. Lee Albright
Robert G. Anthony, Jr.
Mrs. Henry Arthur
Mrs. Eugene Averitte
Raymond Beck
William D. Bennett
W. M. Biggers
Mrs. Miles J. Boyer
James Brawley*
Mrs. Dan M. Busby
Earl Butler
Mrs. C. L. Cade
Dr. Robert J. Cain
Mrs. Spurgeon Canady
Miss Gertrude Carraway
Mrs. Barbara Church
Mrs. J. S. Claypoole
C. Craig Coleman
Mrs. Clark Connelly
Mrs. Robert B. Cooke
Don Corbett
Mrs. Alice Cotten
Miss Beth G. Crabtree
Mrs. A. Berry Credle
Mrs. D. R. Crews
Marc Critcher
Mr. & Mrs. James E. Cross

Dr. Jerry C. Cross
Mrs. James S. Currie
Mrs. Wilbur Debnam
Stephen N. Dennis
Van W. Dillon, Jr.
Mrs. Nannie Dobson
Miss Pattie Doub
G. Wilson Douglas
Mrs. Louisa Duff
Mrs. B. Hampton Ellington
Mrs. Frances M. Farrington
Mrs. W. B. Farr, Jr.
Mrs. Vernon Ferrell
John B. Flowers III
Mrs. Louise Foy
Kirk Fuller
Mr. and Mrs. Charles
   Gignillial, Jr.
Mrs. Jennifer Goldsborough
Mr. and Mrs. Raymond
   Goodman III
Mrs. Charles P. Graham
Mrs. Virginia Grier
Mrs. Thomas R. Gregory
Mrs. Mary Carter Guion
Mrs. Nelson G. Hairston
Mrs. Martha Haney
Mr. and Mrs. J. P. Harris

*Deceased

Mrs. Sue M. Hartsfield
Mrs. Jane Trotter Harvey
Steve Harvey
Lt. and Mrs. R. W. Heathcote
Mrs. Kay Hedgepeth
J. Grover Henderson
Mrs. William N. Hilliard
William Johnston Hogan
Mrs. Muriel Cutten Hoitsma
John A. Holden
Mrs. James H. Holeman
Ron Holland
Mrs. Stamey J. Holland
Mrs. Nell B. Hooks
Fred Hughes
Mrs. Eloise Jackson
Mrs. Marion James
Mr. and Mrs. Bradford Johnson
Mrs. G. Burke Johnston
Hugh Johnston
Mr. and Mrs. Paul Johnston
Abe Jones
Mrs. Craige Jones
Dr. H. G. Jones
Mrs. Coy Jordan
George A. Jones
Mr. and Mrs. Harry Jordan
Weymouth T. Jordan, Jr.
Mrs. William T. Joyner, Jr.
John Kalmar*
M. Keith and Chancy Kapp
Commander Buryl C. Kay
Mrs. Jean B. Kell
Dr. and Mrs. Richard S.
  Kelly, Jr.
Mrs. Henry Kendall
Mr. and Mrs. Charles H. Kesler
Jesse R. Lankford, Jr.
Mrs. Helen F. M. Leary
Mr. and Mrs. Walter Hatch Lee
Mr. and Mrs. Augustus M.
  Lewis
Mrs. Edmund U. Lewis
Mrs. W. E. Lewis
James O. Litchford
Mrs. W. B. Little
Tucker Littleton*
George London
Ralph H. Mann, Jr.
Mrs. Mary Catherine Parrish
  McCoscoe

Mrs. L. W. McCown
Mrs. R. L. McDowell
Mr. and Mrs. Nathan O'Berry
  McElwee
Mrs. John C. Mahler
Ms. Della Mial
Mrs. S. H. Millender
Mrs. Abner H. Miller
Mr. and Mrs. Jesse Miller
Robert K. Miller
Mrs. Memory Farmer Mitchell
Phillip Mitchell
David W. W. Moore
Miss Marie D. Moore
Luke Morgan
Mrs. Catherine Jackson Morris
Mrs. Herbert Morton
Mrs. Elizabeth Reid Murray
Mrs. Ella Murrow
Mr. and Mrs. O. T. Naef
Mrs. Bruce O. Nicholson
Mrs. Gertrude C. Nicholson
Miss Elizabeth Norris
Mr. and Mrs. Thomas L. Norris
Mrs. Thad S. Page
J. Lee Pharr
Mrs. Luciana Poisson Pickrell
Louis Julian Poisson
Mr. and Mrs. Frederick Davis
  Poisson
Du Brutz Poisson
George Pleasants
Mrs. Mary B. McDade Potter
Mrs. Wilson Holden Price
Mrs. John C. Reece
Mrs. Frank R. Reynolds
Mr. and Mrs. Trull Richardson
Miss Mary Rogers
Mrs. C. G. Royster
Joel Ryland
Mr. and Mrs. John L. Sanders
Phillip Scott
Mr. and Mrs. Richard Seawell
Mrs. C. B. Seifert
Mrs. Anna Sherman
Mrs. Flake A. Sherrill
Mr. and Mrs. E. D. Sloan
Carlos Smith
Dr. Claiborne T. Smith
Mrs. F. E. Smith
Mr. and Mrs. John Smith

---

*Deceased

Michael O. Smith
Mrs. Scott Stidham
Horace J. Stepp
Mrs. Andrew Burnet Stoney
Keith D. Strawn
Mrs. Parke Thomas
Mr. and Mrs. Sanford
  Thompson III
Mrs. Ann Thorne
Dr. and Mrs. A. M. Tousey
Miss Hallie Trotter
Mr. and Mrs. William Trotter
Mr. and Mrs. James G.
  Van Story
Mrs. W. A. Walker
Les Warrick, Jr.

Mrs. Helen Watson
Dr. George E. Waynick, Jr.
Miss Sarah Street Whitehurst
Mrs. Harvey Wilhusen
Mrs. Cora Williams
George Burns Williams
Howard D. Williams
Robert Williams
Mrs. Albert Willis
Mrs. Melba Pate Wyche
Mrs. Martha Yarborough
Ramon L. Yarborough
Gary Young
Mrs. Maria Davis Alston
  Young

Introduction

The literature on the subject of American silversmiths is practically devoid of references to North Carolina. In the mid-1940s a somewhat cursory search of all published material was rewarded by only one reference, and that of less than one line. A native, well-informed gentleman, when questioned concerning the possibility of silversmiths ever having worked in North Carolina, said, "No, no, this was a very poor state, and the early people could not afford silver; and besides that, our coastline gave us very few harbors." Since the speaker was not familiar with silversmithing, it is difficult to explain how he realized the importance of harbors to the trade. Nevertheless, the reference to harbors was just as significant as the observation concerning the financial status of the early settlers.

In the first place, the silversmiths were very dependent upon the coin brought in by sea captains and pirates for the material with which to work. Indeed, in the early days there was hardly enough currency to use in transacting necessary business, and certainly there was little to use otherwise. Since practically all early silver produced in America was made from coins, the difficulty of accumulating coins for this purpose naturally restricted the number of silver items that could be made in young North America.

The other British colonies on the Atlantic seaboard had the advantage of trading more directly with the mother country than did North Carolina. Because only the smaller vessels could safely navigate the inlets and enter the harbors of the colony, trans-Atlantic traffic was somewhat limited. Sloops and schooners were used in the coastal trade, while brigs, snows, and other types of colonial ships engaged in a modest amount of oceangoing commerce.[1] In the years 1770-1775 the tonnage of the vessels coming from Great Britain was about 25 percent of the total; the number in later years was far smaller. Nevertheless, some British-made silver was imported directly to North Carolina from England, and some was brought in through the ports of neighboring colonies. In addition, the coastal traffic into North Carolina from as far north as Boston permitted the importation of American-made silver from the more affluent northern colonies as well as European-made pieces; thus, inaccessibility was not really the primary cause of silver's scarcity in North Carolina. Indeed, fine early-eighteenth-century English and American silver has been found in the state. As examples of such pieces, two coffeepots with London date letters of 1727 and 1763 and a chalice of 1725 made in Virginia have been found in Edenton;[2] a London kettle of 1727 and a George II service of 1752 have been found in New Bern.[3]

In addition to coastwise and direct British traffic, an important trade was developed between the Carolinas and the West Indies. While this brought in considerable coin, it was often coin of Spanish and Mexican origin, containing impurities that made it brittle and unsuitable for raising large and important pieces of silver plate. The northern states, which traded more directly with England, received a preponderance of superior English coin. This coin from the time of Richard I down to 1920 was of "sterling" quality and consequently contained a larger proportion of silver; it was alloyed only with copper. Some Spanish money filtered into the northern states, of course, in addition to the English.

There is little doubt about the veracity of the statement that "this was a very poor state." The early settlers did not have the wealth those of the neighboring colonies enjoyed. There were comparatively few large plantations in the colony, and most of the settlers were small farmers. Fine silver was somewhat out of place on small, isolated farms, even if the owners were able to buy it; and since wealth in early North Carolina was measured not in terms of fine household possessions but rather in terms of land and servants, the well-to-do colonists of North Carolina were more likely to invest money in additional land and slaves than to purchase silver.

Nevertheless, owners of silver items were cognizant of the value of their possessions, and perusal of the wills of North Carolinians of early days sometimes reveals silver mentioned in bequests and inventories.[4] Naturally, only the wealthier people customarily made wills, and not all of them did so. In these, bequests of silver were by no means common. Whenever silver is mentioned, it is usually a reference to flat tableware such as spoons, tongs, and strainers or to articles of personal adornment such as stock or shoe buckles. Occasionally, however, teapots, creamers, beakers, mugs, canns, and salvers were bequeathd, showing that silver was both owned and appreciated in the province.[5] Descriptions of these pieces are seldom definite enough to determine whether they were of English or American origin. When markings were mentioned, they usually were the initials of the original owners and not of the makers.

One piece of silver discovered in North Carolina that is of more than passing interest is a gorget made by Barent Ten Eyck (1714-1795) of Albany, New York. It was found in an Indian burial mound at Franklin, Macon County, North Carolina, and is now in the Museum of the American Indian, Heye Foundation, New York. Hanging in place, this piece is 4⅝ inches high and 5⅞ inches wide. In the center, where the silver is 2⅛ inches wide, is a rude engraving of the coat of arms of Great Britain, and across the front are engraved "Danyel Cryn, 1755." A hole is pierced at each end.[6] British line officers and militia officers wore gorgets, although it was contrary to army regulations. Danyel Cryn may have been a British regular officer killed in the battle of Franklin, June 27, 1760, whose gorget was afterward appropriated by an Indian and buried with him when he died.

In many parts of America silversmiths settled in villages shortly after the arrival of blacksmiths. It appears doubtful that many silversmiths came to the southern Atlantic seaboard for the express purpose of practicing their craft. More likely, their chief purpose was to search for precious metals. Both Virginia and South Carolina, however, claim to have had working silversmiths in the seventeenth century: John Brodnax is reputed to have made silver in Williamsburg in 1694,[7] and Solomon Legare was in Charleston in 1696.[8] How do these dates compare with those of North Carolina smiths? Records enable historians to trace a name back to the seventeenth century, but discovering which name conceals a silversmith is the difficult task. The earliest smith who has been traced in North Carolina was Robert Mellyne, who lived in Bath County, Pamtecough Precinct, in 1694, was described as a "quoiner" in 1696, and bought land there in 1702. Although Mellyne is described as a silversmith, no surviving proof of his activity as a smith is available.

The names of more than seventy-five silversmiths who evidently worked in North Carolina in the eighteenth century have been uncovered.[9] Eleven of these men were in Edenton. There is no reason to think that New Bern may not have had as many and as early smiths as Edenton, but the names of only eight who worked in Craven County before 1800 are available—

the earliest one being William Tisdale, in 1770. Fayetteville is thought to have had at least six, and Wilmington at least ten, eighteenth-century smiths.

Three well-trained New England smiths came to this state and settled before 1790. The earliest of these was Roswell Huntington of Norwich, Connecticut, who bought land in Hillsborough in 1786. He was followed soon afterward by John [Tyng] Peabody, also of Norwich, who went to Wilmington, and Peter Strong of Lebanon, Connecticut, who went to Fayetteville. The origin of most of the other smiths is clouded by the obscurity that rests over the times in which they lived.

One of the New England smiths, Roswell Huntington, was involved in a matter of considerable historical interest. On October 12, 1793, William R. Davie, grand master of the North Carolina Masons, laid the cornerstone of Old East Building, the first structure to be erected for the then newly established University of North Carolina at Chapel Hill. This cornerstone was despoiled sometime in the period between 1865 and 1875. Years later in Clarksville, Tennessee, an inscribed brass plate was discovered at a brass foundry, and the inscription proved it to have belonged to the cornerstone of Old East. On October 12, 1916, 123 years after the original presentation, the plate was again publicly and formally presented to the university. The signature at the bottom of the inscription is "R. Huntington, sculp."[10]

It is not easy in the twentieth century to appreciate the role of early silversmiths in the life of the community. They were usually superior craftsmen who fully accepted their responsibilities as citizens. They often acted as bankers in the days when no banks existed. In those times of frequent robberies and inadequate police protection, if a citizen's coin was stolen he could never identify it. If, however, he had the coin made into a tankard or a bowl or a teapot with his initials engraved upon it, the owner not only had the use of the article but, if it were stolen, could also easily identify it. Because of this custom of converting coin into usable articles, the churches of New England have considerable fine early plate inasmuch as a bequest to a church was not so likely to have been in terms of dollars as in beakers or cups or spoons.

If the early housewife wished to purchase a dozen teaspoons, she would not go to the silversmith and say to him, "Please show me some teaspoons," for he would not have any to show her. The purchase was not so simple as that. Neither could her

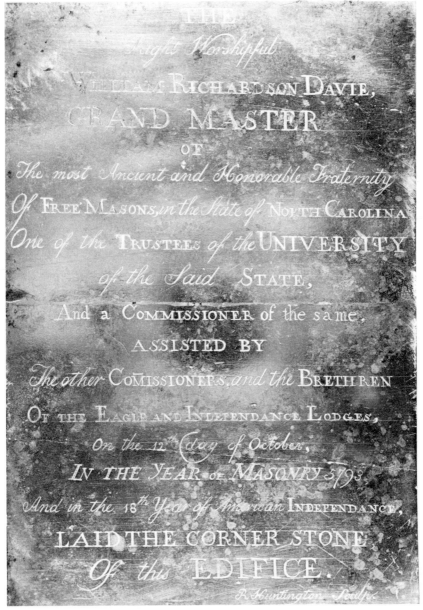

THE
Right Worshipful
WILLIAM RICHARDSON DAVIE,
GRAND MASTER
OF
The most Ancient and Honorable Fraternity
Of FREE MASONS, in the State of NORTH CAROLINA
One of the TRUSTEES of the UNIVERSITY
of the Said STATE,
And a COMMISSIONER of the same,
ASSISTED BY
The other COMISSIONERS, and the BRETHREN
OF THE EAGLE AND INDEPENDANCE LODGES,
On the 12th day of October,
IN THE YEAR OF MASONRY 5793
And in the 18th Year of American INDEPENDANCE,
LAID THE CORNER STONE
Of this EDIFICE.
R. Huntington Sculp.

The inscription on the brass plate originally affixed to the cornerstone of Old East Building on the campus of the University of North Carolina at Chapel Hill bears the name of Roswell Huntington.

husband go to the tailor and ask to be shown overcoats and suits. The situations of the silversmith and the tailor were similar, since neither could write to a large manufacturer and have articles sent to him ready-made. There were no large manufacturers; craftsmen in the villages made their own goods.[11] Since a housewife could not order her silverware until she had saved enough coins to make it, she frequently had at hand a little velvet or silk bag into which she dropped her spare coinage—frequently coinage from many different nations. It sometimes took several months before the colonial lady could save enough. When the bag seemed to be heavy enough, she would take it to the smith and explain her needs. He would weigh the coin, make the spoons, weigh them, credit or charge her for the difference in weight, and then charge her for making the spoons. When she examined the spoons, she would find the maker's name or mark on the back of them and the initials that she had requested engraved on the front.

It is doubtful if many large and important pieces of silver were made in North Carolina, although some of the early smiths were certainly capable of fashioning them. Smiths such as Freeman Woods, who came from New York to New Bern in 1794, undoubtedly produced interesting pieces, but up to the present time only a few items made by him have been identified—among them a very beautiful creamer and a sugar bowl that were found in New York. They were probably made before he left that city. A second Woods creamer was recently acquired by the North Carolina Museum of History, and a third is presently on loan to the museum.

During the period between 1972 and 1984 there has been great enthusiasm among North Carolinians to find and preserve their early handcrafted silver. No styles unique to the state have been discernible, and few pieces of hollow ware have been found. Nevertheless, the actual number of surviving pieces has been greater than anticipated. At the beginning of January, 1983, more than 378 articles had been identified, most of which are pictured in this revised edition: 138 teaspoons, 98 tablespoons, 28 dessertspoons, 9 memorial spoons, 22 punch ladles, 14 sugar tongs, 12 salt spoons (or shovels), 11 sauce (cream) ladles, 8 butter knives, and a few pieces of hollow ware —9 cups, 3 sugar bowls, 5 cream pitchers, a water pitcher, a salver, and various miscellaneous smaller items. Not infrequently a piece of silver made by a North Carolina craftsman not previously recognized comes to light, and it is certain that among the treasured silver of the descendants of old families there are other pieces waiting to be "found." Unfortunately, many pieces undoubtedly have been lost. Silversmiths often advertised for old and broken silver, so some of the oldest silver may have been consigned to the melting pot.

There seems to be an impression among some people that silversmiths and watchmakers were a wandering group, going from village to village and working as demands were made upon their time. Watch and clock repairers were more likely than silversmiths to fall into such a group, but very little wandering actually occurred. It is true that a young man might go to a village for a short time and explore its possibilities as a prospective place for settlement; if the place proved unpropitious, he would try other villages until he was satisfied. Some older men were naturally drifters; and others made excursions to the county seats when court was in session or to the village in which the General Assembly met, for the purpose of selling their wares at that time.

Very frequently a young man would serve an apprenticeship and, after becoming a journeyman, would either go into partnership with his master or open a shop in the same location. It was a time when the country was being settled and some movement was very natural. As might be expected, the migration was from the more populated North to the vacant places in the South, where opportunities were presumably more common. Only one example of a contrary movement is known: Isaac Marquand left Edenton in 1796 and became a somewhat prominent jeweler in New York. John Baptiste Dumoutet, a well-known jeweler of Philadelphia, and afterward of Charleston, South Carolina, traveled in North Carolina, staying a short time in various towns, selling watches and jewelry and taking orders for silverware. As a rule, however, silversmiths were not more peripatetic than men of other crafts.

There was a movement, however, that decimated the ranks of the silversmiths and jewelers—this was the tendency to participate in other occupations or in a more extended line of trade. Jewelers frequently handled fancy goods or military goods in their stores and sometimes branched out and became general merchants, perhaps continuing to engage in watchmaking or silversmithing as a sideline rather than as a main interest. Professionally, silversmiths might become dentists, as dentistry required the filling of teeth with silver or gold and the making of artificial teeth. Paul Revere was a dentist as well as a silversmith; he made artificial teeth for George Washington. John Y. Savage, who worked as a silversmith in North Carolina, later practiced dentistry in Richmond, Virginia; and John Fockel (Fogle) worked as a silversmith in North Carolina and Georgia before he advertised himself as a dentist. Tools that might have been used by a dentist of his day were found among the possessions of John Huntington, leading to the speculation that he, too, might have practiced dentistry.

Particular laws concerning the method of binding apprentices seem not to have been enacted in North Carolina, except such as applied to orphans, deserted children, and children of irresponsible parents; any of these children, white or black, might be bound to masters by the courts. The law on that point was as follows:

> Every male apprentice shall be bound to some tradesman, merchant, mariner, or other person approved by the court, until the age of twenty-one years, and every female to some suitable employment till her age of 18 years, if white, but if colored, till twenty-one.[12]

The common practice of apprenticing boys to craftsmen was apparently as well established in North Carolina as in other colonies and states, but the exact procedure does not seem to have been specifically defined. It was carried out by simple indenture. Most of the apprenticeships of which there is a legal record were those of wards of the court, and it is astonishing to note how few of those apprentices appear later as working silversmiths.

Many Negro boys, wards of the court, were apprenticed, but none, so far as has been found, to silversmiths. Only one reference to a black silversmith has been found. One Daniel, according to the Edenton *State Gazette of North Carolina* (April 8, 1791), who ran away from Abraham Taylor of Bertie County, was described as a blacksmith, silversmith, and cooper who could "read some in print." Records of four such Negro silversmiths were found in South Carolina, all in Charleston, where laws limiting the number of Negro appentices were in force.[13] There was also a black silversmith in Baltimore, Maryland.[14]

Artisans representing different crafts were not uncommon among slaves, although probably none were recognized as master craftsmen. Slaves were evidently taught the different trades by their owners and were used as workmen in the shops of their masters.

Several words of explanation are necessary concerning the list that follows. In the first place, it is incomplete. Undoubtedly there were smiths in North Carolina whose names are not included here, and many facts are missing concerning those whose names are known. The temptation is to defer publication of such a list until all the desired facts are obtained; but then it would never be published. When the known sources are exhausted, as is practically true in this case, publication may be the means of revealing some unknown sources. That is naturally the hope; a pressing invitation for cooperation should therefore be included. If any readers know of silversmiths not listed here, or have further information concerning those listed, or own silver bearing the mark of any North Carolina silversmith, the editors would be under great obligation for the help that such information would furnish. It should also be mentioned that the Division of Archives and History in Raleigh is endeavoring to secure samples of the work of all North Carolina silversmiths to add to its permanent collection in the museum located in the Archives and History/State Library Building.

The second note of explanation is this: Among the names of those included in this list are some of people who were watchmakers and not silversmiths at all. This is inevitable. The terms silversmith, watchmaker, and jeweler were used very loosely. Quite frequently the craftsman was forced to be expert in all three trades. When handwork was the only kind, the jeweler was necessarily a silversmith; but the trades of watchmaker and silversmith were distinct. Sometimes a silversmith advertised that he had hired a competent watchmaker, or a watchmaker advertised that he had employed a silversmith. Partnerships frequently consisted of a watchmaker and a silversmith. In North Carolina, however, as in other states, silver has been found that bears the marks of craftsmen who always advertised as watchmakers. In fact, local custom often dictated whether a craftsman should be designated as a silversmith, a watchmaker, a jeweler, or all three. Moreover, the terms silversmith and goldsmith were used interchangeably. Whitesmiths, however, were not silversmiths but tinsmiths.

It is also recognized by the editor and collectors that the mark of a North Carolina silversmith may sometimes appear

on a piece of silver that was actually made by another craftsman who resided elsewhere. For example, Thomas W. Brown is
known to have retailed some silver made by other silversmiths
whose marks are frequently found on silver along with the
mark of Brown or Brown and his partner William Anderson.
Traugott Leinbach is another craftsman who is now thought to
have availed himself of the opportunity to obtain from others
pieces or parts (cup handles, for example) that he could embellish or combine with his own work and then retail. Some of
these pieces are pictured in this book because they are of historical significance to the state and reflect the taste and practices
of North Carolinians in antebellum days.

Whenever possible, all descriptive terms pertaining to silver
spoons discussed and/or pictured in the following pages conform to the vocabulary established by Louise Conway Belden
and explained in "An Illustrated Glossary of Spoon Terms,"
which accompanies her *Marks of American Silversmiths in the
Ineson-Bissell Collection* (Charlottesville: University Press of
Virginia for the Henry Francis Winterthur Museum, 1980), hereinafter cited as Belden, *Marks of American Silversmiths.*

---

[1]C. C. Crittenden, *The Commerce of North Carolina, 1763-1789* (New Haven:
Yale University Press, 1936), 1-20, 77-84.

[2]E. A. Jones, *Old Silver of Europe and America* (Philadelphia: Lippincott
Company, 1928), 143ff., hereinafter cited as Jones, *Old Silver of Europe and
America.*

[3]Jones, *Old Silver of Europe and America*, 145.

[4]J. Bryan Grimes (ed.), *North Carolina Wills and Inventories* (Raleigh: Edwards and Broughton Printing Company, 1912), hereinafter cited as Grimes,
North Carolina Wills.

[5]Grimes, *North Carolina Wills*, 11, 167, 206, 318, 482, 485.

[6]G. B. Cutten, "The Ten Eyck Silversmiths," *Antiques* 42 (December, 1942),
299-303.

[7]E. M. Davis III, Introduction to *An Exhibition of Silver, Virginia Museum of
Fine Arts* [complete bibliographical data not available], 10; same information
in *William and Mary College Quarterly* [First series], XIV (July, 1905), 53-58,
(October, 1905), 135-138.

[8]E. Milby Burton, *South Carolina Silversmiths, 1690-1860* (Charleston: Charleston Museum, 1942), 105ff, hereinafter cited as Burton, *South Carolina Silversmiths.*

[9]Since Dr. Cutten's research in 1948, the names of other possible silversmiths
have come to light; hence the statistics originally cited in this paragraph have
been revised.

¹⁰*Proceedings of the Grand Lodge of North Carolina*, 1917, University of North Carolina Library, Chapel Hill, 36, 38, hereinafter cited as *Proceedings of Grand Lodge*, with appropriate date.

¹¹The Manowed Watch Factory, located in Tarboro, was advertising in 1835. The *Tarboro' Press* for July 11, 1835, contained a notice that the Manowed Watch Factory in Tarboro had "Palm Clocks and Time-keepers." Also advertised for sale were watches of English, French, German, and Swiss make, "Repeaters," and all material needed for watches and jewelry.

¹²*Revised Code of North Carolina, 1854*, c. 5, s. 2.

¹³Burton, *South Carolina Silversmiths*, 207ff.

¹⁴J. Hall Pleasants and Howard Sill, *Maryland Silversmiths, 1715-1830* (Baltimore: Lord Baltimore Press, 1930), 266, hereinafter cited as Pleasants and Sill, *Maryland Silversmiths*.

SILVERSMITHS
OF NORTH CAROLINA
1696-1860

THOMAS F. ADAMS was a watchmaker and clockmaker on Market Street, Baltimore, in 1804.[1] During October, 1807, he advertised as a watchmaker and clockmaker in Petersburg, Virginia.[2] On December 5, 1809, he announced that he had begun work in his shop on Main Street in Edenton, North Carolina.[3] On June 15, 1809, he asked those who were indebted to him to settle their accounts, as it was uncertain when he would leave the state.[4]

THOMAS AGNIS (AGNES, AGGNIS). A number of items from Thomas Agnis's business files for 1761 and 1762 and two important personal letters from "your Loveing Mother & Sister,

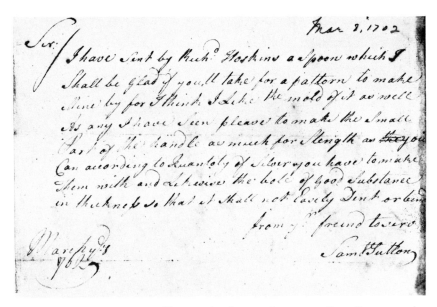

Samuel Sutton's letter to Thomas Agnis contains suggestions for spoons he wanted Agnis to make for him.

Phillis & Mary Cutbird," of London, have been preserved and will be found in Appendix C in this volume.[5] There are letters regarding certain commissions outside his business as silversmith and other items of business significance. The letters are addressed to Agnis with one of the following distinguished amplifications: "Goldsmith in Edenton," "Silversmith in Edenton," or "Jeweler at Edenton." Except for this documentary evidence, nothing is known about Agnis; but his accounts indicate that he was a silversmith of some prominence.

WILLIAM ALBRECHT. The minutes of the Salem *Aufseher Collegium* (supervising board) for 1825 contain an item about "a young man named Albrecht from the Alamance in Guilford County." The February 7 entry notes that Albrecht "wishes to improve himself in his craft as a silversmith." A few months later, it was noted in the diary that Albrecht, "who is working with Br. John Vogler as a silver-smith, was confirmed in the Lutheran Church."[6]

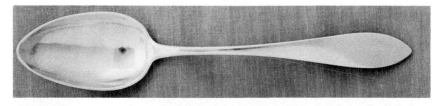

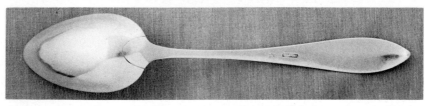

While the maker of this spoon has not been definitely proven to be the Albrecht who worked with John Vogler, there are such similarities to Vogler's work that it must be attributed to Albrecht. Pictured above is a tablespoon 9¼ inches long with an oval bowl 3¼ inches long and 1¹³/₁₆ inches wide. Compare this spoon with the Burmeister spoon described in Appendix A and with the John Vogler tablespoon shown on p. 181. The Albrecht and Burmeister spoons are both in the collection of a descendant of the original owners of the spoons, and there is also a Vogler spoon of the same style in this collection; provenance, the piedmont.

SAMUEL PARKS ALEXANDER (1816-1900) was born July 12, 1816, in Sugar Creek Township, Mecklenburg County, the son of Oswald Alexander and his second wife, Hannah.[7] Samuel was also the grandson of Hezekiah Alexander, a signer of the "Mecklenburg Declaration of Independence."[8] Samuel was apprenticed to Thomas Trotter and after completing his apprenticeship became a member of the firm of Trotter & Alexander. This partnership was formed November 24, 1837, and was dissolved a year later when Trotter took over the business.[9]

This cream ladle, in a fiddle style without shoulders, handle turned down, and engraved *JM* in feathered script, has the mark of Samuel Parks Alexander. It is in a private collection.

In October, 1839, it was announced that Alexander had bought the entire stock of Thomas Trotter and that spoons, among other things, would be made to order.[10] In the *Charlotte Journal* of August 12, 1841, Alexander advertised jewelry he had brought from "the north." On July 8, 1843, Trotter purchased Alexander's stock.[11] The latter then became a member of the firm of Brem & Alexander, which operated a general store. After the Brem & Alexander partnership was dissolved on October 2, 1848,[12] Alexander became a broker who dealt in securities and real estate and amassed a considerable fortune.[13] He acted as executor of the estate of Thomas Trotter. Alexander, who never married, devoted himself to the First Presbyterian Church of Charlotte, serving as deacon and contributing generously for many years.[14]

ZENAS (ZENOS) ALEXANDER (ca. 1771-1826). On July 27, 1787, "Zenos Alexander, son and orphan of Zebulon Alexander dec[d]," was apprenticed to Isaac Price, a gunsmith, to serve until he reached the age of twenty-one.[15] His age at the time of his indenture was not given, and it is not known where he learned the art of silversmithing. Evidently he remained in Mecklenburg County, probably near Charlotte. In the Mecklenburg County estate papers of General Robert Irwin (1800), now filed in the State Archives, is an account paper dated 1799:

1799:   Gen'l Robt Irwin D^r to Zeanus Alexander
             to sundries Work Done   0-5-0
      Sept. 20 to 1 pair Silver Shew buckles   1-0-0[16]

In 1805 Alexander accepted James McRea (McRae) as an apprentice to learn the art and mystery of a silversmith and the stocking and mounting of guns.[17] A bill submitted to Major James Harris for work done in 1807-1811 indicates that Alexander was practicing both crafts:

Maj.^{r} James Harris
1807   To Zenas Alexander   Due
Augt 23   To 2 prs sugar tongs_____5^2/6 $10.50
                   " 1 doz tea spoons _____1 /   12.00
                   " 2 scissors chains_____6 /   12.00

1808
Aug.   " 1 ditto ditto _____   _____6 /   6.00

1811   [not clear] 6 sickles _____1 /   6.00
                 " John Guire's acct _____   3.37
                         Contra Cr $49.87
                         By amt of   37.43¼
                                              due   12.43¾
State of N° Carolina }
Mecklenburg County }   The above balance of twelve
dollars & 43 cents, Sworn to and subscribed before me
according to law this 24th day of Feby—1813

Test   Zenas Alexander
Saul[?] Alexander[18]

In 1810 Henry McBride and Elisha Smartt were bound to Alexander as apprentices in the two crafts.[19] That same year Alexander was appointed guardian of David Vaner Wilson under bond of £1,000.[20] Between 1801 and 1826 Alexander was involved in more than a dozen real estate transactions.[21] His will, dated May 21, 1826, and proved the following August, disposed of considerable property, mostly rural. In the will the silversmith mentioned his wife Margaret, his shop, and his several daughters and sons; he provided that each of the sons should be enabled to receive a half-dozen silver teaspoons.[22] A letter from Mrs. Rose Amanda Coffey to George Barton Cutten dated

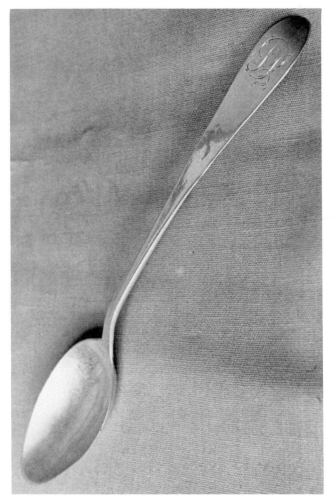

Depicted above is a rare teaspoon that has the mark of Zenas Alexander. The handle, slender and spatulate, is rather sharply turned down at the end. The initials *GS* are engraved longitudinally on the handle. This piece is from a private collection.

July 23, 1949, provided the information that Zenas Alexander and his wife, Margaret, were buried in Steele Creek Cemetery near Charlotte; on his tombstone is the inscription "Zenas Alexander, died May 26, 1826, aged 55 years."[23]

WILLIAM S. ANDERSON (1820-1871), the son of William B. Anderson, was born in or near Wilmington, North Carolina.[24] It seems likely that he learned his trade with T. W. Brown, for he witnessed a deed when Brown bought some land in 1836.[25] At any rate, he went into partnership with Brown and continued in this relationship, under the firm name of Brown & Anderson, until his death in Wilmington on June 15, 1871.[26] In 1868 he refused to act as executor of the estate of Elizabeth Peacock, although named as such in her will.[27] Brown's will named Anderson as executor of Brown's estate, but Anderson died before Brown.[28] No individual mark used by Anderson has been found. See sketch of Thomas William Brown for marks used by the Brown & Anderson partnership.

_____ANDERSON. When David Scott and Aaron Woolworth were competitors in the silversmithing and jewelry business in Greensboro, Anderson appeared on the scene for a brief period and became a member of the firm of Scott & Anderson on June 13, 1829,[29] and of Woolworth & Anderson on November 21, 1829.[30] The latter partnership apparently did not last any longer than the former one. On July 4, 1829, an unclaimed letter addressed to James S. Anderson, Greensboro, was listed in the newspaper.[31]

JOHN ARCHER. The only direct available reference concerning Archer is found in a 1798 advertisement stating that as a goldsmith and silversmith he had opened a shop in the Blue House, opposite Mr. Fleming's store in Halifax, where he proposed to carry on the "above business."[32] In 1790 a John Archer of Halifax County was the head of a large family,[33] and from 1783[34] to 1815[35] a John Archer was involved in real estate transactions in Halifax County. These John Archers appear to have been different persons and to have had different occupations.

WILLIAM ARCHER. A researcher has found evidence that John Whitehouse was apprenticed to William Archer, a silversmith; the apprenticeship was recorded in the Edgecombe County court minutes of May, 1791.[36]

ADOLPHUS ATKINSON. During the Civil War, Private Adolphus Atkinson served in the Confederate army in Company C, Thirteenth Regiment, North Carolina Troops. He resided in Caswell County and was by occupation a silversmith before he enlisted in Caswell County at age seventeen on April 24, 1861. He was present or accounted for until being wounded and captured at or near Gettsyburg, Pennsylvania, July 1-5, 1863. He was hospitalized at Chester, Pennsylvania, until he was paroled and transferred to City Point, Virginia, where he was received August 20, 1863. Atkinson was reported absent wounded through October, 1864.[37] In a private collection are three tablespoons said to have been made by him.[38]

_____ATKINSON. In a letter dated December 21, 1839, from Nathaniel J. Palmer to Governor Edward B. Dudley, Palmer petitioned the governor to pardon John Buckner, a blacksmith, and Johnston Sneed, "a young man the only son of a poor widow of this place who lives with or near her and at the time of his imprisonment was learning the Silversmith trade with a brother-in-law of his who has a shop in Milton."[39] Among the Caswell County marriage bonds are marriage records of four Sneed women:

> Annie N. Sneed to Le Roy Atkinson, 1835
> Frances N. Sneed to Jno. H. Crockett, 1834
> Catherine Sneed to Jas. Lawrence, 1836
> Mary Sneed to Theodorick L. Williamson, 1828[40]

The marriage of a fifth Sneed woman (Frances Sneed to James M. Tucker, January 22, 1839) is recorded in the Rockingham County marriage bonds.[41] If Sneed were a brother of Annie N. Sneed, he would be a brother-in-law of Le Roy Atkinson. Several researchers, including Dr. George B. Cutten, have found references to an Atkinson in Milton who was a silversmith.[42] It is possible that Le Roy may have been this man, but no proof of it has been found.

WILLIAM ATKINSON. In January, 1848, Colonel George Barnhardt in describing the discovery of the Reed Gold Mine in Cabarrus County mentioned a silversmith in Concord, William Atkinson. Colonel Barnhardt's account was used in John Hill Wheeler's *Historical Sketches of North Carolina* (Philadelphia: Lippincott, Grambo and Co., 2 volumes in one, 1851), II, 63-64. According to the story, the first piece of gold was found in 1799 by young Conrad Reed, who took it home to his father, John Reed:

Mr. Reed examined it, but as gold was unknown in this part of the country at that time, he did not know what kind of metal it was: the piece was about the size of a small smoothing iron.

Mr. Reed carried the piece of metal to Concord, and showed it to a William Atkinson, a silversmith, but he not thinking of gold, was unable to say what kind of metal it was.

(Wheeler, *Historical Sketches*, II, 64.)

In 1802 the nugget was recognized as gold by a Fayetteville jeweler unnamed by Barnhardt but who is said to have bought the bar he had fluxed from the nugget, "six or eight inches long," for three dollars and fifty cents!

A watchmaker in Lincolnton by the name of William Atkinson was reported to have been robbed at some time prior to the publication of the *North Carolina Journal* (Halifax) on January 5, 1795:

On the same night was broke open the shop of William Atkinson, watch maker in Lincolnton, and robbed of seven silver watches. . . . Also one hundred ounces of silver of the following description, cut money, filings, one dozen and a half of tea-spoons unfinished, three pair of finished scissors, 40 small files.[43]

This may have been the same William Atkinson who has been identified as a silversmith in Jonesboro, Tennessee, and who designed the Great Seal of Tennessee during the governorship of Archibald Roane in 1802.[44]

R. A. BAIRD. A man named Baird was a member of the firm of Glass & Baird, Raleigh, in 1805.[45] In a private collection is a cream ladle that has the hallmark R. A. BAIRD, with an eagle engraved after the name. On the lower back of the ladle, just above the bowl, is a circle with the initials SJB. Engraved on the front of the ladle are the initials *MB*. Nothing else is known

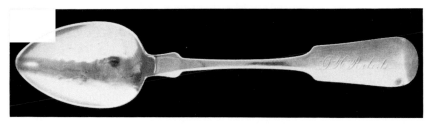

Typically fiddle with rounded shoulders and slightly tapered handles are the R. A. Baird cream ladle and dessertspoon pictured here. The ladle (facing page), from a private collection, is engraved simply *MB* in script. The dessertspoon, 7¼ inches long, is engraved *P A Roberts*; it is in the collection of the North Carolina Museum of History, a gift from the Museum of History Associates.

about the silversmith Baird. There was a David Baird who married Patsy Stanley in Raleigh, the marriage bond being dated June 18, 1805.[46] David Baird was on the Raleigh tax list in 1811, and the David Baird estate was on the list in 1812.

STEPHEN (STEPHENS) BAKER (b. 1791). On November 14, 1791, Stephen Baker was born in Beverly, Essex County, Massachusetts.[47] Just when he came to Wilmington, North Carolina, is not known, but in an advertisement dated March 22, 1817, he returned thanks for the patronage with which he had been favored and solicited a continuance of it. He offered for sale the remainder of his stock of goods "at cost and charges" and emphasized jewelry, watches, and silver teaspoons and tablespoons. He requested his creditors to present their accounts and his debtors to pay theirs.[48] A year later Baker

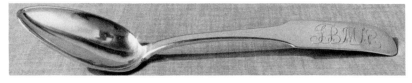

The Stephen Baker fiddleback tablespoon pictured above is 8¾ inches long with *FBMLE* engraved in script on the front of the handle. On the back of the handle *P Messler* is very precisely engraved. From the collection of the North Carolina Museum of History; photograph by Charles Clark.

offered a reward of $20.00 for the return of three watches and a number of keys stolen from his store during his illness. At the same time, he announced that he wished to close his business in Wilmington and offered watches and jewelry for sale. This announcement was still appearing on May 9, 1818.[49] Baker may have returned to New England, as he married Adeline Batchelor of Beverly, Massachusetts, on July 26, 1827.[50] H. W. Belknap says that Baker was a jeweler, justice of the peace, and postmaster in Salem, Massachusetts. Belknap also asserts that Baker in the course of his career lived for a time in Sheffield, Illinois.

JOSEPH BARRINGTON. On July 12, 1792, J. Barrington began business in Dumfries, Virginia; later that year he advertised that he

makes clocks of various descriptions, such as wind up themselves without manual assistance, regulate themselves according to the inclemency of the weather, and show the time of day on all parts of the globe at one time. . . . Watches such as wind up by being carried on a fob, also the key to effect the same being turned either way. At his shop in Salisbury, North Carolina.[51]

In 1826 Joseph Barrington (perhaps the same person) advertised a reward of $5.00 for a watch stolen from his home in Tarboro.[52] In an advertisement in 1832 he asked the following question: "Will the gentleman who called for and received Mr. Jacob Eliot's watch . . . inform me of the reason it has not been delivered . . . ?" This was also from Tarboro.[53] In 1837 a newspaper advertisement indicated that a letter was being held in the Tarboro post office for a J. Barrington.[54] In 1839 T. Barrington, presumably his wife, said she had engaged a good workman and was prepared to repair clocks, watches, jewelry, and silverware. She would also manufacture silver spoons to order and pay highest prices for old silver.[55] Evidently she carried on the business in Tarboro after her husband's death. On August 25, 1839, Peter Nixon and Mary Simmons, daughter of Mrs. Barrington, were married at Tarboro.[56] Apparently Barrington had married a Mrs. Simmons, thereby making Mary his stepdaughter.

GERMAN (GERMON) BAXTER (w. 1768—). On March 16, 1768, Joseph Todd was apprenticed to German (Germon) Baxter to learn the silversmith's trade.[57] In a deed dated October 24, 1774, this transaction was recorded: "German Baxter, silversmith, to James Townsley, silversmith, deed for Lot #4, West Square, town of Salisbury."[58] Since the lot was located on the corner one block south of the main square, it was probably the site of a shop used by Baxter and Townsley.[59]

JOHN M. BEASLEY (1815-1889) was born in Chatham County, North Carolina, October 15, 1815. On October 17, 1838, he advertised that he had opened a shop at the stand lately occupied by Selph & Pyle, in Fayetteville, doing clock and watch repairing and other work in his line.[60] He married Mariah Holmes,[61] the bond being dated January 17, 1837, and in 1841 evidently bought the stock in trade of Warren Prior.[62] In the *Fayetteville Observer* of September 19, 1848, he was advertising that the "subscriber has come home again and has brought with him his watches and jewelry." Among the many real estate transactions in which he was involved from 1838 to 1874 was his purchase in 1852 of the "east wall of his store."[63] In addition to his work as a silversmith and businessman, he served as a Baptist minister.[64] At least two others combined the tasks of silversmith and Baptist minister, namely William Waite (1730-1826) of Little Rest, Rhode Island, and Cambridge, New York,[65] and Elisha Perkins Langworthy (1766-1827) of Ballston Spa, New York.[66] Some early Baptist ministers did not believe in accepting any remuneration for preaching and followed some other occupation to pay their living expenses. A memorial window in the First Baptist Church of Fayetteville carries the inscription, "Rev. J. M. Beasley 1815-1889."[67] Beasley's ministerial activities were devoted principally to country parishes; he gave liberally of his means and devoted his energies to the organization of ten or twelve Baptist churches, among which were Lebanon, Cedar Falls, and Mount Pisgah.[68] In 1886 he retired from his jewelry business; his son, Benjamin Franklin Beasley, and J. C. Houston, who had been his employee for over forty years, organized the firm of Beasley & Houston and continued the business.[69] J. M. Beasley died on August 13, 1889, and five days later his son acquired Houston's interest in the jewelry firm and conducted the business independently for several years.[70]

These sugar tongs and a pair of salt spoons from a private collection have the mark of John M. Beasley. The tongs, 7½ inches long, have arms in a modified fiddleback gracefully scalloped and ending in shell-shaped grips; the salt spoons, 3½ inches long, are also fiddle with tipped ends, rounded shoulders, and the initials *SME* engraved on the front. In the same private collection are six handsome spoons (not pictured) in an early pattern of manufactured silver with the mark of Beasley incised on the backs of the handles. Two additional Beasley spoons are also pictured above. The difference in the size of the bowls and the shape of the shoulders should be noted. One spoon is engraved *JCH*, barely discernible; the second is engraved *AMAJ*. From the collection of the North Carolina Museum of History.

AUGUSTUS BECHTLER (1813-1846) was born in the Grand Duchy of Baden, the son of Christopher Bechtler, with whom he came to America in 1829 and with whom he settled near Rutherfordton, North Carolina, in 1830. Although then only nineteen, he was naturalized as an American citizen in 1832. Augustus worked with his father until the latter's death in 1842 and succeeded him as mint master and gold and silver worker. After a year of minting, he removed to Rutherfordton and devoted himself to the jewelry business, while his cousin Christopher became the mint master. Augustus died in 1846.[71]

CHRISTOPHER BECHTLER, JUNIOR [II], was born in the Grand Duchy of Baden and came to New York in 1829 with his uncle, Christopher Bechtler. With him he moved to a location near Rutherfordton in 1830 and was associated with his uncle as a silver and gold worker until the latter's death in 1842.[72] In 1843 he succeeded his cousin as mint master, and in 1847 he evidently moved to Rutherfordton to succeed his cousin as jeweler, for he advertised that he had commenced the manufacture of medallions, bracelets, crosses, earrings, finger rings, and the like: "The Watch-Making & Gold-Coining business attended to as heretofore."[73] In 1857 he moved to Spartanburg, South Carolina, and started a watch and jewelry business under the name of C. Bechtler & Son, principally for the manufacture of fine jewelry. He was evidently not very reliable, and the business was a failure.[74]

CHRISTOPHER BECHTLER, SENIOR (1782-1842), was born in the Grand Duchy of Baden and with his two sons and a nephew arrived in New York on October 12, 1829. He is listed as a jeweler in the 1830-1831 Philadelphia directory.[75] He came to North Carolina and settled a few miles north of Rutherfordton. His second son, Charles, committed suicide soon after arriving in North Carolina. On July 28, 1830, Bechtler advertised that after long experience in Europe and America he would mend or make jewelry and repair watches and clocks.[76] On July 2, 1831, and subsequently, he advertised that he was ready to coin gold into $2.50 and $5.00 pieces.[77] The first coins were 20k. fine, 2k. below that of United States coinage. After 1831 he coined $1.00 pieces, the first to be coined in the United States. The Bechtler coins passed at par and provided much-needed currency for the time and place. He and his son Augustus were naturalized as American citizens on July 14, 1832. He was "a man of strictest honesty" and was a charter member of the Presbyterian church of Rutherfordton when it was organized in 1835. A local newspaper in 1836 advertised that "Christopher Bechtler, Watch-Maker & Jeweller, RESPECTFULLY informs the public that he has removed to back Street, a short distance West of the Courthouse." He said that he wanted to settle his accounts by September 1.[78]

In addition to their work in gold and silver, the Bechtlers were gunsmiths of great ability and invented a device for firing a rifle eight times a minute. Christopher Bechtler's will was dated November 28, 1842, and he died shortly afterward.[79]

ROBERT W. BECKWITH (ca. 1813-1873). The peripatetic craftsman was exemplified in him. Of his early life nothing is known except that he was a native of Virginia; in 1837 he was a member of the firm of Thomson & Beckwith of Raleigh.[80] (The mark of this firm follows the sketch of Thomson & Beckwith in this volume.) By May 18, 1838, Beckwith apparently had moved to New Bern inasmuch as the *Newbern Spectator* of that date carried this notice:

> R. W. Beckwith Of the Firm of Thomson & Beckwith, Raleigh, N.C. Respectfully informs the citizens of Newbern and its vicinity that he has opened the Store formerly occupied by Mr. Archer Tench, dec'd., adjoining Mr. Sander's Druggist Store, where he is ready to do all repairs on Clocks and Watches, warranted to do well, or no charge made.
>
> Fine Gold and Silver Levers, Swiss and English Watches, and a general assortment of Jewelry For Sale at the above Store.

After the firm of Thomson & Beckwith was dissolved in 1839, he entered into partnership with W. J. Ramsay as Ramsay & Beckwith and worked in New Bern.[81] The partnership did not last long, and in 1843 he advertised that he had taken a shop opposite the courthouse in Tarboro.[82] In 1850 he informed the citizens of Charlotte that he had taken a room in Springs's new building,[83] and in 1858 the firm of Beckwith & Brittain of Charlotte dissolved partnership.[84] His next move is not known, but in 1866 he resumed business at the old stand in Charlotte, where he made rings out of virgin gold;[85] his name appears in *Branson's North Carolina Business Directory, for 1867-8*

(Raleigh: Branson and Jones, 1867). He died December 15, 1873, at about the age of sixty, according to the *Charlotte Democrat* of December 23, 1873.

JOHN BENBOW (w. 1771). A man named John Benbow is described as a silversmith in a deed to land in Bladen County written in February, 1771.[86] Nothing else is known about him.

BERSON & ROBERTS. This firm was advertising in Washington, North Carolina, in 1816. The partners had "commenced business in their various branches" and advertised

Gold and Silver Work, Engraving, & Hair Work executed in the neatest style and at the shortest notice. Clocks, Watches, Patent Levers, repaired and warranted. Also nautical and Mathematical Instruments.
N.B. Cash given for old Gold and Silver.[87]

JOSEPH BISHOP. In an advertisement dated January 13, 1816, and appearing in the *Wilmington Gazette* of that date, Bishop mentioned watches, jewelry, "Table and Teaspoons" for sale and added: "N.B.—All kinds of Gold and Silver work manufactured in the neatest manner. Clocks and Watches repaired as usual." Bishop offered cash for old gold and silver.

The original owner of this Joseph Bishop punch (or soup) ladle was Sara Eagles, wife of Joseph Eagles. Probably made ca. 1816-1822, the ladle measures 13⅞ inches overall, with the width of the bowl 4 inches. The initials engraved on the handle are *SE*. This piece, a gift of the Poisson family of Wilmington, is in the collection of the North Carolina Museum of History.

In the following year, he was advertising in another Wilmington paper.[88] In 1818 he offered $20.00 reward for the return of a silver watch stolen from his shop.[89] In 1819 he continued to advertise watches and jewelry.[90] On August 13, 1821, letters of administration on the estate of Joseph Bishop were granted to Joseph A. Hill and William D. Mosely under $4,000 bond.[91] The following November the administrators were given permission to sell Negroes belonging to the estate.[92] In 1822 a suit against the estate resulted in a judgment for $1,213.40.[93] On August 12, 1823, auditors were appointed by the court to pass upon the administrators' accounts.[94] Bishop was a somewhat common name, and some of these estate items might seem to cast doubt upon the assumption that this was the estate of Joseph Bishop, watchmaker and jeweler. A Joseph Bishop was listed as a jeweler in Philadelphia city directories from 1829 to 1833.[95]

VICTOR G. BLANDIN. In 1831 he advertised in Charlotte that he had recently commenced the manufacture of jewelry from North Carolina gold and had erected a new furnace for that purpose.[96] Two years later he announced that he continued at his old stand to manufacture jewelry from North Carolina gold and that he had just received a large shipment of new jewelry. He also thanked his friends and the public for their kind and liberal patronage.[97] A notice concerning Blandin's estate appeared in 1834. Charles Jugnot, the administrator, announced that he would ". . . expose to public sale, at the residence of the late Victor G. Blandin in Charlotte all the personal property belonging to the deceased, consisting of Jewellry of Various kinds, working tools, beds, and furniture, &c, &c."[98]

GEORGE BLYTH (w. ca. 1772).[99] One document indicates the presence of a silversmith named George Blyth in New Hanover County ca. 1772:

NORTH CAROLINA   ⎱   si.
   Hillsborough District ⎰

(Seal) George the Third, by the Grace of God, of Great-Britain, France and Ireland, King, Defender of the Faith, &c. To the Sheriff of the County of *New Hanover* Greeting. We COMMAND you *as hereto-*

fore that you take the Body of *George Blyth* late afs^d Silversmith (if to be found in your bailiwick) and *him* safely keep, so that you have *him* before our Chief Justice and his Associates, Justices of our Superior Court of Justice, to be held for the District of Hillsborough, at the Court-House in Hillsborough, on the Twenty-Second Day of *September* next; then and there to *Answer James Monro & Comp.^y at a Plea of Trespass on the Law Damages*

Pounds Prov.

Herein fail not, and have you there this Writ, Witness MARTIN HOWARD, Esq. Chief Justice of our said Province, at Hillsborough, the 23^d. Day of March in the *12.th* Year of our Reign, Anno. Dom 1772

Clark [illegible][100]

JAMES BLYTHE (d. 1780). James Blythe has been identified by editors Donald R. Lennon and Ida B. Kellam (*The Wilmington Town Book, 1743-1778* [Raleigh: Division of Archives and History, North Carolina Department of Cultural Resources, 1973], hereinafter cited as Lennon and Kellam, *The Wilmington Town Book*) as a silversmith who had come to Wilmington prior to 1755, possibly from Virginia. He was a Revolutionary patriot and active in local affairs. Apparently prosperous, Blythe owned property in Wilmington on Ann Street between Front and Second streets and a plantation in New Hanover County. The plantation has been incorporated into residential developments, and a street has been named in his honor. Blythe was described in various documents as a "watchmaker" and a "silversmith."[101]

JOHN E. BOGER. On February 8, 1845, he advertised a "New Establishment" in Salisbury and stated that he had recently received from Philadelphia watches and jewelry; he had also obtained a steady and skillful watchmaker.[102] In March of the following year he became a member of the firm of Boger & Wilson;[103] and at Lincolnton on December 6, 1848, he married Mary Ann Ramsour of that place.[104] Boger purchased lots in Salisbury on October 18, 1849.[105] In the census of 1850 he is recorded as a silversmith, aged twenty-nine, born in North Carolina. He sold his interest in the firm of Boger & Wilson to Wilson on April 14, 1853.[106]

BOGER & WILSON (1846-1853)—John E. Boger and William R. Wilson, in Salisbury. The partnership was announced March 20, 1846,[107] and on April 14, 1853, Wilson advertised that he had purchased Boger's interest in the business.[108] This firm was one of the earliest to do extensive display advertising.

BENJAMIN B. BRASWELL (w. 1847). The name of Benjamin B. Braswell is included as number five on the 1847 Descriptive Roll of Companies, Adjutant General's Department, State Archives.[109] Braswell is described in this manner:

[5] Benj. B. Braswell, aged 20, 5 ft. 5½ in., dark complexion, dark hair, dark eyes, native Edgecombe Co. Silversmith by occupation. Enrolled 26 Dec. 1846 at R Tarboro, by L. D. Wilson, for duration of War with Mexico. Cpl. Apt. Sgt 2 Sep 1847.

Aptmts
    1 Cpl 26 Jan 1846 (DOR[?])
    2d Cpl 14 Feb. 1847; Sgt. 2 Sep. 1847

P. N. BRENNAN. In March, 1828, Brennan advertised in Fayetteville that he had for sale an extensive stock of imported jewelry, silver, glassware, household needs, and personal items. The advertisement indicated that Brennan was primarily a dealer involved in selling, but he did offer "the highest cash for Gold and old Silver"; and it is possible that he may have done silversmithing.[110]

N. ALEXANDER F. BREWER appeared in Charlotte in January, 1842, as a member of the firm of Lawing & Brewer[111] and married A. M. Black there, the bond being dated August 1 of the same year.[112] Lawing & Brewer dissolved their partnership the following year.[113] Brewer is listed in the Camden, South Carolina, directory for 1845 as a jeweler, and on January 5, 1848, he announced there that his watchmaker's tools and materials were for sale inasmuch as he was determined to give up the business.[114]

WILLIAM A. (M.) BROOKSHIRE (BROOKSHER, BROOK-SHIER; w. prior to 1862) enlisted as a private in Company K, Thirty-fifth Regiment, North Carolina Troops, on October 15, 1861, in Burke County. He listed his age as seventeen and his occupation as silversmith. The son of R. R. Brookshier, William died of a "fever" at Kinston on May 22, 1862.[115]

DANIEL BROWN. On February 4, 1795, Daniel Brown took an apprentice named George Miller to learn the silversmith's trade.[116] Brown must have lived in Rowan County.

THOMAS WILLIAM BROWN (1803-1872) was born in New York City, the son of James Brown and Elizabeth Adair.[117]

These photographs of a portrait of Thomas William Brown (artist unknown) and Brown's shop shield are used by permission of the owner, Mrs. Charles P. Graham, a descendant of Brown.

Both of his parents were born in Bladen County, North Carolina. He learned his trade in New York City, but in 1823 he opened a shop in Wilmington, North Carolina, where he lived the rest of his life. On November 18, 1822, he married Harriet Sophia Day in New Brunswick, New Jersey; his second wife was Carolina Amelia Marshall, whom he married in Wilmington on January 31, 1828. After the death of his second wife, Brown was introduced by Louis Strite Fellows, a silversmith and jeweler of New York, to Mrs. Sarah Elizabeth Beebe Story, whom Brown married on December 6, 1846, in Norwich, Connecticut. One of their sons was named for Fellows.

Brown advertised in the local papers. On November 15, 1826, he informed the citizens of Wilmington through the *Cape-Fear Recorder* that he had "returned from the city of N.Y. and taken a room in Market Street recently occupied by Gen. Jones" and intended "carrying on the silversmith and jewelry business." In 1840 his shop was evidently damaged in a fire. An announcement carried by the Wilmington *Evening Post* of May 14, 1840, mentioned that he had taken a store nearly opposite his "old stand." By the fall of 1840 he could be "found back at his old stand in a new building since the fire," according to the *Wilmington Chronicle* of November 11, 1840.

About the middle of the century he entered the partnership of Brown & Anderson, which continued until the death of Anderson in 1871. Brown then conducted business under his own name until his death on October 15, 1872. Subsequently the business was known as Brown & Sons, and the firm consisted of his stepson, E. F. Story, and his son, L. S. F. Brown.

These five tablespoons all have the die mark of T. W. Brown in a rectangle with no accompanying marks. The tablespoon at top is rather uncharacteristic in that it is a fiddle with oval bowl but without shoulders. It measures 8⅞ inches and has the engraved initials *AAM*. In the center photograph is a pair of tablespoons in the same style but slightly different from each other in length, width of handle, and shape of bowl; one is engraved *Coxetter*, the other *R*. One has sugarloaf shoulders, the other flared. In the bottom photograph is a pair of spoons 8⅞ inches long, fiddleback with tipped ends and engraved *ES*, believed to be the initials of the original owner, Elizabeth (or Emma) Swann. Center and bottom photographs by Charles Clark.

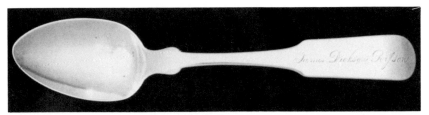

The spoon depicted above was given to the North Carolina Museum of History by the Poisson family. It has the die mark of T. W. Brown. Fiddleback in style, it is 7½ inches long and is engraved with the name of James Dickson Poisson, who was said to have been present at the death of Stonewall Jackson.

Especially lovely is this teaspoon because the "thread" embellishment is used on both front and back. The spoon's handle is tipped at the end, and this feature is emphasized by the "thread." In a private collection, this piece has an oval bowl and measures 5⅝ inches in length; it is marked T. W. BROWN in a rectangle.

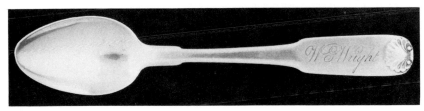

Slender, sleek, and uncharacteristic of T. W. Brown—but with the familiar T. W. BROWN die mark in a rectangle—is this elegant little dessertspoon 7¹⁄₁₆ inches long with straight shoulders, shell embellishment, and engraved W. G. Wright. (From a private collection.)

Brown's obituary pays tribute to his many "deeds of charity" and to his avid participation and high rank in the Order of the Freemasons. The Wilmington Order of the Knights Templars had occasion to befriend Mary Baker Eddy during the 1840s when she lived in Wilmington briefly with her first husband, a brickmason named George Washington Glover. Glover was a contractor and builder who had brought his young wife with him to Wilmington, where he intended to practice his profession. However, he died shortly after the move to North Carolina. Mrs. Glover (later Mrs. Eddy) did not remain; but several years after she moved away, she spoke with high regard of the Wilmington Masonic Order to Harriet Brown Huntington, daughter of Thomas W. Brown. The ladies met again in Amesbury, Massachusetts, where Mrs. Huntington was living at the time.[118]

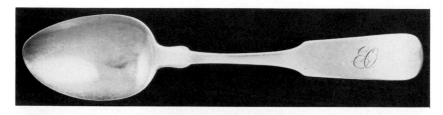

The mark of T. W. BROWN and additional marks of G&H in a lozenge, a circle, and the date 1848 in a diamond are found on this fiddle tablespoon. The spoon measures 8½ inches in length and is engraved *EO* in script on the handle. This piece, a family heirloom, is presently in a private collection. The G&H mark has been identified as one used by William Gale and [Nathaniel] Hayden. (Robert Alan Green, *Marks of American Silversmiths* [Harrison, N.Y.: By the author, 1977], 84, 128; Ralph M. Kovel and Terry H. Kovel, *A Directory of American Silver, Pewter and Silver Plate* [New York: Crown Publishers, eleventh printing, 1978], 106.)

A splendid private collection of T. W. Brown silver in fiddle style is this one, which includes two tablespoons (8½ inches long), a cream ladle (7¾ inches long), a teaspoon (5⅝ inches long), sugar tongs, and a butter knife. Photograph by Charles Clark.

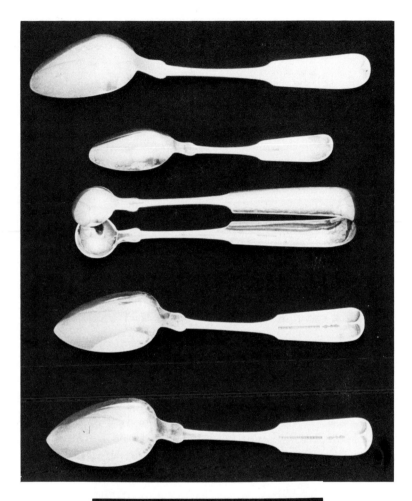

Another fine collection of T. W. Brown and Brown & Anderson silver is the one shown above. The five pieces in this collection include sugar tongs 6½ inches long and engraved *DMAC* in script (for Duncan and Mary Ann Cromartie, married in 1842), a teaspoon 5¾ inches long, a tablespoon 8½ inches long, and two dessertspoons 7 inches long. Four pieces have the additional marks found on some silver retailed by Brown: the date in a diamond, the center circle, and the G&H (Gale and Hayden).

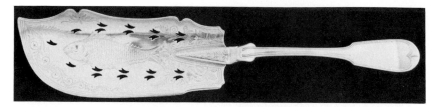

The fish slice pictured above has the mark of T. W. Brown. Its original owner has not been identified. The Museum of History Associates purchased the piece in 1983 for the collection of the North Carolina Museum of History. The handle is in a typical fiddle and thread style with a simulated tipped end, but the blade is quite unique with scroll and leaf ornamentation and a fish, complete with eye and scales, in the center.

BROWN & ANDERSON. The partnership of Thomas William Brown and William S. Anderson, in Wilmington, began about 1850 and was terminated by the death of Anderson on June 16, 1871.[119]

A handsome punch ladle in a classic fiddle style is this one marked BROWN & ANDERSON with three additional marks: G&S, a circle, and the date 1852 enclosed in a diamond. It measures 12¾ inches in length and is engraved *SER*. This family heirloom is in a private collection.

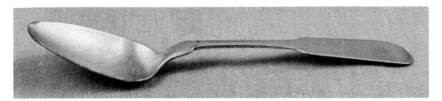

Tablespoons and a pap spoon exemplifying silver with the Brown & Anderson mark are shown above. All three have G&S in a lozenge, a circle, and the date 1852 in a diamond. (William Gale and John Stickler [New York] were partners ca. 1823, but the date 1852 does not coincide: one might conjecture that the S was for William Gale, Jr.; see Belden, *Marks of American Silversmiths*, 181, for William Gale & Son.) The tablespoon in the top photograph measures 8½ inches, has rounded shoulders, an oval bowl, and a tapered handle engraved *HSE*; the center spoon, of fiddle and thread design, also is 8½ inches long, has a simulated tipped handle, and is engraved *BS*, partly obliterated; the pap spoon is 6½ inches long, unengraved, has a handle almost straight, and rounded shoulders. The pap spoon is in the collection of the North Carolina Museum of History; the other two are from private collections. Center and bottom photographs by Charles Clark.

This cup and a collection of four teaspoons marked by BROWN & ANDER-
SON, with an accompanying mark of T.E. & Co., have been found in North
Carolina. Theodore Evans and John Cook used this mark, according to Dorothy
T. Rainwater, *Encyclopedia of American Silver Manufacturers* (New York:
Crown Publishers, 1975), 50, hereinafter cited as Rainwater, *Encyclopedia of
American Silver Manufacturers*. The beautiful cup, now on display in Liberty
Hall, has an overall textured pattern, a reeded trim at upper and lower rims, a
floral and scroll cartouche, and is engraved *Isham F. Hill / Apr 28, 1859 / T. F.
Hill Jr / Sept 28, 1931*. The teaspoons, 6 inches long and engraved *JRE*, were
originally owned by John and Rachel Everitte (m. 1829) and are presently in a
private collection.

These six fiddle tablespoons, with rounded shoulders, oval bowls, and tipped on the reverse of the handle, have the BROWN & ANDERSON mark with the date 1848 in a diamond, a circle, and the G&S. (From a private collection.)

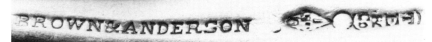

A BROWN & ANDERSON mark with a chevron and an unusual horse's head accompanied by the COIN designation (top) was found by Dr. Cutten on silver in the state. Additional pieces that have come to light have had combinations of the firm mark and those of other makers—G&H, T.E. & Co. Undoubtedly, the two men both made some silver and retailed pieces from other shops.

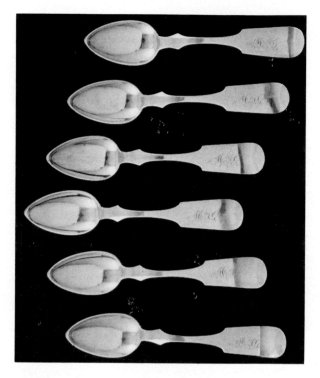

These six teaspoons, 5¾ inches long in a fiddleback style but with pointed shoulders and upturned handles ending in a blunted, triangular effect on the front, have posed a problem in identification. The marks—a horse's head, chevron, and COIN—are the only clues; they are not identical but quite similar to the symbols of one identifying mark used by Brown & Anderson. *MJG* is engraved on these spoons, which are privately owned.

EDMUND B. BURNHAM (d. 1822) was a member of the firm of Elliott & Burnham, which commenced business in January, 1821, in Salisbury. The partners were advertised as clock- and watchmakers from New York. Burnham's name, however, does not appear in New York City directories published between 1814 and 1821. Burnham died March 5, 1822, in Salisbury at the age of twenty-four. An obituary described him as a watchmaker and a native of Litchfield County, Connecticut.[120]

TURNER BURR was the subject of a death notice published in a Raleigh newspaper in 1810. The announcement describes Burr as a "Silversmith of Wilmington."[121] Nothing else is known about him.

ALEXANDER CAMPBELL (1775-1818). One Alexander Campbell is listed in the census of 1790 as head of a household in which there was one free white male over sixteen, five free white females, and one slave.[122] Whether or not this Alexander Campbell was a relative of the silversmith by that name has not been determined. On January 14, 1793, the would-be silversmith was apprenticed to Peter Strong, in Fayetteville, at the age of seventeen.[123] On May 12, 1798, he warned the public against the purchase of two notes of his that had been given to Thomas Green.[124] The following month he advertised himself as a jeweler who had taken a shop in Fayetteville recently occupied by Alexander Torrence, a saddler, where he intended carrying on the business of jewelry.[125] In 1818 a Raleigh newspaper announced the death, in Fayetteville on February 18, 1818, of "Mr. Alex Campbell, silversmith."[126]

JOHN CAMPBELL (1803-ca. 1857?) was born in Scotland[127] on May 6, 1803, and in September, 1818, was apprenticed to John Selph in Fayetteville, North Carolina.[128] Sometime in 1827 he became a member of the firm of Selph & Campbell.[129] After the dissolution of this partnership in 1829 he worked independently. On June 6, 1831, he advertised that he had lost the principal part of his tools in the fire [of May 27];[130] on May 1, 1832, he bought a house and lot "now occupied by said Campbell as a silversmith shop."[131] In 1834 he became a member of the firm of Campbell & Prior,[132] but this partnership lasted only two years. Burton believed that sometime ca. 1835 Campbell was operating a silversmith's shop in Cheraw, South Carolina, having moved there from Fayetteville.[133] Campbell's stay in Cheraw must have been brief, since on September 14, 1836, he advertised that he intended to move to Nashville, Tennessee, in a few weeks.[134] On May 25, 1838, "John Campbell, now of the State of Tennessee, but formerly of Fayetteville," sold to Warren Prior a house and lot "on the north side of Hay Street occupied and long known as a silversmith shop." The lot was 12½ feet fronting Hay Street and 84 feet deep.[135] To

Three spoons quite similar in style and with the J. CAMPBELL mark in a rectangle have been found in different provenances. All are fiddle in style, with a tipped end on the front side, oval pointed bowl, flared shoulders, and slender shaft. The teaspoon in the top photograph is 6 inches long and is engraved *RB*; it is in the collection of the North Carolina Museum of History, but its original owner has not been identified. The spoon in the center photograph is 6⅛ inches long, not engraved, and was found in the Asheville area. The spoon shown in the bottom photograph is unusual because it is marked BATTLE HOUSE, possibly indicating its use in the Battle House tavern, or wayside inn, in Mobile, Alabama. It was purchased in Austin, Texas, and is in a private collection.

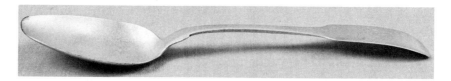

This tablespoon, 8¾ inches long and originally owned by Thomas G. Blewett, is on display at the North Carolina Museum of History. *Blewett* is engraved in script on the front, and a shell embellishment is used on the back of the oval bowl, as shown in the photograph at left. The mark used by Campbell on this spoon is J·CAMPBELL in a rectangle—a pellet, instead of a period, following the J.

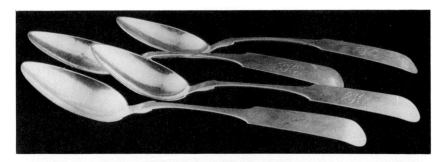

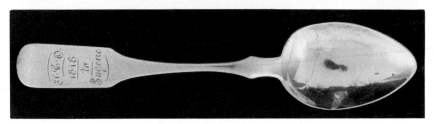

The four tablespoons shown in the photograph at top are from a private collection but were purchased, not inherited, by the present owners. They are 8¾ inches long and engraved simply *K* in script. Distinguishing features of the dessert- (or memorial) spoon in the bottom photograph are the pointed shoulders and the engraving *F.C.O./1818/to/Eugene*. If this spoon was made in 1818, as has been presumed, it would have been during the first year of Campbell's apprenticeship to John Selph. The original owners have not been identified; the spoon was acquired by purchase.

satisfy a judgment of John Campbell against the estate of John Selph, the sheriff sold land to John M. Beasley on May 17, 1843.[136]

From 1836 until 1857 Campbell presumably operated his shop in Nashville, Tennessee, on the southeast corner of Public Square, Union Street. His partners at various times included George Washington Donigan, —— Stevens, and John Peabody.[137]

CAMPBELL & PRIOR (1834-1836). John Campbell and Warren Prior, in Fayetteville. Announcement of the partnership was made on June 2, 1834,[138] and of its dissolution on April 1, 1836.[139]

THOMAS L. CAMPBELL (d. 1810). An advertisement in a Raleigh newspaper in 1809 announced that Campbell "has taken the House lately occupied by Mr. Thomas D. Burch, nearly oposite Mr. Boylan's Printing-Office, in which he intends carrying on the Silver & Goldsmith's Business, in all its various branches. . . ."[140] Campbell's death on February 25, 1810, was noted by the Raleigh newspapers.[141]

ROBERT CARSAN (CARSON?). In the May 26, 1810, issue of the New Bern *Federal Republican* (hereinafter cited as *Federal Republican*), this man described himself as a "Clock and Watch Maker" who had "removed to the house in middle-street adjoining Mr. Wm. Trippe's Taylor Shop, where he intends carrying on the above business in all its branches." He added, "All orders from the country will be strictly attended to."

ANTHONY CASTILE. In the records of the General Court for September, 1754, is a case in which Governor Arthur Dobbs brought suit against Anthony Castile of Chowan County (General Court Civil Papers: 1746-1754, State Archives). Dobbs sought compensation from Castile for enticing away from him a servant named Rosier. In this document is a reference to Castile as a silversmith: "Anthony Castile late of Chowan County in the Province afs. [aforesaid], Silversmith was attached to answer Arthur Dobbs Esquire on a Plea of Trespass on the case. . . ." Again, in the warrant to be served by the sheriff, Castile is described as a silversmith and is ordered to appear "before our Chief Justice, and his Associates, at the General Court, to be held for our said Province, at the Court-house in Newbern, on the Second Tuesday in September next; then and there to answer Arthur Dobbs Esquire on a plea of Trespass on the Case Damage of thirty pounds sterling money of Great Britain."

The case was called (since it is on the calendar in the appearance docket, 1754-1755); but apparently Anthony Castile did not appear, and the final disposition of the case could not be determined from available sources.

CHARLES CLARK. On January 4, 1821, he advertised that all persons having demands against Charles Clark or Clark & Turner of Fayetteville should present them.[142] In May, 1822, he moved his business to the store on Hay Street formerly occupied by Mrs. Rhodes,[143] and on July 22, 1823, he sold his stock in trade to William Widdifield, who had superintended the establishment for three years.[144] Eight days later he signed the marriage bond when Widdifield was married.[145]

CLARK & TURNER. Charles Clark and Franklin Turner were operating stores at Fayetteville and Wadesboro, 1820-1823.[146] William Widdifield superintended the Fayetteville store before he acquired the business.[147]

JOHN CLELAND (CLEALAND, CLALAND, CLAYLAND). The name of John Cleland first appeared in the records when he was on the grand jury list for Chowan County in the year 1743; he also served in this capacity in 1745, 1750, and 1754.[148] In 1753 he was on the venire for the petit jury.[149] He is listed as master of a family in 1747 and 1748,[150] and his name is on a list of tithables in 1746, 1749, and 1753.[151] On October 10, 1752, a bond was filed for his marriage to Rebeckah Wilkins.[152] Moses Wellwood petitioned the court on January 16, 1752, saying that ten months before, he had bound his son,

John Wellwood to John Cleland of Edenton, silversmith, as an aprintice to learn the art and misterey of a silversmith, which he the said Cleland now foloweth; and that the said Cleland has neglected eather to teach his said aprintice, or to find or provide for him sufficient Victuals or Lodging, and that the said Cleland hath unlawfully Beat and evely Intreat his said aprintice. . . .[153]

It should be noted that Moses Wellwood was a carpenter with a somewhat unenviable record and that twice in 1752 he was brought before the court on charges of trespass.[154]

Cleland was a witness in the case of *Smith* v. *Arnall* on October 18, 1753.[155] During that same month John Cooper of

The document reproduced above is the apprenticeship paper that bound John Wellwood to "John Cleland of Edenton Silver Smith As an Aprintice, to learn the art and Misterey of a Silver Smith, which he the said Cleland now foloweth." (Chowan County Papers, VI, 21, State Archives.)

Edenton petitioned the court "to compel John Clayland, administrator of the estate of Humphrey Robinson, late of Edenton, to deliver to him all the blacksmith's tools belonging to the deceased and bequeathed by him to Cooper."[156] But more serious trouble was in store: William Luten complained that John Cleland on March 1, 1757, shot a Negro slave of Luten's named Caesar, wounding him so that he was useless for seven months and was handicapped thereafter. Besides the loss of the slave's labor there were surgeon's fees and other expenses. On October 6, 1757, the jury awarded Luten damages of £30 proclamation money.[157] Cleland and Thos. Lexon gave Colonel William Mackay a joint note for £10 payable in six months with lawful interest. This was dated "Terrell [Tyrrell] County, Oct. 8, 1762."[158] On December 23, 1769, an execution was issued against John "Clealand" to satisfy a judgment of George Laubinger. On the reverse side is the notation "Taken and put in Jale and swore out so says Charles Houghton 1770."[159] In a list of taxable property taken July 24, 1779, is the name of "John McClealand, £4.17 money."[160] The name is spelled Cleland, Clealand, Claland, Clayland.

MATTHEW CLUFF (d. 1845). In 1803 Matthew Cluff was a member of the firm of Ott & Cluff in Norfolk, Virginia.[161] By 1806 the partnership had been dissolved, and in 1811 and 1812 Cluff was advertising for sale an assortment of items—jewelry, shoes, and wearing apparel.[162] In 1814 he was still advertising

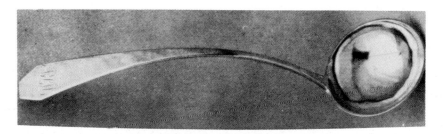

This coffin-end punch ladle with the mark of Matthew Cluff has an additional mark of NORFOLK, indicating that this piece was made during Cluff's residency in that city. No silver made by Cluff during his years in Elizabeth City has been located. Photograph reproduced from Cutten, *The Silversmiths of Virginia*, 90.

dry goods, military goods, clothing, and bonnets, but no jewelry.[163] Sometime in the fall or winter of 1816 Cluff moved to Elizabeth City. Of Cluff's years in Elizabeth City Cutten says:

Late in the year 1816, Cluff moved to Elizabeth City, N.C., and in December bought from Samuel Matthews and Thomas Vaughn, all of Elizabeth City, "a certain message [sic] and a lot of ground in said town." On April 3, 1817 Henry Brown of Norfolk gave a deed of trust of certain household goods to George Ott for the benefit of Matthew Cluff, and about the same time two houses were offered for rent in Elizabeth City, for particulars of which application could be made to Matthew Cluff of Elizabeth City or to George Ott of Norfolk. In 1819 Thomas C. Martin of Elizabeth City sold to Mary C. Cluff, a messuage of ground for $2,500, Matthew Cluff being a witness. Apparently this was not Cluff's wife, for she is not mentioned in the deeds he granted, or in his will. In 1826 Matthew Cluff gave a deed of emancipation whereby a negro slave named Mary, which he bought two weeks before from Charles Branda, was freed. Branda and George Ott, both silversmiths, were witnesses.

Cluff was involved in other real estate and legal transactions ending in his will which was presented at the June term of the court in 1845. Evidently he had no family. In a codicil he gave "to William Allen the profits that have been made in the store during the time he has been my agent or clerk." It seems evident he conducted some kind of a store in Elizabeth City, but we are not sure that it was a silversmith or jewelry store.[164]

_____ COCKE. An item found in the Cameron Family Papers indicates that Richard Bennehan gave a "Mr. Cocke" 45 silver dollars in May, 1776, with which to make various pieces of flat silver: one dozen tablespoons, one dozen teaspoons, four salt spoons, one soup spoon (probably a ladle).[165]

AARON COLEMAN (d. 1797) practiced his trade in Edgecombe County.[166] He probably was the son of Charles Coleman, Jr., who died in 1761. Although he had little education, Aaron Coleman owned a plantation and had three slaves. By his will of July 6, 1796, he left his silversmith's tools to Bartholomew Brown, a kinsman of his wife, Hardee Coleman. Coleman's widow inherited one silver tankard, six silver spoons, and twelve teaspoons, as well as other items. When she died in October, 1807, the widow left one pair of silver shoe buckles, two rings, one gold brooch, and one pair of gold sleeve buttons. Apparently, no children survived.

JOHN COPELAND (d. 1773). Virtually his sole claim to repute as a silversmith is represented by a surviving toddy ladle and a bill (fortunately preserved) that he rendered to Thomas Jones late in 1769.[167] Apart from these items, there is an undated record that St. Paul's Parish ran survey lines between Copeland's property and that of James White, presumably in Edenton, and that both men were present and in agreement with the action taken.[168] In his will, dated April 7, 1773, Copeland left all his property to his wife, Sarah, and appointed her as executrix.[169] His estate papers indicate that he was affluent: in addition to fine furniture, books, flat silver, and slaves, the inventory of his estate included silversmith's tools and 40 pounds of silver and gold.[170]

This photograph of a toddy ladle made by John Copeland and owned in 1948 by Mrs. John G. Wood of Edenton is reproduced from Cutten's *The Silversmiths of North Carolina*, first edition, 28.

The itemized bill from John Copeland pictured above includes services which indicate that he was a versatile silversmith. (Account of Thomas Jones with John Copeland, Chowan County Miscellaneous Papers, State Archives.)

JAMES CRAVEY (MACRAVEY; d. 1768). Only one item found in the Edgecombe County estates records suggests that this man may have been involved with silversmithing: he owned "silversmith's instruments" and a "peace of paper with silver dust."[171]

NATHANIEL DANA. In the *Wilmington Gazette* of December 1, 1807, "Nathaniel Dana, Watch-Maker," advertised "All kinds of gold and silver-smith's work done in a neat manner." On June 28 and August 9, 1808, the following advertisement appeared in the *Wilmington Gazette*:

> [Nathaniel Dana], Watch maker, Goldsmith, and Jeweller, . . . Respectfully informs the inhabitants of Wilmington and its vicinity, that he continues to carry on his business at his old stand at the corner of Dock and Front Streets, where all kinds of Gold and Silver work are made and repaired in the neatest manner, and warranted to be the best Gold and Silver. . . . One dollar and twelve and a half cents will be given for old Silver per ounce.

Dana added that because he was being "called upon by his creditors, for payments, he is under the necessity of requesting all who are indebted to him to call and settle their accounts."

On June 20, 1809, the following notice appeared in the Wilmington *True Republican or North Carolina Whig*: "Two apprentices Wanted, to the Gold and Silver Smith's business; Who will also be taught the Knowledge of Watch-repairing, if required. N. Dana." During the following year, 1810, an item dated June 19 and appearing in the *Wilmington Gazette* of that date stated: "N. Dana requests those who have left work to be done to call for it at Mr. Dick's Hotel."

DANIEL (a slave; w. ca. 1791). Daniel, a blacksmith, silversmith, and cooper, ran away from Abraham Taylor of Bertie County in 1791. Daniel could "read some in print." He took several suits of clothes and "silversmith tools" when he escaped, according to the Edenton *State Gazette of North Carolina* (April 8, 1791).[172]

GEORGE C. DANIEL. On March 11, 1829, he informed the inhabitants of Pasquotank County that he had opened a shop next door to Mr. Asa McCoy's in Elizabeth City for the purpose of carrying on the business of watchmaking and clockmaking. Two years later he had moved to Halifax and had employed a watchmaker. He made spoons to order.[173]

JOHN DAUGHTERY (ca. 1783—).[174] A notice of army deserters published in several newspapers in 1815 suggests that this man was a silversmith:

DESERTERS—The following soldiers of the 3rd Regiment of Riflemen are hereby published as Deserters. . . .

CAPT. CAMPBELL'S COMPANY

John Daughtery, born in Northampton county, N.C., aged 28 years, 5 feet 9½ inches high, ruddy complexion, blue eyes, dark hair, and by occupation a silversmith, latterly accustomed to the sea. He is remarkable for his extreme silence and downcast appearance, addicted to intoxication, and when drunk is both sullen and stupid—deserted from Rowan County, N.C. 20th November, 1814. . . .[175]

This is likely John Daughtery II, since an earlier John Daughtery, who died ca. 1810, had silversmith's tools listed in his estate inventory. This man could have been the father of the deserter John. The inventory listed "10 tablespoons . . . 1 pair bellows, silversmiths tools, two gimblets, two hammers. . . ." The administrator of the estate was William Daughtery. Provision was made for the widow, Sarah.[176] William, no doubt a relative of both John Daughtery the deserter and the elder John, died ca. 1815. When William's estate was sold on June 19, 1815, the inventory included "1 box Silversmiths tools" sold to Jesse Smith, Sr.[177] Nothing indicates that William was a silversmith; it seems likely that the tools sold to Smith were the same tools mentioned in the John Daughtery inventory. A record of accounts kept by the guardians of Penelope and Littleberry Daughtery, "orphans of John Daughtry," can be found in Northampton County Guardians and Other Fiduciary Accounts 1811-1818, p. 323, June court, 1817, State Archives.

JOHN DAVENPORT (fl. 1731-1740). Presumably born, bred, and trained to the craft of a silversmith in London, Davenport appears to have been one of the several artisans encouraged by Governor George Burrington to settle at Cape Fear as part of the governor's program to develop that portion of North Carolina. There are references in the New Hanover County and the General Court records to John Davenport of Cape Fear as early as October, 1731. On May 20, 1734, Davenport presented to a New Hanover County merchant a bill of exchange for £20 sterling drawn on a London goldsmith named Isaac Davenport. The assumption is that the two were close kinsmen. Isaac, however, refused to honor John's bill. Thereupon, the firm of Reynolds and Hepburn sued to recover that amount in the

General Court of North Carolina in July, 1736, and simultaneously brought suit against John Davenport, silversmith, in order to collect an outstanding account of £173 13s. 0d. for debts incurred by Davenport at Brunswick Town. The only other references to Davenport in the records of the colony relate to additional suits for debt or to wills and deeds that he witnessed. A lawsuit of October, 1736, locates Davenport at Wilmington (then called Newton). By September 19, 1740, he had left Wilmington and North Carolina, according to an entry in the New Hanover County court minutes of that date. There are no known examples of Davenport's work.

The foregoing sketch is based on information found in the following sources: General Court Civil Papers, 1720-1745; will of Charles Milliard, 1735, Secretary of State Records, Wills, 1663-1790; New Hanover County Deed Book AB, pages 41, 50, 58, 59, 60, 76, 79, 80, 96, 100, 133; New Hanover County Minutes of the Court of Pleas and Quarter Sessions, September 19, 1740—all in State Archives. (George Stevenson, researcher.)

DAVID DAVIES (DAVIS; Mecklenburg County, w. 1784-1792). On November 30, 1791, John Davies swore to the validity of his account against the estate of Alexander Lewis. He acknowledged payment of the account on July 21, 1792. The itemized bill indicates that Davies distilled rum and did blacksmithing and harness making. In addition, there are two charges for making silver items in 1784—"one Silver Shoe Buckle" by Son[?] David and "a silver stock Buckle by Son[?] David."[178]

JOHN DAVIS (Carteret County, w. 1750s). In Craven County Deeds, Book 5, p. 178, John Davis is referred to as a silversmith. He is also mentioned in the will of Ann Winwright of Beaufort, North Carolina. The will, dated March 7, 1751/52, mentions "the silver in the hand of John Davis to be made in 2 large silver spoons." One spoon was to go to Sarah Benners [Banners] and one to Penelope Lovick.[179]

RILEY A. DAVIS notified the people of New Bern on January 15, 1850, that he had taken a stand opposite the Washington Hotel, where he was prepared to do all kinds of work as a clockmaker, watchmaker, and jeweler.[180]

EDWARD CORNWALLIS DEBRUHL (EDWARD CORN-WALLACE DEBRULE; w. 1777-1784). In a deed dated April 24, 1784, Edward Cornwallace Debrule, identified as a silversmith of Duplin County, sold to John Matchet for £104 two tracts of land (100 acres in each) in Onslow County on New River.[181] This in all probability was the Edward Cornwallis Debruhl who had been involved in a counterfeiting case in 1777. The case concerned the counterfeiting of bills of credit in the District of Edenton and is described in detail in a letter from Judge Samuel Spencer to Governor Richard Caswell, June 1, 1777, recorded in the governor's letter book, I, and reproduced in Clark, *State Records*, XI, 481-482.

CATON DECOSTA. In a Raleigh paper of June 1, 1809, Decosta claimed that he worked in the shop of Jehu Scott for two or three years prior to going into business for himself:

CATON DECOSTA

Jeweller & Silver-Smith, from Europe, Informs the Public, that he has commenced business for *himself* in Raleigh, where he solicts patronage.—Having acquired a thorough knowledge of his business, under the first masters in Europe, and having considerable experience in some of the principal Work-shops in America, he is confident in being able to give satisfaction to those who may employ him. For specimens of his skill he refers to the *difficult*, *fine*, and *elegant* work which has been done for two or three years past in Mr. Jehu Scott's shop in this city, which has been done by C. D.

As the advertiser is master of the business he professes, he deems it unnecessary to enumerate the kinds of work which he will undertake. All Gold and Silver, table beaufet [*sic*] furniture, Ladies ornaments, and every thing appertaining to his business will be neatly and expeditiously executed, and on *reasonable* terms.

Raleigh, June 1, 1809

N. B. Cash given for old Gold and Silver[182]

DE ST. LEGER. In New Bern, on April 15, 1790, he removed to a house on Pollock Street and continued the watchmaking business in all its branches.[183]

JOHN DICKEY (DICKSY, DUKEY; d. 1808). Mrs. Margaret D. Choate of Danville, Virginia, a descendant of John Dickey, has provided information that her Rowan County ancestor was by trade a silversmith. Dickey is included in Francis B. Heitman's *Historical Register of Officers of the Continental Army during the War of the Revolution, April, 1775, to December,*

1783 (Washington, D.C.: N.p., 1914; reprinted Baltimore: Genealogical Publishing Company, 1973), 197, and in a *Roster of Soldiers from North Carolina in the American Revolution* (Durham: Seeman Press for the North Carolina Daughters of the American Revolution; reprinted Baltimore: Genealogical Publishing Company, 1967), 33. He was a captain in the North Carolina militia from 1779 to 1781. Captain Dickey, who had been granted land in Rowan County in 1775, served as executor of the will of Lieutenant Colonel William L. Davidson and undertook other civic responsibilities.[184]

A. M. DORET. Whether or not Doret resided in Charlotte for any length of time is not known. He was at Boyd's Hotel, apparently, when the following item appeared—leading to the conjecture that he was only passing through the town:

> To Miners and others, A. M. Doret, of New-York, takes this method to inform the public, and those having Gold in the impure state, that he is capable to determine the purity of the same by the process of quartation on a small scale. He will take 12 grains from any quantity, and by the process of quartation determine the value of the whole amount of gold. If sufficient encouragement is received, he will erect the necessary apparatus for carrying on the business more largely, when he will be enabled to free any quantity of gold from the baser metals. In connection with the same, he will also make and repair Gold and Silver Watch Cases, &c.
> At present, he can be found at his room, at Boyd's Hotel.[185]

WILLIAM DRAKE (b. 1767). On May 27, 1783, James Darnal was apprenticed to William Drake to learn the silversmith's trade.[186] Presumably, Drake lived in Edgecombe County. This apprentice may have been the James Darnal of Georgetown District, Prince George's Parish, who was listed in the South Carolina census of 1790.[187] He is not included by E. Milby Burton as a silversmith in South Carolina.

IMMANUEL DRESEN (b. 1754). In the minutes of the *Aufseher Collegium*, Salem, for February 18, 1783, there is an item about Immanuel Dresen, who had asked to become a resident after working in Salem for two years. "From his father he learned the trade of a silversmith. He also worked as a watchmaker."[188]

GEORGE C. DUFF. In the Philadelphia city directory for 1837 Duff was listed as a watchmaker. On May 5, 1846, he advertised watches, chains, pencil cases, and the like in New

Bern.[189] Two years later he announced his removal to a location one door from the corner of Pollock and Middle streets, where he offered to repair and clean watches, clocks, and jewelry. He claimed a thorough knowledge of the business in all its branches.[190]

JOHN BAPTISTE DUMOUTET (DOUMOTET, DU-MONTET, DUMORTE, DOUMOUET, DUMONTET; 1761-1813). There is no evidence to indicate that Dumoutet was ever a resident of Raleigh or any other place in North Carolina, but he did advertise in the Raleigh *Minerva* of December 3, 1804, and evidently had a shop or some arrangement for soliciting customers in the area. Perhaps he was a traveling salesman.

J. B. DUMOUTET, jeweler from Philadelphia next door to S. Wheaton's shop. Informs customers that he has an elegant assortment in the watchmakers and his own line. Intends to leave the city next Tuesday. Orders thankfully received and executed in the best manner.

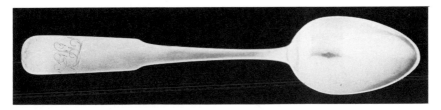

Pictured above is an example of a teaspoon that might have been ordered by customers in the Raleigh area from John Baptiste Dumoutet. It is 6 inches long, has an oval pointed bowl, no shoulders, and is engraved *EL* in script. On the back is the maker's mark DUMOUTET within a serpentine banner.

E. Milby Burton in *South Carolina Silversmiths* (pp. 49-50) says that Dumoutet, born in Cher, France, worked first in Philadelphia but was established in Charleston as a jeweler in 1802 and that by 1806 was listed as a goldsmith and jeweler. Dumoutet died in Philadelphia on July 20, 1813, and his business in Charleston was carried on by his wife, Elizabeth. A few pieces of silver made by Dumoutet have come to light in both South Carolina and North Carolina.

STEPHEN DUNN. George Dunn was apprenticed to Stephen Dunn on September 14, 1786, to learn the goldsmith's trade.[191] Dunn apparently lived in Craven County.

BERNARD DUPUY. Dupuy, primarily a silversmith, must have been established in his trade in Raleigh prior to autumn, 1827, since the *Raleigh Register* for October 12, 1827, mentions that "He [Dupuy] hopes that by his punctual and assiduous

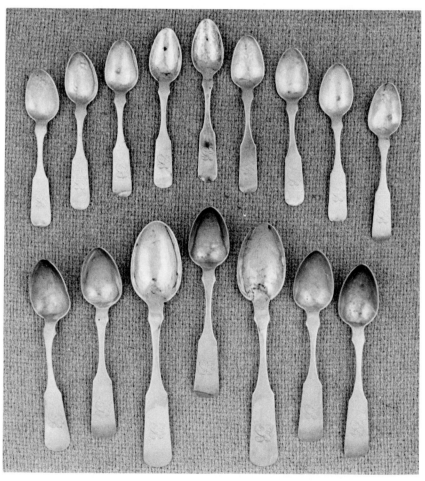

This remarkable private collection of Bernard Dupuy silver consists of nine teaspoons, two tablespoons, and five dessertspoons. According to family tradition, the first owner was Bennett Taylor Blake, who served on the first board of trustees of Greensboro Female College; he was also a member of the faculty. The Reverend Mr. Blake had the flatware made from Mexican silver. The initial *B* in script is engraved on the handle of each piece.

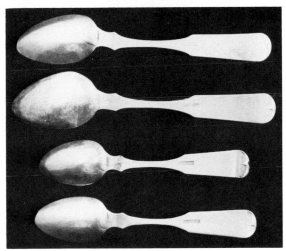

Since the publication in 1973 of the first revised edition of *Silversmiths of North Carolina*, four additional pieces of the Blake Collection have come to light. All the pieces in this important collection have the B.DUPUY mark in a scalloped rectangle. The tablespoons are 8⅝ inches long, the dessertspoons 6⅞ inches long, and the teaspoons 5½ inches long. They are fiddle in style, have oval bowls with short drops, pointed shoulders, and handles with tipped backs.

attention to business to merit a continuance of that liberal encouragement he has received since he commenced business." His advertisements appeared during the following year, 1828.[192] On June 22, 1833, he advertised that he had again been burned out but had reopened his store two doors below the post office.[193] He moved his location in 1835[194] and on November 14,

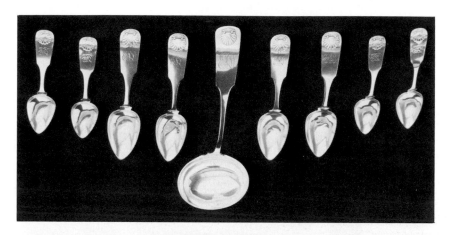

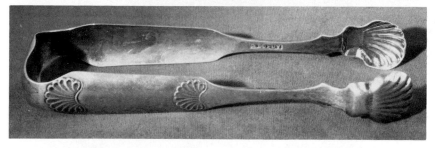

Handsome indeed is Dupuy silver with shell motif. The collection of four tablespoons, four dessertspoons, and a punch ladle pictured in the photograph at top is in the collection of the North Carolina Museum of History. The dessertspoons are classic fiddle distinguished by the shell, with large, pointed shoulders, oval bowls, and engraved *ELD*; each is 7 inches long with a bowl 1¾ inches long. The four tablespoons are 9 inches long and have bowls 1¾ inches in length. The ladle is 13¼ inches long with a bowl 4½ inches across. The pieces shown in the center and bottom photographs are in private collections.

1836, announced his "SPLENDID NEW STORE!!" at 10 Fayetteville Street.[195] He advertised all kinds of gold and silver work manufactured to any pattern. He continued his business until November 15, 1843, when he sold it to C. B. Root, who had worked for him for five years.[196] A deed dated November 16, 1844, designated Dupuy as a citizen of Raleigh,[197] but another

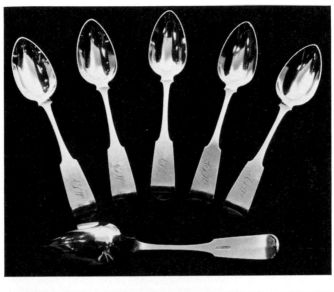

Other fine pieces of Dupuy silver include the six tablespoons shown above (top). Nine inches long, they have pointed, oval bowls with drop measuring 3 inches and downturned, tipped handles engraved *ATW* in script. The cream ladle (center), in perfect condition, is 6½ inches overall with a bowl 3¾ inches long and 1¾ inches across. The baby (or memorial) spoons (bottom) were originally in the Davenport family and are family heirlooms; they are 5⅜ inches long and are engraved *IRD* in a feathered script. All pieces shown on this page are marked B.DUPUY in a scalloped rectangle.

A seal executed for the Hertford County Court of Equity by Bernard Dupuy is pictured above. (From the files of MESDA; used by permission.)

dated June 16, 1847, referred to him as a citizen of Philadelphia.[198] He may have come from Philadelphia, where the name Dupuy was not uncommon.

Research on the Polk family by Dr. Jerry Cross, researcher on the staff of the Division of Archives and History, Raleigh, has also brought to light information about Bernard Dupuy. Dr. Cross writes:

In 1836 a portion of Lot 162 in the Raleigh town plan was sold to Sarah Polk by William and Mary J. White. Sarah was the daughter of Col. William Polk and sometime between 1836 and 1847 married Bernard Dupuy. Dupuy sold the property to William Thompson on June 16, 1847. At that time the Dupuys were residing in Philadelphia. Part of the deed reads as follows:

Beginning at the North West corner of the said Bernard Duprees [sic] House now occupied by Charles B. Root as a Jewelry Store. . . .

It is interesting to note that Root occupied the same house as Dupuy; the house also doubled as the silversmith and jewelry shop. Dupuy built his house on a section that he bought from Rufus Haywood in 1832. This portion adjoined that which he acquired through his marriage to Sarah Polk. Root rented the house for several years before purchasing it from Dupuy in 1853. He resided there for about thirteen years and appears to have moved about the time he became president of the Raleigh Gas Company.

I did not find an actual record of Dupuy's marriage to Sarah Polk, but the circumstantial evidence is so strong that I am convinced that such a wedding did take place. I have all the documentation including maps, wills, deeds, etc. The exact location of Dupuy's house and shop on Fayetteville Street can also be pinpointed.[199]

An incident involving Dupuy occurred in 1831 when the State Capitol burned. Dupuy was credited with being one of several men who saved the famous Sully portrait of George Washington that hung in the building.[200]

Rare in North Carolina is a piece of hollow ware such as this small footed tray, or salver, struck twice on the back with the mark B.DUPUY within a straight rectangle flanked by an eagle at each end. The piece is 14 inches overall with an elaborate, raised rim banded by floral and foliage repoussé. It has cast handles. In the center is a wreath of flowers, very simply executed, with *WLP* (William Lyon Polk?) engraved in script. At a later date was added *Presented to/Frank Lyon Polk/by/Troop "A" U.S. Volunteers/January 27th 1908.* In the center of the back is the family name *Polk.* (From a private collection.)

This handsome cann with the mark of Bernard Dupuy was purchased in 1982 by the Museum of History Associates and is now in the collection of the North Carolina Museum of History. The cann is distinguished by a flared base embellished with a low relief floral and fruit design and a bulbous body tapering to a wide mouth with an applied banding that repeats the design of the base. The scrolled handle has an acanthus leaf thumb grip. Dimensions of the cann are: width, 15.5 cm.; height, 14.9 cm.; diameter of base, 8.3 cm.

BENJAMIN EASTMAN (EASMAN) enlisted on July 21, 1777, for three years in Gregory's Company, Tenth Regiment, North Carolina Militia; he was a sergeant in June, 1778, and a private on November 7, 1778.[201] Benj. Eastman received a grant of land on December 18, 1783, that consisted of 319½ acres in Pasquotank County.[202] On March 21, 1787, in Pasquotank County he accepted Benjamin Ward, aged ten years, orphan of Thomas Ward, as an apprentice to the art of a silversmith.[203] In the census of 1790, as in the land grant, his name is spelled "Easman."[204]

JOHANN LUDWIG EBERHARDT (1758-1839) was born on May 17 at Stadtilm in Thuringia, southeast Germany.[205] When he was fourteen he began his study of clockmaking with his father, Johann Gottfried Eberhardt, who sometimes took his family with him when he traveled about repairing clocks in the towns and castles of the region. From 1783 until 1788 Johann Ludwig worked in the Moravian community of Gnadau and then stayed for almost a year at Zeist, where he probably learned about clockmaking, silversmithing, and watch repairing.[206] For several years he worked in southeast Germany and in 1798 became master of the Single Brothers' clockmaking shop at Gnadenfeld in Silesia. During the following year he received and accepted an invitation to become clockmaker at Salem, North Carolina.[207] When he arrived in Salem he was expected to make "watchglasses at a lower price" and "He also thinks to make a supply of silverware. . . ." It was arranged for him to work in Christoph Vogler's gunsmith shop until he was well enough established to devote his full time to his clock, watch, and silversmith work.[208] On June 2, 1800, Eberhardt married Julianna Michel; the couple had four children— Carolina, Lewis Ferdinand (who also became a clockmaker), Christian Thomas (who died in childhood), and Carl Theodore.[209]

Eberhardt's chief interest was clocks, not silversmithing, and no silver has been found that can be attributed to him. His clocks, on the other hand, were superb. Nevertheless, he displayed an interest in silversmithing by requesting in October, 1801, that he be given responsibility for the sale of silverware; and there is a record of his selling a tablespoon for $4.00 in 1804.[210] In addition, he protested when John Vogler became a competitor in silversmithing. The minutes of the *Aufseher Collegium* for July 15, 1806, record:

Br. Eberhardt sends word that the single Br. John Vogler is making silverware and repairing clocks, and that this work rightly belongs to him and he wishes the congregation boards to forbid Vogler to do it. Against Br. Eberhardt it is noted that he does not do either as well as Vogler: also that it is often impossible to get the work done by him; also that his charges are too high. The Collegium thinks that Br. Vogler may be allowed to make silverware and repair clocks in addition to his regular craft.[211]

ALEXANDER PERRY ECKEL (1821-1906) was born in Jefferson County, Tennessee, January 10, 1821, and moved to Greensboro, North Carolina, from Front Royal, Virginia.[212] On April 12, 1845, he advertised that he had taken a house on North Street, nearly opposite McAdoo & Scott, which he had fitted up for the purpose of carrying on the clock, watch, and jewelry business, of which he had a thorough knowledge.[213] He lived in Greensboro for the remainder of his life. In 1847 he married Mary E. Hill.[214] In 1860 Eckel became the second mayor of Greensboro, and he was a justice of the peace for over forty years. He was identified with many progressive business interests and was a prominent member of the Methodist church. According to tradition, some of the treasure of the Confederacy was buried on his property and thereby escaped confiscation by Federal authorities; it was subsequently returned to Confederate officers. Eckel died in Greensboro on December 17, 1906.[215]

ZEBULON ELLIOTT was listed in New York City directories as a watchmaker from 1814 to 1821, and in 1821 he was a member of the firm of Elliott & Burnham, Salisbury, North Carolina.[216]

This tablespoon by Zebulon Elliott, 8¾ inches in length and a modified fiddle in style, is on display at the North Carolina Museum of History. It has an oval bowl, no shoulders, and is engraved *HTH*.

ELLIOTT & BURNHAM. Members of this Salisbury firm were Zebulon Elliott and Edmund B. Burnham. On January 2, 1821, they advertised as clockmakers and watchmakers from New York who were starting in business a few doors from the courthouse on Main Street. They also advertised silverware.[217]

ISAAC EMMONS (d. ca. 1852) lived on Mulberry Creek in Caldwell (now Burke) County. He is known to have made spoons at Walnut Grove, one of the oldest homes in North Carolina.[218] Emmons is the subject of Chapter XI, "Emmons, the Silversmith" (pp. 91-94), in W. W. Scott's *Annals of Caldwell County.* "As side crop to his farming," Scott wrote, Emmons "did a little silversmithing for his neighbors, in which art he was quite . . . adept in a small way."[219] Robert Glass, quoted at length by the author of the sketch, said that Emmons was in the county prior to 1850 and

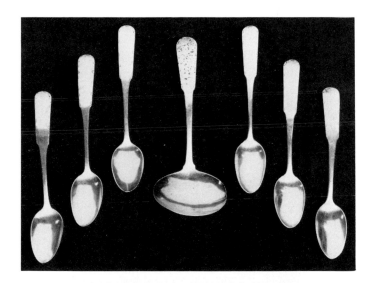

A unique Emmons collection consists of six berry spoons and a cream ladle. The spoons are 5¼ inches long in a modified fiddle without shoulders and drop. The bowl is oval, the stem slender. The small ladle is 5⁷⁄₁₆ inches long with a bowl 2¹³⁄₁₆ inches long and 1¹¹⁄₁₆ inches in width. Shown in the bottom photograph is an enlargement of the crude but charming decoration used on all the pieces. The private collection came to light in the provenance of the maker.

bought the Reuben Coffey farm. . . . [H]e and his wife died on Mulberry; he had some children . . .; he also owned some slaves. He was a silversmith and I [Glass] have some spoons he made for my grandmother [Eliza Dickson (Mrs. Moses T.) Abernathy] and one Mrs. Emmons gave to her; they are marked "IE" on the handle.[220]

The census of 1850 describes Emmons as eighty-five years of age and married, a native of New Jersey, and the owner of real estate valued at $700; his occupation is shown as "farmer." His wife, Mary Emmons, is described as forty-five years of age and a native of Virginia.[221] Emmons's estate inventory included "Silversmith Tools" bought by Jessey Gragg on February 14, 1852, for $1.80.[222] The inventory was filed April 27, 1852; the executor was Charles Emmons.

THOMAS EMOND. Emond had migrated from Edinburgh to Petersburg, Virginia, by 1802. On September 3, 1806, he informed the public that he had started business in Raleigh.[223] The same year, when the Presbyterian church was formed in Raleigh, he was one of three elders chosen.[224] In 1811 he was selected one of the captains of the watch.[225] On December 18, 1812, he advertised that he had resided longer in the city than anyone who followed his line of business.[226] According to the Orange County court minutes of February 4, 1812, Charles Henry Collier was bound as an apprentice to Emond. Emond offered for sale "one likely young negro woman" on February 19, 1813, "to someone who is accustomed to treat negroes well."[227] In August, 1816, he accepted Stephen Pilly, an orphan aged twelve, as an apprentice to be taught the trade of silversmith,[228] and the same year he served as one of two executors of the will of George Hall.[229] From 1816 to 1819 he was involved in several lawsuits, instigated principally by him for the collection of bills.[230] He advertised gold and silver work regularly through the year, and in 1817 he offered for sale his new frame house and several other pieces of property.[231] In a deed dated August 13, 1821, he is referred to as a citizen of Raleigh;[232] and on November 21, 1821, John W. Thomas obtained a judgment against him, which he appealed.[233] Emond apparently moved from Raleigh about this time, as no further record of him has been found.

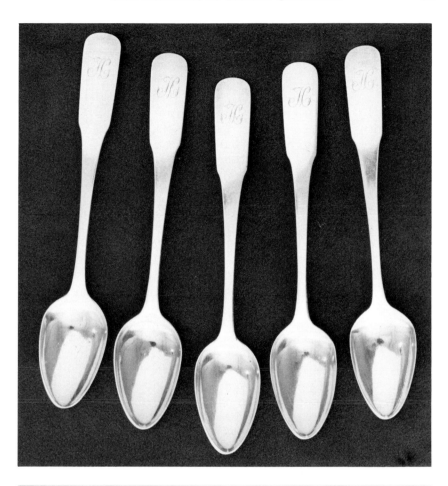

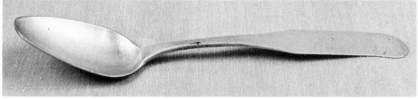

Six spoons marked T.EMOND have been found in North Carolina. The five dessertspoons shown in the top photograph are 7¾ inches long with oval bowls that measure 2⅜ inches in length and 1⅜ inches in width. The engraved *H* is for the Hinton family of Wake County, who owned extensive property on the Neuse River. William Hinton (1768-1836) was the original owner of these spoons, two of which have been given to the North Carolina Museum of History by Mrs. Thad S. Page. The teaspoon in the bottom photograph is also in the museum's collection; it is 5½ inches long. All of these spoons are in a modified fiddle and have oval bowls, no shoulders, and no drop.

WILLIAM FARIS, JUNIOR, was born in Annapolis, Maryland, on December 5, 1762, the eldest son of William Faris, a silversmith and watchmaker in Annapolis, and Priscilla Woodward. He was brought up in his father's shop, where he made some silver; but after quarreling with his irascible father he left Annapolis. He worked in Norfolk, Virginia, sometime prior to 1790 and in 1792 and 1794 was in Havana, Cuba. According to his father's diary, in 1798 he had recently opened a shop in Edenton, North Carolina, where he had some "40 or 50 watches in the window."[234] Little is known about Faris except that a bond dated December 11, 1803, was given for his marriage to Kesiah O'Neill[235] and that a certificate of James Hathaway, J.P., indicates that he had married them at Edenton on that date.[236]

ELIJAH FERGUSON. The first extant record of Ferguson is in connection with a marriage bond dated May 11, 1833, in which he proposed to marry Elizabeth Hamilton of New Bern.[237] In 1845 there is a reference to his jewelry store,[238] and in 1848 his place of business is called "The Old North State Jewelry Store";[239] evidently, he had then been in business for some time. The same title is used for his store in 1850, at which time he advertised that he continued to keep gold and silver jewelry and to repair watches, clocks, and jewelry.[240]
A receipt found in the Kenan Papers, Kenansville, was for payment received by Furguson for silver spoons:

Newbern June 25th [1845?]
Recd of Dr. J. G. Tull in ful for one Set
of Silver Table Spoons warrented pure Silver $18.00

E. Ferguson[241]

ALLEN FITCH, the son of Nathaniel and Mary Fitch, was born in New Haven, Connecticut, in 1785. He advertised there as a silversmith in 1808 and in 1811 bought land with a frontage of 18 feet on the south side of Crown Street and built a shop on it. The same year, he went into partnership with Joshua Hobart under the firm name of Fitch & Hobart; this partnership was dissolved in 1813.[242] He was working as a silversmith

in New Bern in 1817; in the *Federal Republican* Fitch advertised that he had many articles for sale "in the Silver-smith's
line" and that he had taken the shop formerly occupied by Mr.
Perret—"spoons, Silver-plate, &c. cyphered and watches repaired. . . ." Fitch offered cash for old gold and silver.[243] During
the same year he married Harriet Morning, the bond being
dated September 29.[244] On October 1, 1818, he announced that
he had taken the shop he had occupied the previous year.[245] On
October 5, 1821, Fitch informed the people of New Bern that he
had just returned from New York and had commenced business
at his former stand.[246] In 1826 he was referred to as a resident
of New Bern,[247] and in 1828 he became trustee of some bank
stock.[248]

THOMAS FLERE (d. ca. 1781). E. Milby Burton in *South
Carolina Silversmiths*, pp. 63-64, wrote that Flere and Charles
Harris departed London together and arrived in Charleston in
1767; shortly afterward, the two men opened a shop on Broad
Street. In 1768 Harris was advertising that he was in business
but did not mention Flere, so it is assumed Flere had moved
away from Charleston. Two researchers, Mr. Fred Hughes and
Ms. Alice Abel, working independently of each other, have
found evidence that Flere worked in Wilmington after leaving
Charleston and that he later moved to Guilford County. Ms.
Abel, in a letter to Ms. Betty Tyson, August 3, 1982, writes:

In the course of abstracting the wills here in the county [Guilford], I
found Thomas Flere, who made his will in 1781, and listed himself as
"silversmith." . . . According to his will, although living in Guilford, he
was "late of Wilmenton" and he left to his wife, Jane, one half of a
house and lot "No. 52" on Front St. in Wilmington, the other half of
his property to his daughter Judith who was a minor and the residue
of his estate. He did not mention the tools of his trade or anything else
in his will.

JOHN JACOB FOCKEL (FOGLE) was born September 4,
1803, at Bethabara, North Carolina, the son of Gottlieb Fockel
and Elizabeth Beroth (the widow Vogler).[249] In September,
1817, he went to Salem and on March 9, 1818, was apprenticed
to John Vogler. In the Salem Diary it is recorded that on May
14, 1821, Fockel "is learning the craft of a silversmith from Br.
John Vogler."[250] Just when he left and moved to Milledgeville,
Georgia, is not known, although the Salem Diary includes this
entry of April 27, 1829, in mentioning a visit from Fockel: "For

58   DIVISION OF ARCHIVES AND HISTORY

five years he has been working as a silversmith in Milledgeville, South Carolina [Georgia?].''[251] At some point he changed
his name to Fogel, and from 1837 until 1842 he was a silversmith in Milledgeville; he subsequently advertised himself as a
dentist.[252]

These four teaspoons marked J. FOGLE (the trio at top marked within a serrated rectangle, the single spoon at center and bottom marked within a straight
rectangle with accompanying marks) have been found outside North Carolina.
The date and origin of these spoons have not been determined. All are fiddle in
style, 5¾ inches long, with rounded shoulders, oval bowls, broad drop, and
handles tipped on reverse. The single spoon is engraved C in script.

THOMAS H. FOWLER enlisted in the Confederate forces on May 21, 1861. He was then forty-two years old, a resident of Wake County, and by occupation a "silverplater." Fowler was a private in Company K, Fourteenth Regiment, North Carolina Troops, and was present or accounted for until discharged on October 10, 1862, by reason of being overage.[253]

JOSEPH GALE. On January 28, 1788, he was apprenticed to Peter Strong[254] and was probably a member of the firm of Lord & Gale in Fayetteville in 1792.[255] He advertised in Fayetteville on October 13, 1798, that he was in a low state of health, and he requested all those who had watches lying for any length of time in his shop to call or send their orders for them immediately.[256] On April 15, 1797, John Kelly gave a deed to Joseph Gale.[257] In April, 1799, Joseph Gale gave a bill of sale to John Kelly and John Naylor, and Joseph and Eliza Gale gave a deed to Stephen Beck.[258]

BARZILLAI GARDNER, the son of Barzillai Gardner and Jemima Macy, was born May 23, 1778, at New Garden, a Quaker settlement in Guilford County, North Carolina.[259] When sixteen years of age he evidently went to Pennsylvania, for on April 26, 1794, the New Garden Monthly Meeting granted him a certificate to the York, Pennsylvania, Monthly Meeting.[260] He married Mary Long.[261] On April 21, 1807, he announced that he had moved from Guilford County to Charlotte, where he had commenced the watchmaking and clockmaking and goldsmithing and silversmithing businesses in partnership with Andrew McBride.[262] When McBride was appointed guardian to Nancy H. Armond on April 10, 1810, Barzillai Gardner was one of his bondsmen.[263] Little more has been discovered about Gardner except that he was involved in real estate transactions in Charlotte in 1812 and 1813[264] and that his two daughters, Delphinia and Flora, were born in Mecklenburg County in 1811 and 1814 respectively.[265]

JOHN R. GARLAND worked in Greenville, South Carolina, Macon, Georgia, and Memphis, Tennessee, prior to settling in North Carolina. He was in Greenville in 1826-1827 and at one time announced that he intended to make Greenville his permanent home. He was embarrassed by unpleasant publicity stemming from a robbery at his store and seemed to feel that his integrity had been questioned.[266] Just when he actually left Greenville is not clear, but during 1828-1829 he was working in Macon, Georgia, as a partner of Alexander Menard (1828-1829) and of Peter P. Rockwell (1829).[267] After residing in Georgia, Tennessee may have been his next stop.[268] On January 13, 1843, he advertised that he was permanently located in Greensboro and would do clock and watch repairing and engraving.[269]

These two teaspoons with the mark of John R. Garland are in a private collection; provenance, Winston-Salem. They are ca. 5½ inches long, modified fiddle with no shoulders, blunted coffin ends, no shoulders, no drop, and rather crudely made but with an indefinable, primitive charm. The engraving on the imperfectly matched pair is *MW*. Photograph by Charles Clark.

In October of that year he notified the public that he was equipped with all the necessary apparatus for the manufacture of gold and silverware and would make any article at the shortest notice.[270] In 1844 he expressed his gratitude for the patronage he had received;[271] and on June 28, 1845, he said that he had been in Greensboro nearly three years, during which time he had cleaned and repaired 742 watches.[272] About this time he reduced his prices.[273] On December 18, 1845, he advertised watch repairing and engraving in Charlotte,[274] and on July 23, 1846, he said that after a temporary absence he had returned to Charlotte and would resume the business of watch repairing.[275]

EVERARD GARRETT. Bonds for his marriages in Chowan County to Leah Speight and Sarah Hurdle were dated January 30, 1758, and August 3, 1763, respectively.[276] In a bill against the estate of Mrs. Clement Hall, attested January 16, 1760, work (beginning January 1, 1759) for which he charged consisted of such items as "making 5 silver canns, 18 silverspoons, 7 pr. buckles, making 2 rings; repairing 6 spoons, mending earring, making pr. gold buckles"—twenty-nine items in all.[277] On March 5, 1761, he wrote to Thomas Agnis, jeweler at Edenton, saying that he would go to the town the following week and apologetically asked Agnis to have the money ready for him for the two past months, as he was much in need of it.[278] On the following July 22 Garrett gave Evan Skinner an order on Agnis for £1 7s. 6d.[279] In 1763 he was one of three men appointed to divide the estate of Joseph Goodwin[280] and in 1764 one of three to divide the estate of James Smith.[281] On March 5, 1777, he deeded 200 acres of land to Jeremiah Mizell of Chowan County.[282] It seems likely that Garrett worked for Thomas Agnis—he was, perhaps, his former apprentice.

THOMAS GATLIN (b. ca. 1835) was listed in the census of 1850 as being a member of the household of Julia Pender and Thomas Gatlin in the town of Tarboro, Edgecombe County. He was described as "a silversmith."[283]

JOSHUA GAY, according to the Salisbury *Western Carolinian* of May 15, 1827, died in Salisbury at the age of forty-three; he was a silversmith who had learned his trade in Philadelphia.[284] In 1828 a William Gay offered for sale tools for watchmakers.[285] It is possible that William Gay was a relative of Joshua Gay and that these tools were perhaps once owned by Joshua.

JOHN GEDDY (1748-1799), a native of Williamsburg, Virginia, was the son of James and Anne Geddy and brother of James Geddy, the silversmith whose restored shop is located on

Duke of Gloucester Street in Williamsburg.[286] John Geddy, who married Patience McKinnie of Halifax County, North Carolina, and moved there in 1768, was in 1778 commissioned a lieutenant colonel in the Halifax County militia but resigned that commission in 1779 to become captain of a volunteer company of horse. He was a member of the Royal White Hart Lodge in Halifax, and on June 24, 1772, "Brother Geddy presented a pair of compasses by him made, by order of last Lodge, which was highly approved for the Elegance of its Workmanship. . . . Ordered that the Treasurer apply to Brother Geddy for a Silver Square for use of this Lodge."[287] Geddy was at one time senior warden of the lodge. On July 29, 1773, John Geddy was advertising in the *Virginia Gazette*, as was his brother James in a similar style:

MERCHANDISE FOR SALE; OLD SILVER BOUGHT
   Just IMPORTED, and to be SOLD by the Subscriber in Halifax Town, North Carolina.
   Fine Paste Shoe, Knee, and Stock Buckles; Marcasite, Paste, Wax, Pearl, and Mock Garnett Earrings and Necklaces; Paste Sprigs and Bed Pins for the Hair; all Sorts of Finger Rings; Stone Seals, in Gold, Silver, and Pinchbeck; Ditto Sleeve Buttons in Ditto; a large Assortment of Silver and Goldsmith's work, too tedious to mention—I engrave MOURNING RINGS, ARMS, CRESTS, SEALS, and all other Sorts of Clocks and WATCHES, with Expedition, ENGRAVING, in a neat, cheap, and expeditious manner; also repair all Sorts of CLOCKS and WATCHES, with Expedition, and on the same reasonable Terms.
                                              JOHN GEDDY
N.B. I will give 9s. Proc. or 6s. 8. Virginia Currency per ounce, for good OLD SILVER; and 6£ 13s 4d Proc. or 5£ Virginia *Currency*, per Ounce, for GOLD.

   Significant clues about John Geddy's business transactions in Halifax and his subsequent move, ca. 1790, to Cool Harbor, near Lewisburgh (Louisburg), can be gathered from various items that appeared in the *North Carolina Journal* during the ensuing years. On November 21, 1792, Geddy was advertising "My houses and Eight Lots in the town of Halifax. . . . For further particulars enquire of Mr. William Gilmour, or John Geddy." On January 1, 1794, Holcott Briggs Pride of Montecarllow advertised his plantation "in Mush Island formerly rented by Colonel John Geddy." On August 13, 1794, Geddy advertised for sale "A tract of Land on Fishing Creek adj. the lands of D. Ballard, Wm. Hadley, Thomas Davis and Arthur Davis" containing 642 acres and another tract on the "main road from Halifax to Raleigh." The subscriber declared that

"Injurious circumstances will induce me to give a good bargain in these lands for ready money, or part ready money and the balance well secured. . . . Mr. Willis Arrington will show the lands on application. Enquire of Mr. William Gilmour of Halifax for terms, or of the subscriber, John Geddy, near Lewisburgh." On March 21 and 29, 1796, Willie Jones advertised that he had mortgages on seven slaves to secure a debt owed by John Geddy to the estate of General Sumner, the estate of Benjamin McCulloh, and himself. Geddy was advertising on October 31, 1796, that "The subscriber will repair CLOCKS & WATCHES of all kinds during the setting of the General Assembly in the city of Raleigh. . . . Having completely outfitted himself with instruments & his customers will be executed in the most efficient manner, and on easy terms." One of his customers evidently was Samuel Yeargin or his daughter Sarah, of Warren County. In July, 1797, "Sarah Yancey Yeargin, orphan of Samuel Yeargin," owed £1 5s. 0d. to Colonel Geddy for a pair of gold earrings.[288] Two entries in the Franklin County court minutes for the March term are significant:

Ordered that Administration be Granted to Doct: Richard Fenner on the Estate of John Geddy dec? who entered into bond in the sum of three Thousand pounds with John Foster & Green Hill his Securities.

Order'd that Rich? Fenner Adm: of the Estate of John Geddy dec? sell as much of the Personal Estate of said decedent as he may Judge Necessary to satisfy the debts due s? Intestate.

"An Account of sales of the Estate of Col. John Geddy" was dated as beginning on April 1, 1799. Included in the inventory were many items indicative of his trade: "6 parcels of silver smith's files [bought by James Harvey]/6 parcels of silversmith's tools [bought by John Biddle]/1 draw bench & &c/ 1 pair smith's bellows/ 1 lot watchmakers tools/ 1 parcel watch springs/ 3 silver teaspoons/ 1 parcel of garnet soil[?] /1 pair Silver knee buckles/ 1 silver thimble/ 1 p: gold ear bobs. . . ."[289]
The following document seems to complete the business affairs of Geddy as publicly recorded:

On or before the first Day of January next ensuing we or either of us do oblige ourselves our heirs &c to pay or cause to be pay? unto Richard Fenner adm: of John Geddy dec? his Heirs or order the just & full Sum of twenty seven pounds two shillings & 4 d. Current money to carry Interest from the date if not punctually paid   Witness our hands & Seals this fifth day of April anno Dom. 1799
                    Elisha Lankford
                    Jn° Johnson[290]

John and Patience McKinnie Geddy (d. 1814) were the parents of five daughters: Betsy, who never married; Sally, who married William Hill, a secretary of state of North Carolina; Martha, who married John Marshall of Raleigh; Mary, who married William Gilmour of Halifax; and Anne, who married Dr. Richard Fenner of Franklin County.[291]

JOHN GILL, the son of John and Elizabeth Gill, was born in New Bern in 1798.[292] On March 15, 1814, when sixteen years old, he was apprenticed to David A. Murdock at New Bern.[293] In 1818 a letter directed to him was advertised,[294] and on April 10, 1819, John Gill, goldsmith and silversmith, announced that, having purchased the stand lately occupied by David A. Murdock, he was prepared to do all work in his line.[295] On May 5, 1819, Gill married Elizabeth Tignor of New Bern,[296] and in 1842 he married Frances A. Creekman, the bond being dated February 24.[297] In 1821 William Tisdale announced that he had taken the shop lately occupied by John Gill.[298] In 1827 Gill advertised that he would consolidate and mend tortoiseshell combs with silver, "which will be much neater than the usual way."[299] On August 11, 1828, he accepted Carney Cahoon, fourteen years

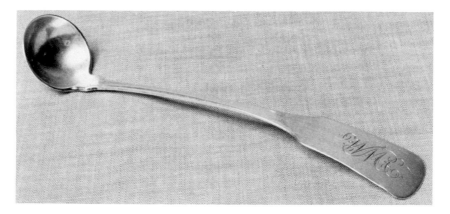

A superbly crafted example of John Gill's work is this mustard spoon, which has descended in the family of the original owner. At left is a detail of the *WMC* so precisely engraved on the handle.

old, as an apprentice.[300] In 1829 "he invented the revolver, first percussion of that kind."[301] (Samuel Colt's revolver was patented in 1835.) In November, 1830, appeared a notice that John Gill, goldsmith and silversmith, had returned to New Bern and opened the shop he formerly occupied on Broad Street and that he would convert common guns into percussion guns.[302] In March, 1839, Gill was advertising that he wanted "apprentices to the Silver, Copper, and White-Smith business."[303] On August 20, 1843, he gave to James Burney, in trust for his two sons, all his tools and mechanical books,[304] and on September 13 he deeded land and a tenement to John Lewis in trust for his two daughters.[305]

DAVID GLASS. Thomas Glass advertised in Raleigh on January 4, 1803, that he was leaving for a few months, and in November of the same year David Glass advertised that he had resumed business.[306] He was probably a member of the firm of Glass & Baird. A certain David Glass, aged seventy-one, died on February 3, 1856, and was buried in the Presbyterian cemetery at Morganton.[307]

THOMAS GLASS. On September 21, 1801, Thomas Glass, a watchmaker, advertised that he sold silver ladles and teaspoons in Raleigh.[308] In January, 1803, he notified the public that he was leaving the state for a few months;[309] in November David Glass resumed business. There was a Thomas Glass who in April, 1771, advertised as a goldsmith and jeweler and opened a shop in Hanover, Virginia.[310] In February, 1773, he advertised that he carried on business as usual in Hanover.[311] One Thomas Glass took the oath of allegiance to the state of North Carolina in 1778[312] in Granville County. The Norfolk, Virginia, directory for 1801 contains the name of Thomas Glass, watchmaker, 21 Market Square.

GLASS & BAIRD. This firm advertised in Raleigh on February 4, 1805, that it had commenced business and would manufacture all kinds of gold and silver work on the shortest notice.[313] The members of the firm were probably R. A. Baird (or David Baird) and David Glass.

EDWIN GLOVER advertised on October 3, 1843, that he continued to repair watches and jewelry at the old stand of C. C. Smith in Fayetteville.[314] On January 16, 1845, he announced that he had moved to a store opposite the Cape Fear Bank.[315]

Edwin Glover's spoons, depicted here, show a noticeable lack of uniformity in size, shape of bowl, and overall length. All are in the same style, however, and are engraved with the same initials in script, *SMB*; these are in a private collection. (Photograph by Charles Clark.) In the collection of MESDA at Old Salem are a ladle, cup, teaspoon, and tablespoon by Glover.

He married Louisa Smith, the bond being dated September 8, 1843; he later married Elizabeth A. Smith, this bond bearing the date May 6, 1856.[316] In a deed dated December 21, 1869, Edwin Glover and his wife, Elizabeth A., were described as residing in Cumberland County, presumably in Fayetteville;[317] a similar deed in 1871 gave their location as Mecklenburg County.[318]

WILLIAM GREENAWALT[319] advertised in November, 1826, and for a few months thereafter as a watchmaker and clockmaker in Halifax.[320] See the Greenewalt & Cover spoon and mark discussed in Appendix A.

JOHN GRIFFEN was a silversmith who worked principally in Staunton, Virginia, but spent from 1794 to 1803 in Germantown (Hyde County), North Carolina,[321] presumably working at his trade there. The first mention of him was in connection with a marriage license granted to him August 30, 1773,[322] when he married Elizabeth Wilson.[323] Shortly after this, on November 27, 1773, he bought Lot 12 in Staunton from Thomas Smith,[324] and on May 2 following, he and his wife, Elizabeth, sold this same lot to Alexander Sinclair.[325] It was in this deed that he was first mentioned as a silversmith. He was one of the patrollers of Staunton in 1776,[326] and on July 20, 1779, John Cowden was bound to him.[327] The streets of Staunton needed repairs in 1779-1780; and in an assessment levied at that time, John Griffen was among the tithables and was taxed $4.00.[328] He was called upon for various civic duties, such as foreman of a coroner's jury,[329] witness to wills,[330] appraising estates,[331] and surety for a marriage.[332] There is no record of his death, and nothing is known of his life while he lived in Germantown. The last court entry in which his name was mentioned was in October, 1813.[333]

JOHN C. GUERRANT[334] served as a private in Companies H and K, Thirteenth Regiment, North Carolina Troops, during four years of the Civil War. When he enlisted in Rockingham County at age twenty on May 3, 1861, he listed his occupation as silversmith. He transferred from Company H to Company K on July 1, 1861, and was present or accounted for until detailed in the "gun factory" at Danville, Virginia, on or about February 5, 1862. He was reported absent on detail through October, 1864.

JAMES BRANDON HAMPTON (1801-1832) was born in Salisbury in 1801, the son of William Hampton and Mary Brandon, a niece of Hugh Horah.[335] In 1822 he advertised watch repairing in the old shop formerly occupied by his father on Main Street and stated that he had employed a competent workman to help him.[336] In 1828 he was still working in the old shop.[337] In 1830 he and his brother-in-law, John C. Palmer, formed the firm of Hampton & Palmer.[338] He married Susan A. Locke on February 2, 1831, one of the bondsmen being Ashbel Smith, who later became surgeon general of the republic of Texas.[339] Hampton bought and sold several pieces of real estate. On August 25, 1832, he died in Salisbury.[340] In his will he left his property to his two sisters, his wife having predeceased him. Hampton's executors were "my friends" William H. Horah, his cousin, and John C. Palmer, his brother-in-law, both of whom were silversmiths.[341]

WILLIAM HAMPTON (d. 1815) was described as a silversmith in an item dated November 6, 1810, in Rowan County Deed Book 20. He was the father of James B. Hampton. A Raleigh newspaper of 1815 contains a notice published by John Travis, the administrator of Hampton's estate. The notice identifies Hampton as a silversmith and former resident of Rowan County.[342]

HAMPTON & PALMER (1830-1832)—James B. Hampton and John C. Palmer, brothers-in-law, of Salisbury. The partnership was announced on April 2, 1830,[343] and was dissolved on March 9, 1832, with Palmer continuing the business in the house formerly occupied by James B. Hampton.[344] They advertised the manufacture of all types of silverware, such as spoons, ladles, and sugar tongs.

J. C. HANNA put his stamp on silver spoons that have been found in the state. Nothing at all can be ascertained about this silversmith, but the fact that his mark includes N.C. after his name strongly suggests that he was in this state.

Who was J. C. Hanna? Where did he work? The four spoons pictured above have the same die mark, J.C. HANNA.N-C. in a rectangle. Surely N-C. indicates that he was in North Carolina. The three spoons in the photograph at top are all engraved *JCP*, although two are 6 inches long and the other only 5¹³⁄₁₆ inches long. The dessertspoon in the bottom photograph is in the same fiddle-back style, has a tipped, upturned handle, and is 6 inches long; it is engraved *AMP* in script.

JOHN BISHOP HARRY was described by historian Lee B. Weathers as "John Bishop Harry, silversmith and gunsmith by trade."[345]

SIMON PETER HAUSER. In the minutes kept by the Moravians, it was characteristic to identify individuals occasionally by adding their occupation in parentheses following the name. For August 18, 1825, there is to be found this entry in the Bethania Diary: "We visited Simon Peter Hauser (Silver), Isaac Conrad, and Jacob Conrad (oil-miller)."[346]

THOMAS HIGHE (d. 1793) resided in Plymouth and had a set of silversmith's tools. Whether he actually was a silversmith or not has not been determined. His widow was named Rebecca.[347]

GEORGE W. HILLIARD. On April 24, 1823, he advertised that he had taken a stand opposite the Mansion House in Fayetteville, where he worked at clockmaking and watchmaking. He also made and repaired gold and silver work.[348] Possibly he was a son of William Hilliard. A certain G. W. Hilliard, perhaps a son of this George W. Hilliard, bravely and somewhat frequently assumed marriage obligations in Fayetteville. The following record of bonds is extant: G. W. Hilliard and Susan Alephant, July 16, 1846; G. W. Hilliard and Catherine Dove, January 4, 1848; Geo. W. Hilliard and Lovedy Briggs, November 8, 1856; George W. Hilliard and Catherine Wade, September 28, 1871.[349]

WILLIAM HILLIARD (HILLARD). In April, 1801, he accepted William Dye as an apprentice.[350] On December 29, 1805, he advertised that as a watchmaker and jeweler he had opened a shop in the house lately occupied by Edwin Jay Osborne, Esq., opposite the post office in Fayetteville, where any work in the above line would be done with neatness and dispatch. He also wanted two or three apprentices of good character.[351] On February 12, 1810, he offered a reward of $50.00 in connection with a robbery. The previous night his shop had been entered and about thirty watches, which he described, had been stolen.[352] In 1809 N. Foster sold to William Hilliard and E. W. Barge rights in certain counties to a patent hemp- and flax-spinning machine.[353] They subsequently advertised for hemp. As late as 1814 Hilliard bought or sold land in Fayetteville.[354] Also in 1814 there was an announcement in a Fayetteville newspaper[355] concerning Hilliard's house: William Gee, a tailor, advertised that he had moved his business "to the house lately occupied by Mr. William Hilliard, silversmith. . . ." The same advertisement appeared in the Fayetteville *American* on November 17, 1814. Hilliard is later identified as a silversmith in Tennessee, perhaps suggesting that he left Fayetteville ca. 1814.[356]

The William Hilliard mark is reproduced from Cutten's *The Silversmiths of North Carolina*, first edition, 35. It was taken from a teaspoon owned in 1948 by Mrs. H. McR. Lutterloh of Chapel Hill. See also the Hilliard mark discussed in Appendix A.

EDWARD HOELL, the son of Elias and Delilah Hoell, was born in Washington, North Carolina.[357] His father had conducted a school in the public schoolhouse at New Bern in 1774.[358] On February 19, 1819, Hoell advertised in Washington for a boy of good character as an apprentice to the silversmithing business.[359] From 1816 to 1828 and again from 1845 to 1850 he bought and sold land in Washington.[360] He has been referred to as "a travelling silversmith, who lived in Greenville,

Experimentation in details of workmanship is evident in these two spoons by Edward Hoell. The example at top is a long coffin-end, 5½ inches long, engraved *JTG*, and marked E·Hoell in a rectangle. The tablespoon in the bottom photograph is a fiddle-coffin 8⅞ inches long with a slender, tapered stem and an oval bowl 3 inches long with no drop and no shoulders; it is engraved *PS*, the mark partly obliterated but obviously in script.

North Carolina, from 1830 to 1847."[361] In a deed dated June 28, 1873, Richard Williams, administrator of the estate of Edward Hoell, deceased, of Pitt County, North Carolina, conveyed two lots of land in Van Norden town and two lots in Washington.[362] Greenville is in Pitt County, so it seems likely that Hoell had transferred his residence from Washington to Greenville.

JOHN HOLLAND (d. 1823).[363] This man was a legislator from Beaufort County. His career is discussed in the *American Recorder* (Washington, N.C.) for May 24, July 12, and July 29, 1823. He died June 20, 1823, at the age of about fifty. In the newspaper is mentioned his inventory, which included silversmith tools.[364]

JOHN HOLLAND. Evidently there were two men of this name who may have been silversmiths. According to the *Tarboro' Press* of December 18, 1847, this John Holland was a working craftsman in or around Tarboro.[365]

WILLIAM HOLLIMAN. In 1783 there may have been a silversmith by this name in Warren County. Two boys, John and Willie Duncan, were apprenticed to him in that year to learn the silversmith's trade.[366]

HENRY HORAH (d. 1789). The will of Henry Horah, dated April 7, 1789, states that he was a silversmith in Salisbury. In the document Horah named his wife Nancy and his daughter Elizabeth as beneficiaries of property he had bought at public auction; the property had, according to the will, formerly belonged to Henry Eustace McCulloch (McCulloh).[367] The Rowan County court minutes for May 6, 1783, record that Henry Horah took John Miller, aged twelve, orphan of Benjamin Miller, as apprentice to the silversmith's trade.[368]

HUGH HORAH (1760-1822) was born in Salisbury in 1760, the son of Henry Horah (probably a Scotch-Irish immigrant) and his wife Nancy.[369] Hugh Horah lived all his life in Salisbury. On January 14, 1788, he married Mary Moore,[370] and he and his wife were two of the thirteen charter members of the Presbyterian church organized in Salisbury on August 4, 1821.[371] His son, William H. Horah, was his apprentice. Hugh was a member of the firm of Wilkinson & Horah,[372] but most of his life he worked independently.

In 1791, when George Washington visited Salisbury, a grand ball was held in his honor at Hughes Hotel. Among the prominent citizens present was Hugh Horah.[373] Horah died in Salisbury on September 24, 1822, "an old and useful citizen of the town."[374] A street in Salisbury is named for the Horah family. At least three apprentices were bound to Hugh Horah: Horatia [Horatio?] Jones, November 11, 1796;[375] Nathan Williams, August 7, 1800;[376] Brice Andrews, August 12, 1809.[377]

JAMES HORAH (1826-1864), the son of William Henry Horah and Louisa Furr, was born May 28, 1826, in Salisbury.[378] On May 17, 1849, he advertised as a watchmaker and clockmaker located opposite Cowan's Brick Row in Salisbury.[379] The census of 1850 lists him as a silversmith. He died July 30, 1864, in Salisbury.

WILLIAM HENRY HORAH (1788-1863) was born in Salisbury, December 31, 1788, the son of Hugh Horah and Mary Moore. He was apprenticed to his father and in early life worked as a silversmith. In 1814 he married Louisa Furr. He was cashier of the State Bank of Salisbury, and when this closed in 1834 he became a clerk in the Salisbury branch of the Cape Fear Bank.[380] He died in Salisbury on May 3, 1863. The census of 1850 lists him as a silversmith.

DAVID HOULTON, according to descendants, was a silversmith in Cabarrus County ca. 1816.[381] He married Leah Barringer, daughter of John Paul Barringer, in 1816.[382] There is believed to have been a relationship between David Houlton and the John Houlton who worked in Philadelphia (1794-1798) and Baltimore (ca. 1800).[383]

NATHANIEL HOWCOTT was born in Chowan County, the son of Nathaniel Howcott and Sarah Norcom.[384] When his mother wrote her will on March 15, 1823, he was not yet of age.[385] The bond for his marriage to Adaline Meredith was filed on April 14, 1828,[386] and on December 30 of the same year Howcott advertised that he had taken the house formerly occupied by Simeon Staudin in Edenton and would work on clocks and watches.[387] On January 9, 1830, he served notice that he had removed to the dwelling house on King Street lately occupied by James Iredell.[388]

JAMES HUGHES (HUES; d. 1809). On May 31, 1808, James Hues advertised that he had taken John McMillan's house in Wilmington, where he intended to carry on his former line of business in making all kinds of gold and silver work and the like.[389] A notice of Hughes's death that appeared nearly two years later in a Raleigh newspaper identified him as a silversmith of Wilmington and indicated that he had died December 28, 1809.[390]

CHARLES FREDERICK HUGUENIN. Huguenin, a native of Switzerland, is listed as a watchmaker in the Philadelphia directories from 1797 to 1802.[391] He took a trip to North Carolina in 1798, appearing first at Halifax in May. He advertised that he would repair watches while he remained there and could be found at Hopkins's tavern.[392] In October he was in Wilmington selling watches, gold earrings, necklaces, and lockets.

He said that while he remained there he would repair watches and clocks for those who applied at Jonathan Jennings's.[393] In November he was in Fayetteville, where he repaired watches and clocks for those who applied at a certain Gross's.[394] During 1836 and 1837 the firm of Roberts & Huguenin [Felix Roberts and Charles Frederick Huguenin?] advertised in the *Tarboro' Press* that they would be present during court sessions in the area and would have for sale "Watches, Jewelry, & Silver ware."[395]

JOHN HUNTINGTON (1808-1855) was born in Hillsborough, the son of Roswell Huntington and Mary Palmer.[396] He probably learned his trade with his brother, William. He was a member of the firms of Wm. & John Huntington in Oxford in 1824;[397] Huntington & Wynne in Salisbury in 1827;[398] Trotter & Huntington in Charlotte in 1828;[399] and Huntington & Lynch in Hillsborough in 1834.[400] He married Salina Gray near Tuscaloosa, Alabama, in 1839, and died at Pontotec, Mississippi, in July, 1855.[401] William J. Hogan, who has done extensive research on the Huntingtons, suggests that John Huntington may also have practiced dentistry at some time inasmuch as tools such as those used by dentists of his day were found among the silversmith's possessions (see Hogan, *Huntington Silversmiths*, Appendix A, 117-119).

HUNTINGTON & LYNCH (1834—). John Huntington and Lemuel Lynch announced a partnership at Hillsborough on October 22, 1834,[402] and probably dissolved it early in 1837 when Huntington went west. The following notice appeared in the *Hillsborough Recorder* on May 5, 1837: "All persons indebted to the firm of Huntington and Lynch are requested to call and settle their respective accounts."

MARTIN PALMER HUNTINGTON (1797-1851) was born in Hillsborough, the son of Roswell and Mary Palmer Huntington. On September 27, 1815, Martin Palmer deeded to his nephew [grandson?], Martin Huntington, 36 acres of land.[403] William Huntington witnessed the deed. In 1819 Martin Huntington was a member of the firm of M. P. Huntington & Co., Milton, North Carolina.[404] On March 24, 1832, Martin P. Huntington deeded land in Hillsborough to William Huntington.[405] The *Hillsborough Recorder* of February 12, 1851, quoted a lengthy obituary from the *Milton Chronicle* that was signed "D. N. S."

According to this obituary, Huntington had lived an exemplary Christian life and had never removed from Milton after his initial move there from Orange County. His death, as noted in this account, occurred on February 1, 1851, at the age of fifty-four. Martin Palmer Huntington had married Susan Holden in 1822; his second wife was Mary A. Donoho, whom he married September 29, 1834. Both marriages are recorded in the Caswell County Marriage Book.

M. P. HUNTINGTON & CO.—Martin Palmer Huntington and probably his brother, William Huntington, at Milton. This firm advertised in 1819 that it had just received an elegant assortment of watches, ladies' rich jewelry, and silverware.[406] In the same advertisement is the statement that William Huntington & Co., of Hillsborough, had just received and offered for sale a complete assortment of the above articles.

ROSWELL HUNTINGTON (1763-1836) was born in Norwich, Connecticut, March 15, 1763, the son of Ebenezer Huntington, Jr., and Sarah Edgerton.[407] When he was fourteen years old, young Roswell joined the American army and served in the defense of New London.[408] He later learned the art of silversmithing with Joseph Carpenter, although it is not clear whether he actually was an apprentice. In 1784 he opened a shop of his own in Norwich.[409] By March 3, 1785, Huntington was in Hillsborough, North Carolina, since on that date an agreement was made between the silversmith and John Ray, chairman of the Orange County Court, whereby the craftsman took an apprentice, Francis Nash, "now of the age of thirteen years . . . to learn the art and mistery of a silver and gold smith"; not until August 25, 1786, however, is there any record of Huntington's purchasing property.[410] He was the fifer in a militia company commanded by Samuel Turrentine, sheriff of Orange County.[411]

Huntington was evidently a skilled engraver. On May 29, 1786, he was paid £4 by James Gillespie, payment "in full for Engraving one set of Margins for the present Emission of money."[412] A second man, John Coleman, was somehow involved in the same transaction because in the same file is his receipt of the same date: "Rec.[d] of James Gillespie one of the com[rs]. for superintending the present Emission of money the sum of seventy pounds for cuting seven sets of margins and Eight Devices." In 1793 Huntington again had an opportunity to demonstrate his competency as an engraver. A brass plate engraved by him was deposited in the cornerstone of Old East, the first building erected on the campus of the newly established University of North Carolina in Chapel Hill.[413]

Mr. John A. Holden of LaPlace, Louisiana, writes of this set of spoons that they are "smaller than a modern teaspoon, which have the unmistakable mark RH of Roswell Huntington on the back and initials *JH* engraved on the front. The initials are those of John Holden, Sr. (1764-1842), who was born near St. Mary's Chapel, east of Hillsborough, lived there all his life and is buried in the cemetery at St. Mary's Chapel. It is not known when the spoons were made, but he was married in 1805 and may have had them made at that time. According to his granddaughter, Catherine (Kitty) Holden (1848-1925), they were made from the silver buckles which John Holden, Sr., wore on his knee breeches and shoes. There were six of these spoons and four of them are owned by other branches of the family." One of these spoons was given to the North Carolina Museum of History by Mr. Holden and his sister, Mrs. Wilson Holden Price.

At the age of twenty-six Huntington married Mary Palmer of Hillsborough, the marriage bond being dated October 12, 1789.[414] In the same year, he was one of nine members of the Orange County Horse [militia] employed to guard the removal of state funds from Hillsborough to Fayetteville.[415] Over a period of years there were several land transactions with which he was connected, the last one in 1799.[416] Among a group of letters remaining in the post office in Raleigh on March 31, 1802, was one for the silversmith.[417] Public notices and records of Huntington's business transactions in 1818, 1820, 1828, and 1832 have been found, and his obituary notice states that he lived in Hillsborough until the autumn of 1833, when he moved to Alabama with four of his children.[418] He died in Marion, Alabama, September 7, 1836, survived by a rather large family, including three sons trained to be silversmiths.

The RH mark at left appears on the spoon depicted. The signature (center) is taken from the brass plate originally affixed to the cornerstone of the Old East building at the University of North Carolina at Chapel Hill. The initials (right) were used by Dr. Cutten in the first edition (p. 35) and are attributed by him to the reverse of the brass plate shown at center. Compare the initials with the RH mark discussed in Appendix A.

WILLIAM HUNTINGTON (1792-1874) was born in Hillsborough, September 8, 1792, the son of Roswell Huntington and Mary Palmer.[419] William learned his trade from his father and established his business in Hillsborough on December 7, 1815.[420] He was a member of the firm of Wm. Huntington & Co., which was active in 1816.[421] The firm was dissolved in 1820,[422] but Huntington continued the business. On December 9, 1819, he married Frances Robeson Howze. In 1821 he was one of the commissioners of the town of Hillsborough and treasurer of the church.[423] He seems to have been a general trader: in 1822 he advertised gravestones;[424] in 1823, a blacksmith shop;[425] in 1828, family flour and medicines;[426] and, periodically, silverware. In 1824 he was a member of the firm of Wm. & John Huntington.[427] Lemuel Lynch was one of his apprentices, and in 1828 Huntington sold his materials and rented his tools to

William Huntington and his wife, Frances R. Huntington, sent to their friends the fiftieth wedding anniversary memento depicted here. On one side was a photograph of themselves; on the other, the greeting pictured below. The original is in the possession of Mr. William Johnston Hogan and is reproduced with his permission. See Appendix A for discussion of two Huntington portraits that have had questionable identifications.

Presented

To

Miss Mattie A. King

MARION, PERRY COUNTY, ALABAMA,
December 9th, 1869.

William Huntington,

AND HIS WIFE,

Frances R. Huntington,

On THIS, *the 50th Anniversary, of their Marriage,—send Greeting : to their Friends :—*

" Bless the Lord, O my soul, and forget not all His benefits:
Who redeemeth thy life from destruction; who crowneth thee with loving-kindness and tender mercies."

We have lived long & happily together :— But we will soon part to meet again!

Wm. Huntington 77.
F. R. Huntington 67.

Marion Ala.
28th April 1870.

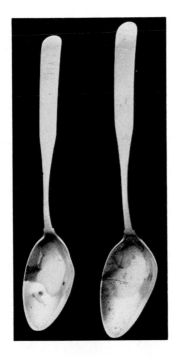

Variations in style and engraving of William Huntington's work are apparent in the seven spoons pictured above. In the photograph at top left are two teaspoons 5½ inches long with disproportionately long handles and diminutive, squared shoulders. One is engraved *WC* in script, the other [?]*M*. (From a private collection.) In the photograph at top right are two small spoons 5¼ inches long and a tablespoon 8½ inches long. The initials *JND* on one memorial spoon and *1820/ND* on the tablespoon were designed to commemorate the wedding of Nancy Cabe Latta to Major Robert Donnell. (From a private collection.) The third photograph depicts a fiddleback spoon 7½ inches long with *MB* engraved with an embellishment—a vinelike motif. (Collection of the North Carolina Museum of History.) A similar motif was used on the *B* engraved on the large tablespoon 9½ inches long (bottom). (From a private collection.)

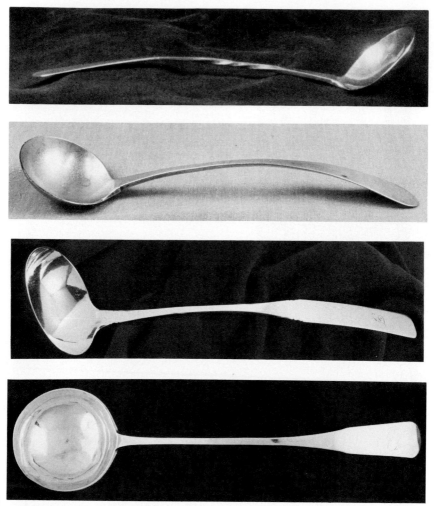

Two cream ladles and two punch ladles—three of these are in private collections—have the William Huntington marks. A twisted, corkscrew handle is a unique feature of the cream ladle in the photograph at top. This 10-inch piece was made ca. 1830 and descended by inheritance to the present owner. In a more conventional style is the cream ladle in the second photograph. It is 7½ inches long and has a graceful downturned handle and diminutive shoulders. The punch ladle in the third photograph has a special charm evoked by the elegant, restrained design of the handle and the single script initial *T* (for its first owner). The punch ladle at bottom is also quite individual with its tapered handle, suggestion of shoulders, and precisely engraved *JES*, rendered in the vine-foliage motif seen on other Huntington pieces. It is 37.2 cm. long, and the width of the bowl is 8.9 cm. Through the generosity of Lieutenant and Mrs. R. W. Heathcote, it is presently on display at the North Carolina Museum of History.

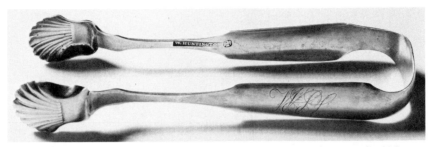

These sugar tongs with the Huntington mark in a barbed rectangle with an accompanying eagle are 6 inches long; they have shell grips and fiddle arms engraved *WSS*.

Lynch and recommended him to the public.[428] He again opened his shop in 1829,[429] and he was continually buying and selling land. This advertisement, dated July 19, 1832, appeared in the *Oxford Examiner* for August 9, 1832:

> William Huntington has from circumstances he could not well control been prevented from attending two or three of the last Granville courts. In future, he will attend the courts regularly, and will have an assortment of watches and jewelry, which he will dispose of at moderate prices. . . . Orders for silver spoons of every description thankfully received.

In 1833 he advertised that he intended to discontinue his business in Hillsborough and move from the state.[430] He offered for sale several lots of land, furniture, farming tools, and livestock. The original minute book of the Presbyterian church of Hillsborough contains the information that he joined the church May 27, 1819, and removed to Alabama in 1833. William Huntington, who died in Marion, Alabama, October 22, 1874, was a very skillful engraver. In testament to his reputation, the Livingstone, Alabama, *Journal* of January 12, 1872, had this item: "William Huntington, jeweller of Marion, has just engraved sixty perfectly formed letters on a finger ring made by himself." Another ring attributed to Huntington was one given to Cornelia Phillips Spencer of Chapel Hill. In a note dated October 19, 1869, she described it as

> a very massive plain gold ring, having been engraved on the inside, and very beautifully done, "In memory of the University of N.C., as it was. Caldwell, Phillips, Mitchell, Hooper, Swain. A tribute to Mrs. C. P. Spencer." 113 letters are engraved on the inside and very beautifully done. I do not think I ever had anything to please me more.

(Selected Spencer Papers, Southern Historical Collection)

WILLIAM HUNTINGTON & CO. (-1820)—William Huntington and John Van Hook, Jr., in Hillsborough. The firm was active in 1816[431] and was dissolved on June 6, 1820, with Huntington continuing the business.[432] Van Hook was not a silversmith.

WM. & JOHN HUNTINGTON. The two brothers opened a shop at Oxford, which was probably tended by John. They advertised in 1824.[433]

HUNTINGTON & WYNNE (-1828)—John Huntington and Robert Wynne, in Salisbury. They advertised in January and May, 1827, as silversmiths[434] and dissolved their partnership on January 21, 1828.[435] According to their advertisement of January 16, the partners were "now well-prepared to manufacture Silverware, and all articles in their line." They also announced that "Arrangement has been made with a gentleman from Philadelphia by whom they will have manufactured Jewelry of every description, and of the best workmanship, of North Carolina gold." In an advertisement dated May 9, 1827, the firm announced in the Salisbury *Western Carolinian* that it "wishes to purchase a considerable quantity of gold . . . on delivery at the silver-smith's shop in Salisbury."
William Huntington, John's brother, evidently provided the capital for the firm; upon its dissolution, the accounts of the firm were transferred to him.[436]

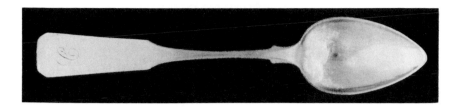

The mark H.&W. in a serrated rectangle (left) and the engraved initial *C* have been found on a teaspoon from a private collection in the provenance of Hillsborough. The spoon (above) is attributed to the firm of Huntington & Wynne; it is executed in a graceful modified fiddle style with a tapered, coffin-end handle. Photographs by Brent Clayton; courtesy of Phillip Scott.

_____ HYAMS. "Mr. Hyams" is identified as a silversmith of Charlotte, North Carolina, in the Tarboro *Free Press* of September 26, 1826.[437]

ELISHA JOHNSON. An advertisement bearing the date July 21, 1841, indicated that Johnson, who worked in Greensboro, repaired clocks and watches and made silver spoons to order. Johnson also thanked the people of Greensboro for the encouragement they had given him. He was still in Greensboro a year later.[438]

JOHN JOHNSTON (JOHNSON). An inventory of his estate includes "Silver Smith's Tools." Randolph County Estate Records, 1781-1928, State Archives; Helen F. M. Leary, researcher.

WILLIAM JOHNSTON (1763-ca. 1812) was apprenticed to William Tisdale of New Bern on September 19, 1778, to learn the art of silversmithing.[439] He was to be fifteen years old on September 24 of that year. He evidently was very active in the St. John's Masonic Lodge of New Bern from a very early age and was "one of the signers of the Lodge's message to President George Washington in welcoming the President here in April, 1791."[440] The cornerstone for a new Masonic temple was laid on April 5, 1801, according to "a small [2 5/8 inches by 4 13/16 inches], oblong, engraved silver plate now in the lodge archives." The plate on one side is engraved:

Grand Lodge of North Carolina instituted Jan'y. 14, A.D. 1771, A.L. 5771. Present officers: William Polk, Esqr., G. Master; John Lewis Taylor, Esqr., D.G.M., Thomas Jefferson, Pres't of the U. States; Aaron Burr, V. Pres't; Benj. Williams, Governor, N.C. Bro. Johnston, Sculp.

On the other side is the inscription:

St. John's Lodge No. 3, New Bern, N.C. Instituted Jan. 10, A.D. 1772, A.L. 5772. Present officers: Francis Lowthrop, Esqr., M. George Ellis, Esqr., S.W. Edw Kean, Esqr., J.W. Isaac Taylor, Esqr., Tr. Revd. Thos. P. Irving.[441]

Johnston was paid for making jewels for Eagle Lodge No. 19 in Hillsborough, the first delivered on January 8, 1793, at which time a special meeting was called to

receive the Jewels which had been purchased in New Bern. The solid silver Jewels and other Apparatus presented at this meeting are on display in a case on the wall of Eagle Lodge. The original bill of the maker is in the archives. Herewith is the statement:

Col. S. Benton to William Johnston. Dr.

For making seal for Eagle Lodge	£2.0
" making Square & Compasses for do	1.10
" making Level for do	1.0
" making Triangle for do	1.0
24 inch guage	0.15
plumb rule	.15
	£7.0
Weight of the above oz.	3.6
Wastage	.4
	3.10

2.0
£9.0

New Bern   Dec. 31st   1792.

Received payment in full
William Johnston[442]

A special meeting was called in March, 1824, to discuss the purported sale of one of the lodge jewels, about which a reporter wrote, "These officers Jewels were made by a silversmith in New Bern and presented to the Lodge January 8, 1793."[443]

Johnston's forte seems to have been engraving. In 1807 he worked with Nathan Tisdale in engraving the seals of the superior courts of the counties. In a letter to Governor Nathaniel Alexander on March 19, 1807, Tisdale acknowledged a letter of instructions concerning the seals.[444] Johnston evidently died sometime later, ca. 1812, inasmuch as an inventory of his estate made on January 20, 1812, included these items:

9 Table Spoons	$13.00
12 Tea ditto	5.00
1 Silver Ladle	7.00
1 Silver Sugar tongues [tongs]	1.00
1 ditto milk pot	5.00
Jack Screws	1.00
Clock Case &c	2.55
Wire tongs	25
One vice	6.35
1 Brace & drill	1.30
Ingots	70
Lott Punches	1.10
One stake	1.15 [445]

William Johnston is credited with making "solid silver Jewels and other Apparatus . . ." for Eagle Lodge No. 19 in Hillsborough. The Eagle Lodge jewels are pictured above. Photograph from Thomas C. Parramore, *Launching the Craft: The First Half-Century of Freemasonry in North Carolina* (Raleigh: Grand Lodge of North Carolina, A.F. and A.M., 1975), p. 153.

MERIDY D. JUSTUS (ca. 1832-1862) was born in Henderson County and lived there prior to enlisting in the Confederate army at age twenty-seven on May 5, 1861. His occupation was listed as silversmith. He served as a private in Company I, Sixteenth Regiment, North Carolina Troops. He was present or accounted for until his death from "disease" at Fredricksburg, Virginia, on March 27, 1862.[446]

PATRICK KELLY bought 150 acres of land in Robeson County with house and buildings for £130 on September 6, 1790; the transaction was recorded at the January term of court, 1792.[447] On March 12, 1792, Patrick Kelly, "planter," sold 100 acres of land to Angus Shaw for £15.[448] In the census of

1800 Kelly was listed as the forty-five-year-old head of a household that consisted of 1 male under ten, 3 females under ten, 1 female between the ages of twenty-six and forty-five, and 7 slaves. The only suggestion that Kelly or someone on his plantation was a silversmith comes from the following provision in his will, dated February 15, 1808: "I order that my executors should sell my mare and all carpenters tools and coopering tools silversmiths tools to be sold and defray all the debts that will arise."[449]

JOHN KILLINGSWORTH. The *Star* (Raleigh) for October 23, 1812, carried the following advertisement:

John Killingsworth ran away and carried with him a son of mine, a free mulatto boy. I apprehend he will try to sell him. Said Killingsworth is a plausible hypocrite about 45 years of age, he is a mill wright, a silversmith, a counterfeiter, a great Liar and occasionally tries to preach. . . .

Johnston Co., Oct. 5, 1812.   Priscilla Caps.

JOHN KIRKLAND (d. before April 2, 1785), of Craven County, is not named as a silversmith in the inventory of his estate dated April 2, 1785, or in the bond of administration given by Jarvis Buxton and James Council Bryan (whose signature is not affixed to the document).[450] However, the inordinate amount of jewelry and silver itemized, as well as a list of supplies and tools for making such items, leads to the conclusion that Kirkland was not only engaged in selling such items but also made them. There is a very large inventory of such things as gold studs, brooches, ear bobs, rings, Masons' "meddels," dozens of buckles—shoe, stock, and knee buckles—snuff boxes, scissors, buttons, spoon molds, watch-making supplies, lockets, weights and scales (bought by William Johnston), plates and spoons, a ladle, a large vise, bellows, a set of draw plates, files, watch tools, and a "lott of sweepings."[451]

JOHN KIRKWOOD. The name of John Kirkwood appears in the minutes of a meeting of the commissioners of the town of Wilmington, North Carolina, held July 25, 1768. Donald R. Lennon and Ida Brooks Kellam, editors of *The Wilmington Town Book,* identify Kirkwood as a watchmaker (p. 183n):

John Kirkwood, watchmaker, served as town commissioner and constable for Wilmington. He died in 1785, leaving a wife, Margaret, and three children: Mary, Anne Jeane, and Robert Alexander Kirkwood.

HENRY KUNSMAN advertised as a watchmaker in Richmond, Virginia, in 1820. Two years later, in an advertisement dated November 12, 1822, and appearing in the *Raleigh Register and North Carolina Gazette* on November 22, 1822, Kunsman announced that he had established a shop in Raleigh, North Carolina. He listed a large number of articles for sale in addition to "Watch-Makers' Tools and Materials of every description, together with a large assortment of files, such as Dentists', Clockmakers', and Gunsmiths' Files." Kunsman emphasized his watch repair business in the advertisement: "having devoted the principal of his [Kunsman's] time to Watch repairing. . . ." Again, in November, 1823, Kunsman stated that every attention would be given to watch and clock repairing.[452] In the *Raleigh Register* of July 23, 1824, this notice concerning H. Kunsman appeared:

Watches and Jewellry at Auction. On the 29th instant, will be sold at the shop of H. Kunsman, in this city, without reserve, at public auction, a general assortment of Watches, Jewellery, Chains, Seals and Keys of every description, Ear-rings, Finger-rings, and Breast pins. Gilt and steel Keys and Seals, Brittannia Tea Pots, Swords and Epaulettes, Silver Lace, Elegant Time-pieces, Watch-maker's files &c.

An excellent Gig, Horse, and Sulkey, household and Kitchen furniture and c. Watch-makers and others would find it to their interest to attend the sale, as the articles will be sold for whatever they will bring—Terms of Sale, Cash.   T. Pullen, Shff.

In an advertisement that appeared in the *North-Carolina Journal* (Fayetteville) on December 6, 1826, the subscriber, Henry Kunsman, announced that he would open a night school. It was to be a "Mathematical School," and students could avail themselves of the opportunity to study "a regular course of Mathematics" or select particular courses. On February 7, 1827, the *Journal* contained this advertisement, with the subscriber listed as H. Kunsman [Henry Kunsman?]:

Watches and Clocks. The subscriber informs the public that he has opened a shop near the South West corner of the market square, next door to Mr. S. Steiart, for the purpose of repairing *Watches and Clocks*. Those who will favour him with their custom, may rest assured that no exertions shall be wanting to give entire satisfaction.

DAIN (DESIRÉ?) LAMBERTOZ. On October 20, 1795, he advertised in Wilmington for an apprentice, to whom every encouragement was to be given and every means used to instruct in the silversmith business as well as in any other art the subscriber might be able to teach.[453] Lambertoz gave notice on

February 16, 1797, that he was leaving North Carolina; he requested all who had watches, silver work, or jewelry in his custody to call for them. He remembered citizens who had for many years "honored him with their friendship and favored him with their custom."[454] In *Hall's Wilmington Gazette* of April 6, 1797, D. Lambertoz advertised a long list of items, including silverplate and jewelry. They were to be disposed of by a "scheme of lottery" and were, according to the ad, "chiefly made by the subscriber. . . ." The following May 31 Henry Melville, watchmaker and clockmaker, advertised that he was located in Wilmington in the shop of L. Lambertoz on Dock Street.[455] Use of the initial *L.* in Melville's advertisement was probably an error; the New Hanover County court minutes for December 21, 1798, refer to "Dain Lambertoz, Silversmith." On June 13, 1797, D. Lambertoz again requested those who had left any goods with him in the line of his business to call for them, as he was leaving the state.[456] By September 17, 1799, Lambertoz probably had moved to Savannah, Georgia, inasmuch as on that date he was advertising in the *Columbian Museum and Savannah Advertiser*: "The subscriber lately from Wilmington, North Carolina, offers his services to the inhabitants of this city and the vicinity, as silver & goldsmith in their various branches. He also mounts swords and executes ornamental military & naval devices . . . at his house in Drayton St., lately occupied by Mr. Darnell Taylor."[457] In the *Southern Patriot* (Savannah, Georgia) of March 10, 1806, there was this notice by Lambertoz: "Stolen or lost by a child—a silver gravy spoon not polished or marked except the French stamp on the handle."[458] Lambertoz died in Savannah in 1817.[459]

WILLIAM LANE, the son of William and Eliza Lane, was born in Nixonton, Pasquotank County. At the time his father's will was written, March 20, 1754, Lane was not of age.[460] A marriage bond was filed on January 15, 1772, for his marriage to Martha Pool,[461] and he represented Pasquotank County in the assembly in 1782 and 1783.[462] On September 22, 1785, he accepted William Sylvestre, orphan of John Sylvestre, as an apprentice "to the art and calling of a silversmith."[463] In a deed dated July 9, 1787, Lane's residence was given as Nixonton,[464] and on August 17, 1789, William and Martha Lane gave Lot 25 in Nixonton to their daughter, Betty Stanton.[465] In a deed dated July 7, 1790, Lane was referred to as "William Lane (Inn Holder)."[466] The census of 1790 referred to him as "William

Lane, Esq."; at that time his household consisted of 2 white males over sixteen, 4 white males under sixteen, 3 white females, and 4 slaves.[467] On November 1, 1790, Lane was entry taker for Pasquotank County.[468] He was involved in many real estate transactions; in one instance, land was deeded to him on April 9, 1801.[469]

CHARLES LaPLACE. A newspaper notice dated July 9, 1795, declared that Charles LaPlace, a watchmaker from Paris, had taken the store lately occupied by Alexander Young in a certain Jones's house in Wilmington.[470] On March 23, 1796, P. Maugeon advertised that Charles LaPlace, watchmaker, after having left that town, had written to him giving him certain instructions.[471]

SAMUEL LAWING (1807-1865) was born May 3, 1807, probably in Mecklenburg County, and married Susan Means on September 23, 1834.[472] On June 1, 1841, he opened a shop for clockmaking and watchmaking in Charlotte, nearly opposite the Carolina Inn.[473] He became a member of the firm of Lawing & Brewer, and after the dissolution of the firm in 1843 worked independently. The will of Biddy Lawing, dated March 2, 1844, indicated that she held a note of her son, Samuel Lawing, for about $200, on which she allowed him a credit of $50.00.[474] He died on December 13, 1865, and was buried in Paw Creek Cemetery.[475]

LAWING & BREWER (1842-1843)—Samuel Lawing and N. Alexander F. Brewer, at Charlotte. The partnership was formed on January 18, 1842,[476] and was dissolved about a year later,[477] with Lawing continuing the business. The two men made jewelry and silverware to order.

JOSEPH LEE on January 24, 1767, was granted 185 acres of land on the waters of Garrison's Creek in Mecklenburg County. The grantor was George Augustus Selwyn, and the amount of money involved in the transaction was £18. In the deed Lee was described as a silversmith.[478]

TRAUGOTT LEINBACH (1796-1863), the son of Ludwig Leinbach and Anna Barbara Lauer, was born in Salem on July 7, 1796. He was apprenticed to John Vogler in October, 1811. On March 6, 1820, he asked permission of the church to go to

Shown above are five pieces of silver from the shop of Traugott Leinbach, who sometimes spelled his name Linebach. Top to bottom, the five are: a small teaspoon 5½ inches long, fiddle with pointed shoulders, engraved on the handle *SLV/from/CG*, pointed oval bowl with an incised drop; a dessertspoon 7 inches long with a bowl 1⅝ inches wide, 2¹⁵⁄₁₆ inches long, no engraving, long and gently pointed shoulders; a tablespoon 9 inches long, engraved *FSB* (or *FTB*), an eagle facing inward at the right of the maker's mark; a tablespoon 8⅝ inches long with a bowl 1¾ inches wide by 2⅞ inches long, engraved *NES*; a punch ladle 13 inches long with a bowl 4½ inches across and 3¼ inches long, engraved simply *H* in script for the original owners, Mr. and Mrs. Peter W. Hairston of Cooleemee plantation. (All from private collections.)

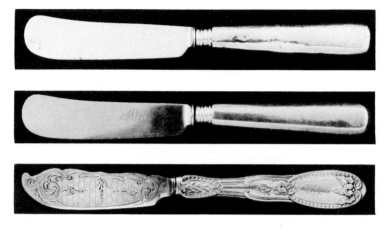

Pictured above are three butter knives and a fish slice marked by Traugott Leinbach with the three special die marks found on his hollow ware and unusual pieces: an eagle with head facing inward, a diamond enclosing an *L*, and an oval enclosing a head. The knives shown in the two topmost photographs are very similar butter knives. The one at top is 6¾ inches long with a handle of hammered silver, not engraved; beneath it is a knife 7 inches long engraved *MAM*. In the third photograph is a very ornate butter knife, Victorian in style, with several types of embellishment: a diapered surface on the blade, scrollwork, a foliage and wreath motif on the handle; three of this type have been found, all quite individual in detail. Of particular interest is the fish slice shown in the two bottom photographs. It is 11½ inches long, with very elaborate floral scrollwork on the front side of the blade, and is engraved *R.C.S. from Mrs Mayberry Brooks/Nov. 3rd 1858*. The handle is hexagonal, tapered, and ornamented with bright-cut engraving. The fish slice and two of the butter knives are on display at the North Carolina Museum of History. One of the butter knives was a gift from the Museum of History Associates; the fish slice was a gift from Commander Burl C. Kay.

Five important cups with the three special die marks of Traugott Leinbach have been found. Two of these, not pictured, have been the subject of an article by John Bivins in the *Old Salem Gleaner* (a publication of Old Salem, Inc.), XVII (Fall, 1974), 4. The two shown in the photographs at top are in private collections; the mug (marked T. LEINBACH & SON) shown in the two views at bottom is in the collection of the North Carolina Museum of History. At top left is an unusual footed cup that has an oriental appearance derived from a tree in the foreground with a structure in the background. The banding at upper rim and base is identical. The cup is 4⅜ inches high, 3⅜ inches in diameter, and is engraved *ACL* in script. The footed cup at top right is 4½ inches high and 2⅝ inches in diameter. It has a Greek key banding around the upper rim, beading at the base, and elaborate repoussé floral and foliate decoration on the body. (Not shown is the engraving *MH To/MSH*, enclosed in a wreath directly opposite the handle.) The presence of concentric rings in the footed cups, which indicates the use of a spinning technique, has given rise to questions about whether Leinbach was equipped to make these cups or whether they were produced elsewhere.

Bethlehem, Pennsylvania, and to work as a silversmith on his return to Salem. In January, 1821, he returned and opened his shop. On March 15, 1821, he married Maria Theresia Lange in Bethlehem, Pennsylvania. He worked continually in Salem until 1860, when he asked permission to transfer his house there to his son, Felix. He then went to Bethlehem, where he died on April 30, 1863.[479] Another son, Nathaniel Augustine, born in Salem on August 28, 1832, was a silversmith; but he later studied medicine and transferred his residence to Bethlehem in 1861. An entry made by Heinrich Leinbach, brother of Traugott, in his diary on August 22, 1834, suggests that the silversmith may also have been a pioneer in the field of photography: "I saw my brother's [Traugott's] Galvanic battery in operation, he has also got a Daguerreotype Apparatus, all of which he bought of a gentleman who also instructed him how to operate [them]. . . ."

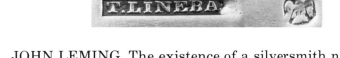

JOHN LEMING. The existence of a silversmith named John Leming in the Bertie County area is indicated by this notice: "John Leming takes Jeremiah Cullipher as apprentice to the silversmith's trade." The notice has the word "shoemaker" struck through and corrected to read "silversmith."[480]

LORD & GALE—[Joseph?] Gale and———Lord. On November 5, 1792, this firm advertised in Fayetteville a watchmaking and jewelry business. The two men offered silver-spangled and plated buckles and silver spoons—large and small—to the public.[481] It is likely that Joseph Gale was one member of the firm; Lord has not been identified.

JOHN A. LUKEMAN. An apprentice, Willis Smith, was bound to John A. Lukeman in March, 1791, to learn the trade of silver-smith.[482] Lukeman apparently worked in Carteret County.

LEMUEL LYNCH (1808-1893), the son of Moses Lynch and Susan Dickey, was born April 15, 1808, at Back Creek in Orange County.[483] He learned his trade with William Hunting-ton in Hillsborough. In 1828 Huntington advertised that he had sold his materials and rented his tools to Lynch and recom-mended him to the public.[484] On September 25, 1828, Lynch married Margaret W. Palmer of Hillsborough;[485] she was a niece of Mrs. Roswell Huntington. On June 10 he advertised that he had opened a shop in Greensboro, where all kinds of silver work were made;[486] and in September of the same year he announced that he had moved to another shop in Greens-

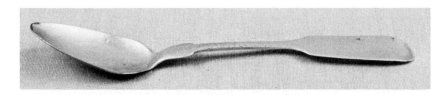

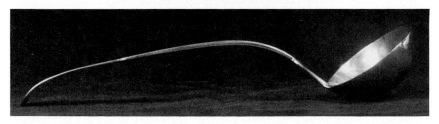

Two teaspoons made by Lemuel Lynch are on display at the North Carolina Museum of History. The spoon in the photograph at top was part of the wed-ding silver of Rebecca Waddell in 1848. It is 5⅞ inches long and fiddle in style, with rounded shoulders, a handle almost flat, and no engraving. The double-tipped end adds interest to the spoon in the center photograph. This piece was a gift to the museum from Mrs. Mary Catherine Parrish McCoscoe. The very handsome punch ladle (bottom) descended in the family of the late Mr. Robert B. Cooke of Durham and has been retained in a private collection.

boro.[487] On April 23, 1832, he advertised that he had commenced business in Concord;[488] but on March 18, 1834, he announced that he was again operating a business in Hillsborough.[489] The partnership of Huntington & Lynch was formed on October 22, 1834,[490] but it did not last more than two years. Lynch operated his own business in Hillsborough for the rest of his life. In 1841 he was appointed a justice of the peace and held court in Hillsborough. When the Orange County Courthouse of 1844 was built, Lynch repaired a treasured cupola clock and thereafter kept it regulated. In 1846 his bill for repairing (and possibly installing) the clock was $250.[491] He had three sons to whom he taught the silversmith craft: Thomas M. Lynch (1829-1881) of Oxford; Seabourn Lynch, who worked intermittently as a silversmith; and L. George Lynch, who worked with his father in Hillsborough. Lemuel Lynch died in Hillsborough on September 19, 1893. Evidence indicates that he kept at least three ledgers (A, B, C). Ledger C, covering the period 1861-1881, lists repair work and sales; it is in the Duke Manuscript Collection of the Duke University Library.[492] Lynch left his silversmith's tools to his son Seabourn J. Lynch, who died intestate in 1903. The Orange County Historical Museum has the original copper plate used for Lynch's watch papers and several pieces of Lynch silver.[943]

Three marks known to have been used by Lemuel Lynch are pictured here. The mark at top was taken from the back of the McCoscoe spoon; the mark at center is from the Cooke ladle; and the one at bottom is reproduced from Cutten's first edition, p. 35.

THOMAS M. LYNCH (1829-1881) was the son of Lemuel and Margaret W. Palmer Lynch. Trained by his father, Thomas was living in Oxford in 1868 inasmuch as on September 11 of that year Lemuel Lynch wrote a letter to his wife, who was then visiting her son, Thomas, in Oxford. Portions of that letter,

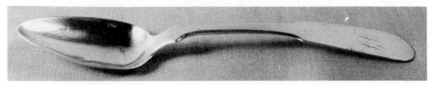

A teaspoon with the mark of Thomas Lynch has been identified. Presently in a private collection, it measures 5½ inches long, is fiddle with pointed shoulders, and is engraved *JS* (or *TS*) in script.

given to the Hillsborough Historical Society by Mrs. Virginia Gattis, were quoted in the *News of Orange County* (Hillsborough), November 11, 1965.

GEORGE LYON (LYONS). On January 30, 1819, he advertised that he had commenced the watch- and clockmaking business on Market Street in Wilmington.[494] Burton reports that in June, 1844, George Lyons, a watchmaker, was brutally murdered in his bed in Charleston;[495] although the evidence is not conclusive, the George *Lyon* reported to have worked in Wilmington may have been this George *Lyons*.

ANDREW McBRIDE. The first reference to him as a silversmith is as a member of the firm of McBride & Gardner, Charlotte, in 1807,[496] but he was involved in real estate transactions in Charlotte from 1804 to 1815.[497] In January, 1810, he was appointed guardian to the heirs of William Wilson and to the minor heirs of William McCord.[498] On April 24, 1810, McBride was appointed guardian to Nancy H. Armond, and his partner, Barzillai Gardner, was one of his bondsmen.[499] In May, 1813, McBride was elected high sheriff of Mecklenburg County and continued in that office until November, 1814.[500] He evidently left Charlotte shortly after this, probably in 1815, and settled in Newberry, South Carolina. On June 29, 1816, and September 6, 1816, from his new home he gave powers of attorney to John Black[501] of Mecklenburg County, North Carolina; and the following year Harriet McBride, wife of Andrew McBride of Newbury (Newberry) Village, South Carolina, is mentioned in a deed.[502] McBride, described as a native of

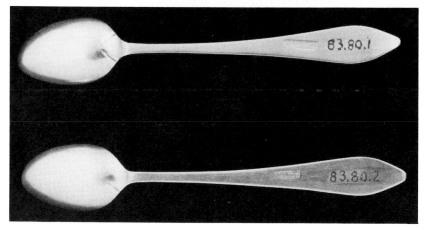

A recent acquisition for the collection of the North Carolina Museum of History is this pair of very graceful McBride spoons, each measuring 14.3 cm. in length. It is interesting to compare the decorative bright-cut decoration with that used by Freeman Woods. The initials *AF* are engraved on the handles, and the blunted oval of the handle ends is repeated in the shape of the drop.

Charleston, South Carolina, a former resident of Salisbury, and former sheriff of Mecklenburg County, died August 12, 1826, in Montgomery, Alabama.[503]

McBRIDE & GARDNER (1807-   ). On April 20, 1807, A. McBride and B. Gardner announced themselves as clockmakers and watchmakers, goldsmiths and silversmiths, in Charlotte. They thanked the public for past favors and offered cash or work for old gold, silver, or brass.[504]

JOHN McCLENAHAN of Granville County died November 26, 1826. He is described in his obituary, in the *North Carolina Star* of December 1, 1826, as being a "planter and silversmith, an old and respectable inhabitant" of the county. The large inventory of his estate includes many items that would suggest that he had considerable business in silversmithing:

1	Clock case	$ 8.77
1	musical clock	51.99
1	card of clasps	1.00
1	card Ear Drops	.22
1	" " "	.25
1	" " "	1.95
1	Pair scales & Weights	2.00
3	Harmers [*sic*] & 3 weights	2.55
1	vise	1.05
1	stack weights	.80
1	stack weights	.85
1	Box of Crusables [*sic*]	.02
1	Pair Tongues [tongs]	.15
1	Stones Judge [a device for appraising]	.60
½	Doz Tea Spoons	4.00
1	Ladle	1.26
"	" [bought by John C. Palmer]	.99½
½	Doz. Tea Spones [*sic*]	4.75
½	Doz. " "	5.36
2	Pair Spectacles	1.16
1	Watch	1.25
1	brass Watch	2.00
1	" "	1.50
1	silver watch	8.00
1	Lot old Silver [bought by Wm. McClenahan]	3.02
1	Lot old Gold [bought by Wm. McClenahan]	3.25
1	Lot old Gold [bought by Wm. McClenahan]	6.81
1	Lot old Gold [bought by Jn°. P. Smith]	14.00
1	Lot old Silver [bought by Wm. McClenahan]	6.66
1	Lot Castings [to Judith McClenahan]	.05
1	oven	.25
1	Kettle	1.00
1	lot of Castings	.25
1	Ladle [bought by John C. Palmer]	1.10
1	Ladle [bought by John C. Palmer]	1.25
1	Coker nutt [cocoanut?]	1.05
2	Sissors [*sic*] Chane [*sic*] [bought by John C. Palmer]	.75[506]

In addition to these excerpted items, there were many articles of jewelry, thimbles, buttons, a set of watch papers, spectacles, tweezers, etc., some of which were purchased by another silversmith, John C. Palmer. The total sum realized by the estate sale was $2,478.45¼, which for that day was rather impressive in North Carolina.[507]

DREWERY McGEE. Mrs. W. H. McGee of Germanton, North Carolina, has provided the information that Drewery McGee (1828-1895) was a silversmith who lived in Surry County, near Mount Airy.

NEIL McKAY. A notice in the Iredell County court minutes for August 23, 1804, indicates that there was a silversmith named Neil McKay in the Iredell County area in the early nineteenth century. Neil McKay bound Alexander McKay, orphan of Robert McKay, as an apprentice to the silversmith's trade.[508] In the *Raleigh Minerva* of February 5, 1813, there was a second item about the McKays:

TWELVE-AND-AN-HALF-CENTS REWARD

ABSCONDED from the subscriber, ALEXANDER McKAY, an indented apprentice to the silversmith's business. The above reward, but no charges, will be paid for his delivery to me, on my premises, in Iredell.
    N.B. All persons are hereby forewarned not to harbor the said apprentice at their peril.

January 11, 1813[509]

ANGUS McLEAN was described as a silversmith in notices of his death that appeared in two Raleigh newspapers. He died of pleurisy on March 13, 1810, "at his seat in Robeson County . . ." and left a "widow and three small children."[510]

JOHN McLEAN (ca. 1755-1829) came to North Carolina from Scotland and settled in Cumberland County in 1772. In 1779 he moved to Rowan County in what is now part of Iredell County, settling in a community about nine miles west of present-day Statesville. With other Scotch families in the area, McLean established an ARP church in New Starling. He became known as "Silversmith John" and evidently prospered, acquiring a number of slaves. According to a notice of his death in the October 6, 1829, issue of the Salisbury *Western Carolinian*, McLean, of Iredell County, died September 16, 1829, at the age of seventy-four. There are several pieces that are reputed to bear his mark (IM) and which are still in the hands of his descendants or the descendants of his friends.[511]

JAMES McRAE is said to have made at least two spoons and to have put his own mark on them. McRae was an apprentice of Zenas Alexander, the apprenticeship papers having been processed in 1810 by the Mecklenburg County Court. Whether or not the apprentice McRae was related to the Reverend James McRae (1782-1820), pastor of Steele Creek Presbyterian Church, has not been determined.[512]

THOMAS WALE MACHEN (ca. 1774-1839). The *Newbern Gazette*, September 26, 1800, contained a notice of Machen's removal to another location, and he described himself as a "Gold & Silversmith." In the *Morning Herald* (New Bern), September 17, 1807, Machen advertised "Watches and Clocks Cleaned and Repaired." Again he especially solicited business as a clock and watch repairman in the *True Republican or American Whig* (Wilmington), May 2, 1809. In this notice Machen emphasized his special ability to repair "Mariners Compasses" and to do engraving at reasonable prices. He also announced a move to a different location in New Bern.

On January 25, 1812, Machen was advertising a long list of silverware and jewelry he had just received from New York;[513] and in 1813[514] and again in 1821[515] he gave notice of his removal to another location in New Bern. In his frequent advertisements he mentioned silver articles prominently. In 1824 the silversmith advertised tablespoons, dessertspoons, sugar tongs, and soup ladles of superior quality.[516] A new line of goods appeared in his advertising in 1826 and subsequently: fancy goods, lemon syrup, soap, starch, quinine, Sedlitz powders, dry goods, and books.[517] He never entirely ceased handling watches and silverware, however, and in 1830 he continued to advertise the cleaning and repairing of watches and clocks.[518] He married Betsy Banks, the bond being dated January 25, 1822.[519]

The *Newbern Spectator*, October 25, 1839, had an account of Machen's death "in the 65th year of his age"; thus, his birthdate apparently was 1774. The obituary further stated that "Mr. Machen had been in a declining state of health for several years." A valuable find in the 1970s was a gorget made by Machen, which was found by Mr. John P. Hart of York, South

Carolina, in an Indian grave on the South Carolina side of the
Broad River near the town of Van Wyck. The gorget is now in
the MESDA Collection at Old Salem.

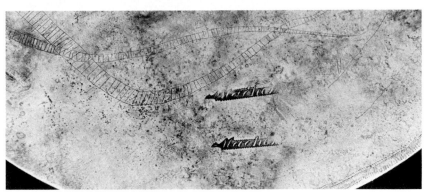

The ornamental piece of armor pictured above (front view at top, detail of
back segment at bottom) is described in the *Old Salem Gleaner,* XV (Spring,
1972):

"This silver gorget, marked by Thomas W. Machen of Newbern, has been
added to the MESDA collection through the generosity of G. Wilson Douglas,
Jr. . . .

"The crescent-shaped ornament, Ca. 1800, was made for a Catawba Indian,
Finey George, whose name is engraved on its face. George added some engraving of his own—two millipede-like devices at the corners and two snakes on the
rear.

"Gorgets were used as a badge of rank by military officers during the 18th
century, and they proved to be excellent trade items when bartering with the
Indians. This one was found in an Indian grave near the Catawba River South
of Charlotte." (Photographs courtesy MESDA.)

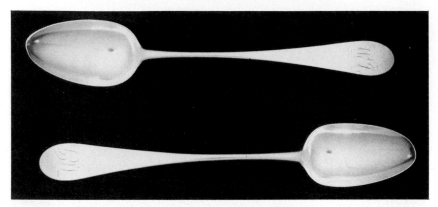

These two tablespoons with the rare mark of Thomas Machen are exciting additions to the collection of the North Carolina Museum of History. Purchased by the Museum of History Associates in 1982, both have flat, spatulate handles but slightly different proportions. The ends of the handles vary in width, and the bowl of one spoon is eliptical, while the other is oval. Both are engraved *MEJ* in script. The mark is the same as that on the gorget.

H. MAHLER (1832-1895). Henry Mahler emigrated from Osnabruck, Germany, to Raleigh ca. 1852. His two older brothers, Frederick and Christian, had preceded Henry in coming to America; Frederick had also come to Raleigh, where he operated a general store "next to Pomeroy's" and allowed his younger brother to have his silversmith's shop. Henry Mahler's apprenticeship as a silversmith and engraver had been served in Hanover, Germany. By November 15, 1854, the craftsman was advertising his trade in the Raleigh *North Carolina Standard* of January 3, 1855:

H. Mahler takes pleasure in informing the ladies of Raleigh and the public in general that he still continues to manufacture Gold Earrings, Breastpins, Bracelets, Fingerrings, Silver Spoons, Mugs and Goblets, Tea Sets, and all articles in Gold and Silver that can be had at a Jewelry establishment.

Engrave and chase on Gold and Silverware and all materials where engraving can be executed.

Repair in the neatest manner and at the lowest rate that will ensure universal satisfaction.

The workroom is in the rear of F. Mahler & Company's store where orders may be left any time during the day.

P. S. Court and other Seals executed in a manner not surpassed at the North.

Nov. 15, 1854   H. Mahler

Spoons with the mark Henry Mahler used on his handcrafted silver are pictured on this page. The two shown above have a variation of a double-swell handle not typical of North Carolina silver. The dessertspoon in the top photograph is 7¼ inches long with a stylized engraving of *CI* (?); the mark used is MAHLER in a rectangle. In the bottom photograph is a tablespoon 8⁹/₁₆ inches long engraved *GNP* in script; the mark is H. MAHLER N C, the N and C separated by a pine tree.

Three of the spoons pictured are traditional fiddle in style, 5½ inches long, engraved *Belle*, and stamped on the back with Mahler's die mark and N C with the pine tree. The serving spoon is elaborately engraved—not handcrafted but in an early Victorian silver pattern. On silver he retailed, Mahler used an incused mark. (From a private collection; photograph by Charles Clark.)

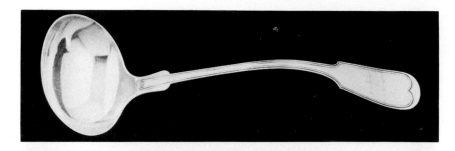

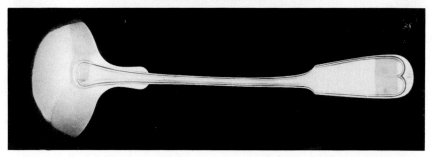

Shown here are front and back views of a handsome fiddle and thread punch ladle simply marked H. MAHLER in incused letters and engraved *Mother To Hannah* in script. It is 13½ inches long with a bowl 4¼ inches across. (From a private collection.)

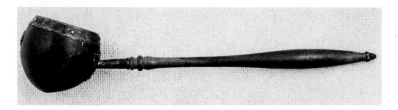

Pictured here is one of two dippers known to have been made by Mahler. Both have bowls made from coconuts, but this one is trimmed with brass and has brass studs and a brass plaque in front with elaborate engraving—*LM*(?). It is 18 inches overall, with a bowl 3⅝ inches deep and 3⅛ inches across. (From a private collection.) The dipper not pictured has been described as having silver trim.

Three important small pieces of hollow ware found in North Carolina have
Mahler marks. Two views of a cup made for Frances Iredell Johnson, granddaughter of Governor James Iredell, are shown at top. The cup, slightly pear-
shaped, is 4 inches in diameter, 12½ inches around the top rim, and 3¼ inches
deep. It has a molded rim and cast scroll handle. On the front is a repoussé
wreath of flowers and foliage with the name of the original owner engraved
within. The die mark is MAHLER in a rectangle. (From a private collection.) At
bottom left is a handsome cup distinguished by its round, globular body on a
round, stepped foot. The rim and base are molded with beading beneath the
upper molding and above the base molding. The family name *Warters* is
engraved in black lettering on the front in free form. This cup is presently on
display in Harmony Hall, Kinston. At bottom right is an unusual beaker with
tapered body, incised banding at median, molding at lip, and decorated by a
unique motif of moon and stars on the lower half of the body. It is 9.3 cm. in
height, 8 cm. in diameter. A gift from Mr. G. Wilson Douglas, this piece is presently on display at the North Carolina Museum of History.

These pieces, a "silver matching creamer and covered sugar bowl" attributed to "H. Mahler, N.C., c. 1840," were advertised in the catalog (New York: Tabard Press, 1971) compiled for the American Heritage Society's Auction of Americana, conducted by Sotheby, Parke-Bernet Galleries on November 12 and 13, 1971. The silver was described as being "of Lobed Vase shape with borders of flowers and foliage, engraved with a monogram, double-scroll handles, 40 ozs. 10 dwts. Heights 8½ and 9 inches." (From a private collection; photographed by Taylor and Dull for Theresa and Arthur Greenblatt.)

Mr. and Mrs. John C. Mahler, Raleigh descendants of Henry Mahler, have provided the following additional information:

During the Civil War he gave much time to helping the Confederate government in various ways, making ammunition, belt buckles and other articles of vital importance.

The business he established grew to be probably the largest jewelry concern in eastern North Carolina. During H. Mahler's forty or so years of residence in Raleigh he also engaged in many community projects. He was appointed one of the commissioners of the city by Provisional Governor Holden. Later he was on the board of aldermen for two or three years and was instrumental in effecting city improvements, especially the lighting of the streets and the care of the market. He was interested in the city's welfare, and the Democratic County Convention of 1872 named him as head of the Board of Commissioners; his name went on the ticket, but, having little interest in politics, he declined to run for office.

In the bound volumes of legislative proceedings and state officers' reports, prior to and during the Civil War, the itemized statements of receipts and expenditures contain constant mention of H. Mahler as maker of county seals or presses, these being paid for by the state of North Carolina.

Henry Mahler died November 19, 1895. The funeral was held at Christ Church, with the last rites conducted by the Masons. Interment was in Oakwood Cemetery, Raleigh.

In the autumn of 1971 Parke-Bernet Galleries of New York City advertised that "a silver matching creamer and covered sugar bowl" attributed to "H. Mahler, N.C., c. 1840," would be sold during the American Heritage Society's "Auction of Americana" on November 12 and 13, 1971.

A granddaughter of Henry Mahler, Mrs. Stephen Farrington (Mary Frances Mahler Farrington) of Lake Placid, New York, has provided information about handsome flat silver that bears the incused mark "H. Mahler." Its style and the fact that "Sterling" is marked on this magnificent silver would indicate that it is late nineteenth-century work; Mahler was obviously a very skillful engraver. Mrs. Farrington says:

Henry Mahler married a widow in 1865 [Fanny Kramer Mahler, d. 1913]. There were four Mahler children—Louis August, Frederick Wilbelur, Julius Henry, and Francis. Louis and Frederick went into business with their father and the name [of the firm] changed at his death to H. Mahler's Sons.

ISAAC MARQUAND (1766-1838) is referred to as a goldsmith from London.[520] On November 11, 1791, he advertised himself as a goldsmith and silversmith, clockmaker and watchmaker, and opened a shop on Broad Street, Edenton, adjoining Henry Niel's store. He proposed to carry on the silversmith's business in all its branches and wanted "a boy, between the age of 14 and 16, as an apprentice."[521] On November 16, 1792, he announced that he had returned and had again commenced business in Edenton.[522] On February 11, 1796, he gave to Jonathan Maltbee a bill of sale for "two buildings joined together making a shop where I formerly worked, . . . all my silversmith and watchmaking tools, one negro boy by the name of Sam."[523] (Three years earlier, he had bought Sam at a sheriff's sale for £130.)[524] Six days later, on February 17, 1796, he informed the people of Edenton that he intended to leave the state and requested all persons indebted to him to make payment to Jonathan Maltbee.[525] His name is to be found in the New York City

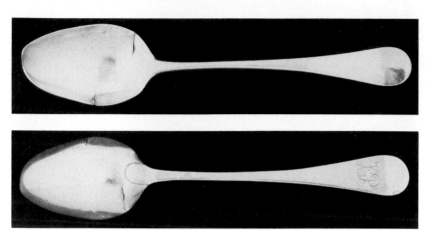

Pictured above are front and back views of a tablespoon attributed to Isaac Marquand. The spoon, from a private collection, was one of several pieces of North Carolina silver held by a single family in the Edenton area. The bowl is oval with a rounded drop; it is damaged and unrepaired. The spatulate, tapered handle has a front midrib with IM in an oval cartouche on the back and *JCPN* (or *HP*) engraved on the back.

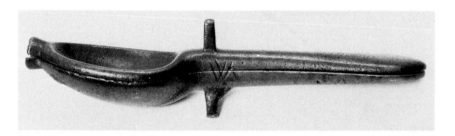

This mold for making tablespoons is believed to have belonged to Isaac Marquand. It is presently in the collection of the North Carolina Museum of History.

directory for 1804-1805 as a merchant; and the following year the address of his store is given as 183 Front Street. For the next five years his name does not appear, but it was continually present from 1811-1812 to 1838-1839. He was always designated as a merchant, but his brother Frederick, at the same address, was classed as a jeweler; and those with whom he entered into partnerships were known as jewelers. His store was opened at 166 Broadway in 1810; and in 1815 an English jeweler, Erastus Barton, became his partner at the same address under the name of E. Barton & Co.[526] This partnership was dissolved by the death of Barton in 1823. In 1825 Marquand's brother Frederick entered the business with him. In 1830 at the same address was the firm of Marquand & Brothers (Isaac, Frederick, and Josiah P.). In 1833 it became Marquand & Company when the business was moved to 181 Broadway, at which time former apprentices William Black and Henry Ball joined the firm.[527] Isaac Marquand died in Brooklyn on November 24, 1828;[528] the following year the Marquands withdrew from the firm, which then became Ball, Tompkins & Black.[529]

The IM maker's mark at left is from the tablespoon attributed to Isaac Marquand; the one at right is from the tablespoon mold believed to have belonged to him. Note that the two marks are not identical.

Isaac Marquand was in Edenton, 1791-1796. In 1833 the name of the firm of Isaac, Frederick, and Josiah P. Marquand was changed from Marquand & Brothers to Marquand & Co. The business was moved to 181 Broadway, and William Black and Henry Ball joined the firm. (Rainwater, *Encyclopedia of American Silver Manufacturers*, 102.)

PLEASANT HENDERSON MARTIN of Guilford County was a silversmith, according to information provided by his great granddaughter, Mrs. Ruth Martin Decker of Summerfield. Nothing else is known about this man's craft.

JOHN M. MASON. The Wake County court minutes for November 20, 1826, record that John M. Mason had taken Anderson B. Williams, an orphan of seventeen, as an apprentice to the silversmith's trade. Again, on February 20, 1832, the minutes reveal that William Adams also was apprenticed to Mason to learn the silversmith's trade.[530]

CHRISTOPHER N. MASTERS. The Craven County court minutes for September 10, 1810, indicate that Christopher N. Masters bound as an apprentice to the silversmith's trade the orphan George Bruce. This would suggest that Masters was working as a silversmith in the area during the early 1800s.[531] Ten years earlier, a Christopher Masters had been apprenticed to Freeman Woods,[532] which further substantiates the suggestion that Masters was a working silversmith.

ROBERT MELLYNE (Moline, Mellyn, Morlines, Meline, Mulline, Mullines, Mollyn, Moliones, Moloines, ca. 1666-ca. 1708/9) was living in North Carolina for some years prior to 1702. His name, with all its variations of spelling, appears numerous times in Saunders, *Colonial Records, The Colonial Records of North Carolina, Second Series,* and the Beaufort County Deeds, Book I. Mr. George Stevenson, archivist in the Division of Archives and History, has found evidence to support the belief that this man was by trade a silversmith, possibly the first in North Carolina. Although the name was spelled in so many ways—most often "Moline" in the public records—the man himself spelled it "Mellyne" and was consistent in doing so. His signature, for example, is on the wills of David Makee and Edward Wood; both documents are in the North Carolina Wills, 1663-1790, Secretary of State Records, State Archives. An interesting deed of land was made to Mellyne in 1702:

> Know all men by these Presents that I, John Lawson, do bargain, sell, alienate and make over to Robert Mellyne a Tract of Land containing six hundred and forty acres, be the same more or less, lying and being up the north dividing creek in Pamtico River relation being had to the entry will more largely appear, to have and to hold the aforesaid tract of land. . . .

> Witnesses   Narrows
> Levi Truewhitt   the legal Attorney
> Richard Smith   of Jo." Lawson
>   July 1, 1702

(Beaufort County Deeds, Book I, p. 20, State Archives.)

On the same page is a reference to "land I now live upon" being deeded to William Price by "Robert Mollines of Pamtico, Silversmith." In the same deed book (p. 43) is an entry dated

July 5, 1703, giving rights of entry to his property—"Robert Mellyne of Bath County, Silversmith, rights to entry of land on North Dividing Creek [Moline's Creek?]"—made by Mellyne on June 12, 1703, to Philip Howard.

Mellyne's will was made on December 29, 1708, and he had died by January 4, 1708/9, when the will was probated. This is also in the Beaufort County Deeds, Book I, p. 98. Since there were no children, Mellyne willed his property to his sisters still living in Ireland and to their heirs upon the death of Ellinor Mellyne, his wife. Edward Mackswine, a nephew, claimed the property in 1720. (Saunders, *Colonial Records*, II, 377.)

An identification of "Mollines" as a "Quoiner" (coiner) in 1696 is found in the *Crown* v. *Fewox* case (Mattie Erma Edwards Parker [ed.], *North Carolina Higher-Court Records, 1670-1696*, Volume II of *The Colonial Records of North Carolina, Second Series*, edited by Mattie Erma Edwards Parker and others [Raleigh: Division of Archives and History, Department of Cultural Resources (projected multivolume series, 1963—), 1968], 308-309). In November, 1693, "Robert Mulline" was called to serve on the grand jury; and in the court records of the council for September, 1694, "Robt. Moline" was subpoenaed as a witness. Subsequent documents reveal that both Mellyne and his wife Ellinor were involved in several cases brought before the court. Except through these court records, little is known about him; but Robert Mellyne of Bath County may well have been the first silversmith to live in North Carolina.

HENRY MELVILLE. Present-day knowledge of him is confined to less than two months of the year 1798. On May 31 he advertised that he, a watchmaker and clockmaker from London, had taken the shop lately occupied by Lambertoz on Dock Street, Wilmington.[533] On July 4 a bond was furnished for Melville's marriage to Nancy Browne,[534] and on July 19 he advertised for an apprentice.[535]

JOHN BRYANT MILLS was married to Cynthia Twigg, the bond being dated July 18, 1827.[536] On January 1, 1830, he advertised in Fayetteville as a goldsmith and silversmith and announced to the public that things needing repair might be left with John Campbell, goldsmith, and when repaired would be left there again for their owners.[537] In August, 1831, he complained that the public had forsaken him; notwithstanding this, he advertised for an apprentice.[538]

WILLIAM R. MONTCASTLE settled in Warrenton in 1844 and was still there in 1856, at which time he thanked the public for the support given him for nearly twelve years as a jeweler.[539]

CAMERON (CAMM) MOORE (1755-1845), a Quaker craftsman in Guilford County, was born on March 22, 1755, the son of John Moore, Jr., and Elizabeth Sanders, whose marriage had taken place in the Cedar Creek Meetinghouse, Hanover County, Virginia, in 1750.[540] The silversmith's paternal grandparents were John and Anne Moore of Louisa County, Virginia, and his maternal grandparents were John and Jane Sanders, very active members of the Hopewell Friends Meeting at Opekon in Frederick County.[541] The Cedar Creek meetinghouse was built by John Sanders in 1739, and in 1742 the family moved to that community.[542] In 1778 Camm Moore was accepted as a member of the New Garden Monthly Meeting in Guilford County on a certificate from the Cedar Creek Meeting; and during the same year he was married to Sophia Benbow, by whom he had seven children who were born between 1779 and 1799.[543] Sophia died on July 16, 1821. The first record of Moore's buying land is dated September 24, 1799, at which time he acquired 173 acres from William Dillon.[544] The tract extended upstream from Dillon's Mill on both sides of Reedy Fork and was apparently the same tract on which Moore was living at the time of his death at the age of ninety in July, 1845. At some point, the Moore family moved their membership to Dover Meeting. Moore's executor was his daughter Hannah, and one paragraph of his will has an unusual request: "It is my will that all my moveable property be sold as soon as convenient, except my tools [if his son Joshua did not want them], which I will should be advertised two months or more, and described what they are for in some suitable newspapers. . . ."[545] This provision gives rise to speculation as to what unique tools these may have been. Although only one article signed by Moore has yet come to light, that one is of significance. It is a surveyor's compass now on display at the Greensboro Historical Museum. Unfortunately, there is no information available about either the original owner or the donor.

Certainly, Moore was reputed to have been a silversmith, but he may also have been making other instruments comparable to the compass. Hughes says: "Cameron Moore represented another branch of technology—a more precise and exacting one. He was a maker of precision mathematical instruments,

This surveyor's compass with the mark of Cameron Moore "represents a high state of the art for the period and may be equal to those of the Rittenhouses of Philadelphia," writes Fred Hughes. This instrument, presently on display at the Greensboro Historical Museum, is made of cast brass with a cast brass cover and sighting posts. The face is engraved and signed C. MOORE, GUILFORD, N.C. The needle is of a high quality of steel with built-in compensation. The ring is made of silver or silver-plated brass. There is no sign of wear, and the compass is in an excellent, usable state. A comparison of Moore's compass with the one made by John Vogler reveals a number of remarkable similarities, Moore's being the older of the two. Photograph courtesy Archives Division, Greensboro Historical Museum, Greensboro.

and a very good one."[546] He had at least one apprentice, Samuel Short, son of Moses and Sarah Short. Moses died or was killed in 1781, and there were four children besides Samuel—Sarah, Aaron, William Oldham, and Jonathan Bird.[547] In the Guilford County County court minutes for the May term, 1787, is the record that "Samuel Short, age 12 years, 11 months, 3 weeks was bound to Cameron Moore to the age of 21 to learn the trade of silversmith."

JOSEPH MOORE is identified as a silversmith in Edgecombe County Deeds, Book 2, p. 2, according to information from the files of MESDA. The deed containing this information bears the date December 10, 1750.

DAVID A. MURDOCK on April 25, 1812, informed his friends and the public that he had opened a shop on Middle Street in New Bern, where he intended carrying on the goldsmith and

silversmith business in its various branches.[548] In the advertisement, which can be found in several of the extant issues of
the *Carolina Federal Republican*, Murdock offered the "highest
prices" for old gold and silver. He married Maria Dewey, the
bond being dated May 20, 1813.[549] On March 15, 1814, Samuel
Fisher and John Gill were apprenticed to the silversmith Murdock.[550] In 1819 John Gill advertised that he had purchased the
stand lately occupied by David A. Murdock.[551] Murdock himself
had been apprenticed to Freeman Woods on June 10, 1805.[552]

HENRY NIEL opened a goldsmith's, jeweler's, and hair
worker's shop in Edenton in August, 1811. He then advertised
that he would work gold according to the alloy the customers
should propose.[553] There was a certain Henry Niel, or Honore
Niel, designated as a merchant and active in business in Edenton from 1792 until the time of his death in 1810, when he left
property to his wife, Peggy.[554] These presumably were the parents of Henry Niel, goldsmith. There is some indication from
the Cupola House Papers that ca. June 17, 1813, the goldsmith
was involved in financial trouble and left town.[555]

JAMES S. NORMAN advertised in 1840 that he would repair
clocks and watches in Lincolnton and claimed to have had long
experience.[556]

MARTIN NOXON (1780-1814), born May 12, 1780, at Oswego,
Duchess County, New York, the son of Pasco Noxon and Anna
Harris, was baptized at the neighboring village of Hopewell. He
came to Edenton in 1800 or soon afterward, and on February
28, 1804, a bond was given in connection with his marriage to
Hannah Carpenter.[557] Noxon advertised in the *Edenton Gazette*
of February 26, 1806, that he had jewelry for sale, mentioned
"watches repaired as usual," and offered to accept old gold and
silver in payment. In a September, 1807, issue of the *Edenton
Gazette* was another advertisement. The date of the extant
Gazette is missing, but the notice was dated June 30, 1807. In
this notice Noxon urged prompt payment from those indebted
to him but said that he was "intending to leave this state for a
short time"; evidently, he truly expected to return, since he said
"that in consequence of some additional assistance, he shall be
enabled to serve them [his customers] with more punctuality, in
future, in all the branches of his business. . . ."

These coffin-end spoons with the NOXON mark were photographed by
MESDA for its files. The initials *FRL* in script with a single *S* beneath are
engraved on the handle. The bowls are oval with a shallow drop. Photograph
courtesy MESDA. A Noxon spoon has recently been acquired by the Museum
Associates for the North Carolina Museum of History.

In 1808 Martin Noxon of Edenton and Miriam Carpenter had
three different dealings involving bills of sale, two of which
were for slaves Noxon bought from her and the third involving
Lot 14 in Edenton.[558] On April 21, 1809, Noxon was advertising
in the *Gazette* that "in addition to his usual business of repairing Clocks and Watches, making gold and silver work, &c. he
has furnished himself with everything necessary for Repairing
and Touching the Mariner's Compass." In 1810 he advertised
as a clockmaker and watchmaker and thanked the public for
past favors.[559] On February 8, 1811, he announced that he had
employed a gunsmith.[560] The *Republican Herald* (Poughkeep-
sie, New York) announced Noxon's death in its issue of November 9, 1814. At the October term of the court of equity in
1815, Nathaniel Bond, guardian of Martin and Elizabeth,
orphan children of Martin Noxon, deceased, late of Edenton,
asked permission to sell "a lot of land on King St. occupied by
the deceased as a silversmith shop."[561]

GIDEON OLMSTEAD. In Charlotte on June 18, 1832, he
advertised a "New Establishment." He commenced business as
a clockmaker, watchmaker, and jeweler.[562]

PHILIP OTT advertised on October 2, 1792, that he continued to carry on the goldsmith and jewelry business in Fayetteville.[563] Two weeks later he said that he intended to carry on plating also.[564] In June, 1793, the advertisement was still running.[565] On October 15, 1793, he deeded land to James Beard.[566] At a meeting held September 15, 1786, at the Golden Ball, Petersburg, Virginia, a certain Philip Ott voted.[567]

JOHN C. PALMER (ca. 1800-1893), silversmith, daguerreotyper, and churchman, was the son of John B. and Sarah Rich Palmer.[568] The Palmers removed to Rowan County from New Jersey, and various members of the family were involved in a number of land transactions in Rowan County.[569] John C. Palmer learned the art of silversmithing from John Y. Savage, a silversmith in Raleigh. It was during his years of apprenticeship that he became a very active member of the Edenton Street Methodist Church there.[570] In 1826 Dr. Robert Vance, a physician in western North Carolina, was defeated for Congress by Samuel T. Carson. Some words uttered during the campaign resulted in a duel in which Carson was killed at Saluda Gap, South Carolina. The pistols used on that occasion "belonged to Mr. Palmer, a jeweler in Raleigh."[571]

About 1827 Palmer left Raleigh to work for some time in Oxford, Granville County, and in Haywood, Chatham County. On October 16, 1827, Palmer (whose middle name could not be determined) married Maryann (Mary Anne) Hampton, daughter of William Hampton of Salisbury and sister of James B. Hampton and Mrs. Philo White (Mary Hampton).[572] Palmer and James B. Hampton operated a jewelers' and watch repair firm known as J. Hampton & Palmer until Hampton's death in 1832.[573] Two years later, on August 9, 1834, Palmer was advertising a branch business in Concord, with the Concord office being operated by a "Mr. Bagby" of Lynchburg, Virginia.[574] The two men combined the jewelry and watch repair trades, and Palmer made silver to order.

On October 23, 1840, John Palmer advertised in the Salisbury *Western Carolinian* that he planned to sell at auction most of his household furniture since he planned to remove from Salisbury to Raleigh. By November 18, 1840, he had returned to Raleigh and was operating a jewelry business and watch repair shop in a new building erected by Richard Smith on Fayetteville Street.[575] By 1845 he had added a daguerreotype gallery to his business operation.[576] Two years later Palmer acquired a

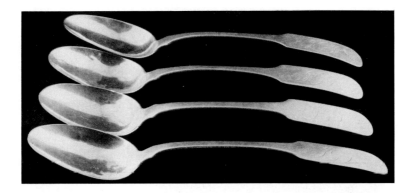

Two styles of spoons made by John C. Palmer are illustrated on this page. In the photographs at top and center are six tablespoons, all approximately 8⅝ inches long. Fiddle in form, they have chamfered shoulders. All are engraved *JGL* in script, suggesting one original owner (although the spoons are presently in two different collections). Two have been given to the North Carolina Museum of History by Mr. and Mrs. Walter Hatch Lee. The mark used is J.C.PALMER in a barbed rectangle. In the photograph at bottom are teaspoons with tipped-front handles and chamfered shoulders. There are four other spoons in this collection in addition to the two shown. They are engraved *WHW* in script and are marked only by the pseudomarks (an eagle, a *W* in a diamond, and a monarch's head) found on other silver, which also has J.C.PALMER in incused letters.

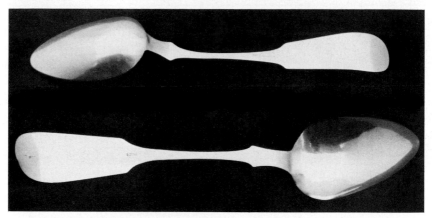

One of the two tablespoons shown above has the mark of J. C. Palmer, and the other has the mark of Palmer & Ramsay. Both are 8⅝ inches long, but they differ in other dimensions. The Palmer is a tipped fiddle with no engraving, while the Palmer-Ramsay has a wider, more shallowly tipped handle and is engraved with an *A* in script. Two other spoons, evidently from this set, have been found.

partner, Walter J. Ramsay, and from 1847 until 1855 the two maintained this partnership; upon its dissolution Palmer purchased Ramsay's interest and continued the business until he retired in 1889. Palmer was listed in the *Raleigh Register* of March 30, 1859, as one of the directors of the North Carolina Institution for the Education of the Deaf and Dumb, and of the Blind.[577] The craftsman, who had been instrumental in the organization of a Methodist church in Salisbury, resumed his activity in the Edenton Street Methodist Church following his return to Raleigh. In 1868 the *Milton Chronicle* ran advertisements for Palmer and O. Salzman, "watchmakers and Jewelers, Milton."[578]

These two spoons show a difference in form in that the handle of one is more definitely downturned than the other, although both measure 8¼ inches in length. Both are Palmer-Ramsay.

Palmer was married twice, but the death date of his first wife, Mary Ann(e) Hampton Palmer, is uncertain. The frequent occurrence of the name Mary Palmer in county records and newspapers causes confusion. There was in the *Western Carolinian* of January 17, 1840, this notice: "Departed this life at Hillsborough very suddenly on the 9th inst. Mrs. Mary A. Palmer in the 60th year of her age." The name Mary was common in the family of Martin Palmer of Hillsborough, and it cannot be determined whether or not this was the first Mrs. John C. Palmer. The *Charlotte Democrat* of August 22, 1871, carried a notice of the death of Mary Ann Hampton Palmer in Raleigh, and it is noted in another source that she was "age 60 years 8 months 8 days." In the *Carolina Watchman* of March 4, 1875, was an announcement of John C. Palmer's marriage on February 25, 1875, to Mrs. Mary Alphia Young of Chatham County. The fact that both wives were named Mary adds to the confusion.

John C. Palmer died in 1893 at the home of Mrs. M. J. Brown on North Person Street in Raleigh. The funeral service was conducted at his church, and burial was in the Raleigh City Cemetery.[579] Palmer's grave, evidently unmarked, is believed to be in what is known as the "family plot" wherein Charles W. Palmer and his wife Sarah J. Palmer also are buried.[580] Their relationship to John C. Palmer has not been determined. No survivors are named in Palmer's obituary, and it is believed there were no surviving children or spouse. In Raleigh during his final years he was affectionately called "Uncle Johnny."

In partnerships with other craftsmen and working alone, John C. Palmer handcrafted much silver flatware of exceptionally fine quality during his long lifetime; many pieces have

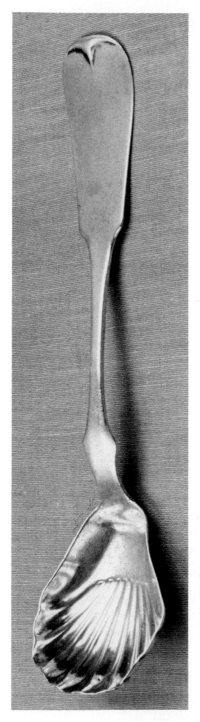

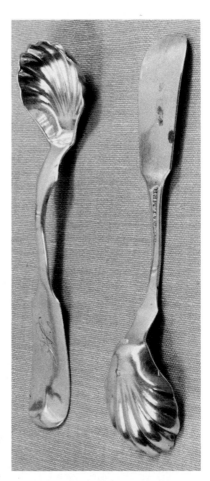

Shown at left is a sugar shell made by John C. Palmer. Pictured above are two salt spoons, also made by Palmer. The Palmer hallmark accompanied by additional marks following the name was taken from the sugar shell. All three pieces are in private collections.

been identified in the Salisbury and Raleigh areas—all over the state, in fact—and undoubtedly other pieces will eventually come to light.

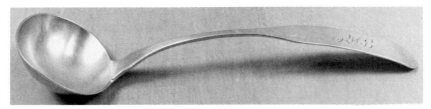

The handle of this graceful punch ladle is engraved *RHB* for the original owners. Presented as a gift, the ladle was used at the wedding of Richard and Harriet Blacknall. On the back is J. C. Palmer's mark and his name in a rectangle, which is plain on three sides but beaded at the top.

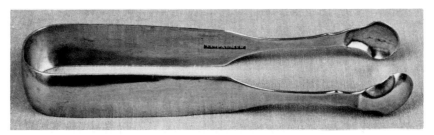

These sugar tongs, made by J. C. Palmer and presently on display at the North Carolina Museum of History, are plain with no engraving and measure 6¾ inches in length.

This handsome silver mug with the Palmer-Ramsay mark on the bottom is a rare find. The mug has a molded upper rim with beading, wide banded molding at the base, and double scroll handle. (In the collection of the North Carolina Museum of History.)

PALMER & RAMSAY (1847-1855)—John C. Palmer and Walter J. Ramsay, Raleigh. The partnership was announced November 24, 1847,[581] and dissolved June 1, 1855;[582] Palmer purchased Ramsay's interest and continued the business.

JOHN W. PAXTON and William C. Paxton were both in Milton, Caswell County, ca. 1850-1863. (See sketch of William C. Paxton.) No silver with the mark of William C. Paxton has yet

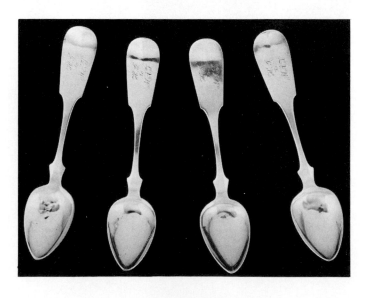

These teaspoons (above and at bottom of facing page), found in Georgia, have the incused mark of J. W. Paxton & Son. They are 5½ inches long, fiddle in style, and have pointed shoulders, short front midrib, a broad-based drop, and an oval bowl. On the front of the handle is script engraving, *H.J. to M.A.T.*

come to light, but the location of four teaspoons with the mark of J. W. Paxton & Son raises the possibility that William C. may have been the son of John W. Paxton.

J.W.PAXTON & SON

WILLIAM C. PAXTON, according to the Caswell County census of 1850 (p. 195), was a silversmith. Paxton's name was found by Mrs. Henry Kendall, who also was able to determine that Paxton, who was thirty-three years old in 1850, came from Pittsylvania County, Virginia. Three Caswell County deed books reveal that Paxton was deeded a lot in Milton, which he sold in 1863. This was a plot that fronted on the west side of the public square; it was first sold by George Williamson and William Price to John W. Paxton for $125.[583] John W. Paxton deeded the same property to W. C. Paxton.[584] In December, 1863, W. C. Paxton sold the same lot to A. A. Mitchell and evidently moved away.[585]

ROBERT PAYNE (PAINE). Payne, or Paine, may have worked as a silversmith in Caswell County during the latter part of the eighteenth century. The county court minutes for September 21, 1779, record that "Robert Payne takes James Thomason, aged 8½, orphan of Gentry Thomason, as apprentice to the silversmith's trade."[586] In the Caswell County indentures for June 4, 1782, there is an entry stating that Payne had another apprentice to the silversmith's trade, John Brown, aged twelve, orphan of Shadrack Brown.

ASA PEABODY. On December 15, 1821, this clockmaker and watchmaker, silversmith and goldsmith, informed the citizens of Wilmington and vicinity that he had taken the house adjoining Casaux's '76 Hotel, where he intended to carry on the above business in all its branches.[587] It is assumed that Asa was a son of John Peabody of Wilmington and that he was named for his grandfather Asa. On February 12, 1823, he sued James F. McRae and obtained judgment for $6.70.[588]

JOHN PEABODY was a watchmaker and clockmaker, jeweler and silversmith, who acquired the stock and trade of Alvan Wilcox of Fayetteville in 1823.[589] On October 3, 1825, he asked those who had left watches with A. Wilcox for repair to call for them before January 1. His advertisement listed an elegant assortment of watches, clocks, jewelry, silver, and fancy hardware.[590] Peabody married Julia Booth, the bond being dated February 11, 1825.[591] Presumably this silversmith was a son of John [Tyng] Peabody of Wilmington. In an advertisement dated December 13, 1826, but still appearing as late as February 7, 1827, in the *North Carolina Journal* (Fayetteville), J. Peabody was advertising for sale "watches, Jewellry. . . ."

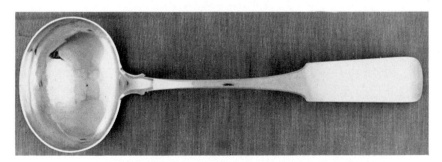

This very fine punch ladle with the mark J.PEABODY in a rectangle is in the ever-popular fiddle style and has short, rounded shoulders. (From a private collection.)

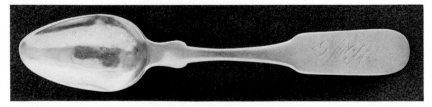

Pictured here is a Peabody teaspoon 5⅝ inches long and in the classic fiddle pattern, with rounded, flared shoulders and a pointed, oval bowl with drop; *CMH*(?) in feathered engraving appears on the handle. The maker's mark that appears at right at the conclusion of the sketch is taken from this spoon. (From a private collection.)

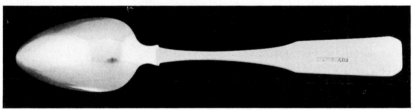

This pair of teaspoons, in a fiddle, coffin-end style and with squared shoulders, have the mark of John Peabody. The spoons are 6$\frac{1}{16}$ and 6$\frac{1}{8}$ inches long respectively, and their bowls are oval and pointed, with crescent, incised drop. The initial *H* is engraved in a cross-hatched script on the front of the handles. One of these spoons was purchased by the North Carolina Museum of History Associates for the museum's collection. The Peabody mark that appears at left following the sketch is taken from these spoons.

The Masonic emblem engraved on this tablespoon leads to the question of who was the original owner. With the J.PEABODY mark in a rectangle on the back, there is no question about the maker. The tablespoon is a fiddleback with drop but no shoulders and a pointed, oval bowl; it is 9$\frac{1}{2}$ inches in overall length. (From a private collection.)

JOHN [TYNG] PEABODY (1756-1822) was born in Norwich, Connecticut, October 27, 1756, the son of Asa Peabody and Mary Prentice. On May 7, 1778, he married Elizabeth Strange of Norwich.[592] In 1779 he advertised as a silversmith in Enfield, Connecticut.[593] After his wife's death in 1787, he moved to Wilmington, North Carolina. There he married Catherine Jessup on June 5, 1789. On May 8, 1787, John Williams gave a power of attorney to "my trusty friend John Peabody of Wilmington, in the county aforesaid, gentleman."[594] He advertised in 1798, thanking people for past favors and telling of a large supply of materials imported from Europe, among which were two or three silver-mounted swords.[595] He died in Wilmington in October, 1822. Evidently he did not use his middle name in North Carolina.

LEWIS PERRET. Two newspaper advertisements seem to indicate that Perret was primarily a watchmaker who worked in Fayetteville in the early 1800s but moved to New Bern at some time before his death ca. 1817. In an advertisement of May 2, 1809,[596] Perret said he would conduct the business of "Watch Making, &c." in the house "lately occupied by Mr. Canu." On March 15, 1817, this notice appeared in the *Carolina Federal Republican* (New Bern):

> Notice. Will be sold by the Subscriber on Monday the 31st inst. at the Court House in Newbern, all the property of Lewis Perret, deceased, consisting of a complete set of Watch-maker Tools, and materials for Watchmaking. . . .
>
> Joseph Bell   Adm'r

DAVID L. POOL (1810-1861) was born April 26, 1810, in Salisbury. In November, 1832, he advertised that he had returned from Philadelphia, where he had acquired a competent, practical knowledge of his art, and had established himself in Salisbury in the tenement recently occupied by Benj. Fraley, a tailor.[597] Through the years Pool advertised as a clockmaker and watchmaker, jeweler and silversmith, and engraver. He moved in June, 1839, into the building formerly known as the post office.[598] In 1832 David L. Pool was one of the executors of the estate of John Pool, presumably his father.[599] He married Angelina Bolen,[600] and he died in Salisbury on March 9, 1861.

JAMES M. POOL advertised in Washington, North Carolina, on July 21, 1846, a long list of articles for sale. He also advertised clock and watch repairing and the repairing of jewelry.[601]

The following February he again offered the public a list of articles.[602] In a deed dated March 29, 1849, he was referred to as "formerly of the County of Pasquotank, now of the County of Beaufort."[603]

WILLIAM T. PRATT. Calvin Howard gave a deed of trust to William T. Pratt in Beaufort County on January 24, 1834.[604] Another deed of trust was given to Pratt in 1840.[605] In 1843 Pratt advertised clocks, watches, and jewelry carefully repaired

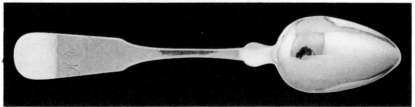

The three teaspoons pictured above (top) have been identified as the work of William T. Pratt. Fiddle with tipped backs, they have rounded shoulders, oval bowls with drop, and a shell embellishment on the back. The spoons are 8⅝ inches long and are engraved *MSV* in feathered script. They came from the Kinston area and are in a private collection. The W.T.PRATT mark that appears at left following the sketch is taken from one of these spoons. The dessertspoon in the photograph at bottom is quite similar but without the shell motif. It was given to the North Carolina Museum of History by the Museum of History Associates. The maker's mark that appears at right following the sketch is taken from the dessertspoon.

at the building formerly occupied by the post office in Washington, North Carolina.[606] During the same year two additional land transactions in which he was involved were recorded.[607] It has not been ascertained if this was the W. T. Pratt who was in Black Rock, New York, in 1826 or the William T. Pratt who was in New York City ca. 1828.[608]

WARREN PRIOR (1811-1909) was born in Northfield, Massachusetts, on December 21, 1811, the son of Isaac Prior and Roxanna Stebbins.[609] He moved to Fayetteville in the winter of 1833 and became a member of the firm of Campbell & Prior in June, 1834.[610] After the dissolution of this firm two years later, he worked independently. On March 29, 1837, he married Louisa McIntyre in Fayetteville,[611] and on October 3, 1838, Fellows, Cargill & Co. of New York appointed him their agent to take over the accounts of Selph & Pyle.[612] Among the large number of real estate transactions in which Prior was involved was one on May 25, 1838, in which John Campbell sold him a house and lot "on the north side of Hay St. and well known as a silversmith shop."[613] This same property Prior sold to J. M. Beasley in 1845. It appears that Prior may have sold his stock to Beasley,[614] but if so he was soon in business again. He conducted his store in Fayetteville until 1887, when he retired; the business was subsequently conducted by his son, John N. Prior, under the firm name of Warren Prior & Son.[615] At the time of his death, January 5, 1909, the elder Prior was said to have been the oldest Mason in the United States. As a young man he led the music in the Presbyterian church with a bass viol; and in later years, although totally deaf, he was an unfailing church attendant.[616] He was a man of strictest honesty and punctual habits and was most highly esteemed.

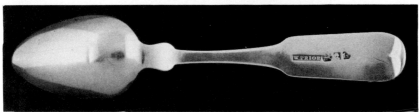

Five Warren Prior teaspoons, two sauce (cream) ladles, and possibly a lady's chatelaine have been found in the hands of descendants of the original owners. In the photograph at top are two teaspoons, one 5¾ inches long, the other 5½ inches. They are fiddle with rounded shoulders and tipped backs and have oval bowls with no drop. The W.PRIOR within a rectangle is accompanied by three pseudohallmarks—a lion passant, a head, and a G. The elaborately engraved *JLAEM^{C}K* represents the initials of the original owners, John Lloyd and Ann Eliza McKoy. This gift to the North Carolina Museum of History was made by Mrs. W. D. Sherman. In the photograph at bottom is a teaspoon in the same style and with the same marks but engraved *HW*.

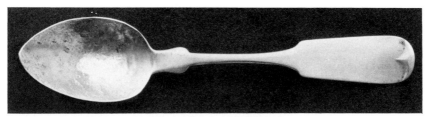

This small teaspoon (memorial), 5½ inches long, is tipped, has no engraving, and is marked W.PRIOR within a rectangle; there are no pseudohallmarks, but the Prior mark is accompanied by an incused TE&Co. in a lozenge and the date 1853 in a diamond. This suggests that Prior was sometimes a retailer for silver made by Theodore Evans (see *New York Silversmiths* [Eggertsville, N.Y.: Darling Foundation of New York State Early American Silversmiths and Silver, 1964]).

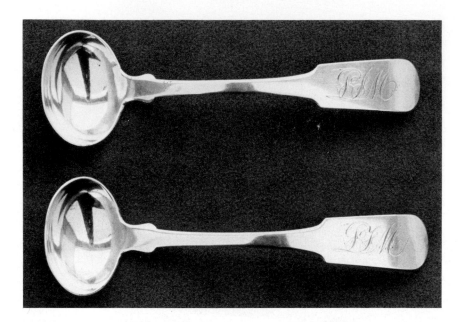

Pictured above is a handsome pair of cream ladles 6 inches long, fiddle with tipped back, rounded shoulders, and engraved *LFM* in feathered script. At left is a close-up view of engraving on a spoon not depicted, a gift to the North Carolina Museum of History from Dr. George Burns Williams. It was one of a set of wedding silver (teaspoons and tablespoons) belonging to the donor's great grandparents—Mary Clegg and Mark Bynum—who were married February 18, 1839. The spoon is marked W.PRIOR in a rectangle without pseudohallmarks.

BENJAMIN PYLE I (d. 1812). At the December term of Beaufort County Court in 1812, letters of administration were granted to Joseph B. Hinton in connection with the estate of the late Benjamin Pyle, watchmaker and silversmith of Washington, North Carolina.[617] Hinton advertised a sale, on February 4, 1813, in the town of Washington, of all the goods and chattels of Benjamin Pyle, deceased, consisting of an excellent set of clockmaker's and watchmaker's tools and also a set of silversmith's and jeweler's tools, watches, jewelry, teaspoons, sugar tongs, and the like.[618]

BENJAMIN PYLE II appeared in Fayetteville in August, 1837, as a member of the firm of Selph & Pyle.[619] Selph died, and Pyle advertised on September 18, 1838, the sale of the remaining stock on hand, as he was going west.[620] In October J. M. Beasley opened his shop at the stand formerly occupied by Selph & Pyle.[621] Evidently Pyle had already left Fayetteville and had set up a business on the southeast corner of the public square in Jackson, Madison County, Tennessee, where he advertised his business and said he was "late from Fayetteville, N.C."[622] On November 8, 1841, three years after his departure from Fayetteville, he annouced that he had commenced clock and watch repairing in Fayetteville and that he had had long experience.[623]

A tablespoon made by Benjamin Pyle II has been photographed, and eight teaspoons that have not been photographed are known to exist. The spoon depicted is 9 inches long and has a pointed handle and an oval bowl. The mark B.PYLE is enclosed in a rectangle with serrated ends.

WALTER J. RAMSAY (1802-1856) went to Raleigh in 1826 or 1827 as an apprentice or employee of John C. Stedman. There he married Martha Ann Pulliam, the bond being dated July 2, 1831.[624] Immediately following the death of Stedman he formed the firm of W. J. Ramsay & Co.[625] On the dissolution of this partnership he worked independently for a while but then became a member of the firm of Ramsay & Beckwith, which in 1840 moved to New Bern.[626] This partnership did not last long,

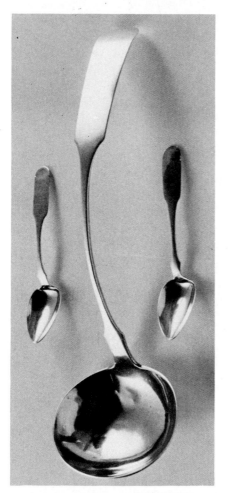
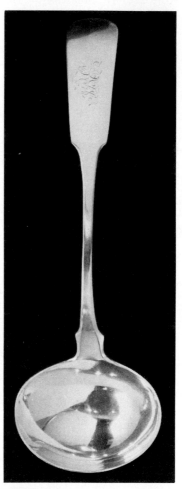

At left are three pieces of W. J. Ramsay & Company silver from a private collection. The punch ladle, 14 inches long, is in a fiddle style with no engraving; its bowl is 4⅜ inches across. W.J.R & Co. in a serrated rectangle is struck twice on the back of the ladle. One of the teaspoons is 5¾ inches long, the other 5⅝ inches; both have pointed shoulders and no drop. The ladle at right is marked W.J. RAMSAY & CO. in a straight-sided rectangle. It is 13 inches long, is also in a fiddle style, has pointed shoulders, and is engraved on the handle in script *JRE* (for John and Rachel Everitt, married in 1829). The mark that appears at top at the conclusion of the sketch is taken from this piece. (From a private collection.)

and Ramsay was soon back in Raleigh, where he worked independently until he became a member of the firm of Palmer & Ramsay in 1847.[627] He retired from this firm in 1855 and died in Raleigh on February 23, 1856.[628] (See Appendix A for an unidentified Ramsey mark found on North Carolina silver.)

W. J. RAMSAY & COMPANY (1833-1836)—Walter J. Ramsay and Dirk Lindeman, in Raleigh. Lindeman was a bookbinder and bookdealer. The partnership was announced on November 15, 1833,[629] and was dissolved on September 15, 1836,[630] after which time the business was continued for a brief period by Lindeman.

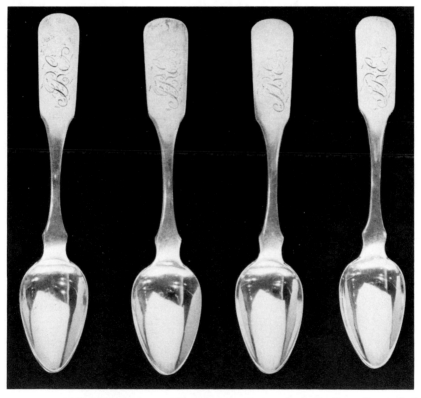

Four teaspoons with the W.J.R. & Co. mark are pictured above. In perfect condition, they measure 5⅝ inches in length and are engraved *JRE* for the original owners, Mr. and Mrs. John Everitt of Everittsville.

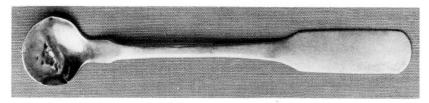

This mustard ladle in fiddle style with pointed shoulders and a round bowl has no engraving; provenance, LaGrange. The W.J.R & Co. mark that appears at bottom following the sketch is taken from this ladle. (From a private collection.)

Walter J. Ramsay had a succession of partners. The tablespoon depicted is marked W.J. RAMSAY & Co.; the teaspoon is marked W.J.R. & Co. Six other teaspoons are known to exist. The original photograph, used in Cutten's first edition, depicted spoons owned in 1948 by Mrs. D. L. Corbitt.

RAMSAY & BECKWITH (1840-   )—Walter J. Ramsay and Robert W. Beckwith, in Raleigh and New Bern. A newspaper advertisement bearing the date May 2, 1840, announced that the firm, "formerly of Raleigh," had relocated in New Bern.[631] The partnership was of short duration.

ANDREW READ. The only evidence of a silversmith by this name is an item in the Rowan County Deeds, Book 10, p. 382 (February 4, 1785): "Andrew Read, a silversmith, and wife Elizabeth, convey to David Beall a tract of land on Fifth Creek, Rowan County."[632]

JOHN ROBERTSON (ROBINSON; d. ca. 1765).[633] Several subpoenas for Daniel Mulford, administrator of the estate of John Robertson (also spelled *Robinson*), were issued during court sessions of 1765 and 1766. William Ball was attempting to collect a debt of "Sixty three Pounds sixteen shillings and ten-pence Pensilvania Currency of the value of Eighty pounds proclamation money which he the said Daniol [*sic*] Mulford unjustly detains from him & Damage ten pounds Proclamation money." A second man to whom John Robertson had been indebted was Joseph Hilborn, who made a claim for amounts of "Sixty-nine pounds three shillings and Six pence Pensilvania Currency of the Value of eighty pounds proclamation Money of North Carolina which to the said Joseph he owes and unjustly detains from him . . . Damage ten pounds proclamation money." There is a reference in this writ to "John Robertson of Philadelphia in the Province of Pensilvania—Mariner." In another of the writs Robertson is described as being "lately of Cape May County in the Province of New Jersey," a "Silversmith [and] mariner." Judge Samuel Johnston issued writs of attachment on Robertson's property in Currituck County in an effort to force Mulford to appear in court. The writs were ordered to be served on Mulford by the sheriff of Currituck County, William Bray.

WILLIAM ROBINSON.[634] It has not been definitely established that this man worked in North Carolina, but Dr. Cutten suggests that he did (see Cutten's *Silversmiths of Virginia*, 128-129). After working in Portsmouth, Virginia, from ca. 1840 to 1841, Robinson announced that he was forced to discontinue his business. It was at this point that he moved to North Carolina, Cutten concluded. It seems that Robinson must have then moved from North Carolina to Maryland. This assumption is based on an advertisement that appeared in the *Chronicle and Old Dominion* (Portsmouth, Virginia) of December 9, 1844:

William Robinson, practical watchmaker and dealer in fine watches, jewelry, &c. Corner of Calvert and Baltimore Streets, opposite the Museum, Baltimore. William Robinson informs his friends in Virginia and North Carolina in addition to goods for sale, he repairs. He solicits patronage.

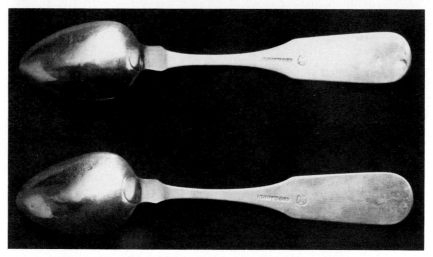

Attributed to William Robinson, these teaspoons are 5¾ inches long, have classic, downturned fiddle handles engraved *IEF* in script, pointed shoulders, and pointed, oval bowls. One, a gift from the Museum of History Associates, is presently on display at the North Carolina Museum of History.

CHARLES BOUDINOT ROOT (1818-1903), the son of Elihu Root and Sophia Gunn and grandson of Samuel Gunn, patriot soldier of the American Revolution, was born October 31, 1818,

at Montague, Massachusetts. After attending school at Green-
field, Massachusetts, and a brief stay in New York, he went to
Raleigh, North Carolina, in 1837.[635] He was employed by Bernard Dupuy for five years and then bought Dupuy's business
on November 15, 1843.[636] In 1847 Root married Annie Freeman

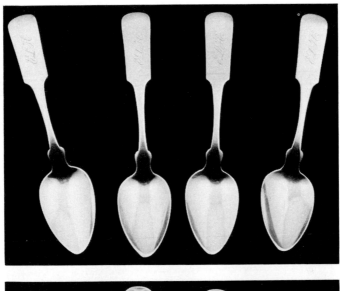

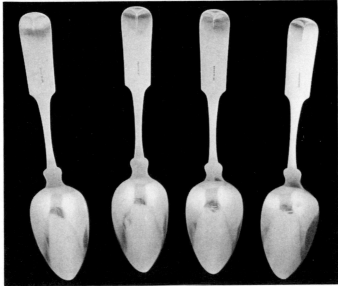

These four dessertspoons made by C. B. Root provide a good example of the
nicety of his work. They are classic fiddles, 6¹³/₁₆ inches long, with oval, pointed
bowls, rounded shoulders, short back midrib, no drop, and *ELH* engraved in
script. C.B. ROOT in a rectangle is the mark. (From a private collection.)

Still in the hands of descendants of the original owners is this graceful butter knife, 7½ inches long, fiddle, tipped on the reverse of the handle, and struck twice with the Root mark. Provenance, Franklin County.

The romantic story of this lovely Victorian creamer is told in detail in Appendix B. It is one piece of an important tea service and is displayed at the North Carolina Museum of History through the courtesy of Mr. and Mrs. J. P. Harris, who inherited the set from Miss Daisy Green. The creamer is 6¾ inches high, with a round, inverted, pear-shaped body on a round, stepped foot. Note the repoussé foliage cartouche, the motif repeated at lip and base of body, the acanthus leaf and shell banding around the upper body and foot, and the double scroll handle.

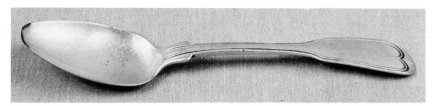

On display at the North Carolina Museum of History is one of three such spoons known to have been made by C. B. Root and to have survived. This one is 5⅝ inches long, has a slightly worn oval bowl, and the stem is almost straight.

This splendid sugar bowl was photographed and identified by the late Mr. John Kalmar. The bowl has a round, inverted, pear-shaped body on a round, stepped foot with repoussé banding at shoulder, bottom of lid, and base. The Root mark is struck three times on the bottom.

This lady's snuffbox has an interesting history. Made by C. B. Root from scraps and discarded silver objects, the box still bears the marks of the smith who made an original item and not the mark of Root, who gave the new box to Miss Martha Gorman, whose father worked for the *Raleigh Register*. (The original marks, N.M. in a rectangle with an anchor, lion passant, profile, and date, suggest that the earlier smith could have been Nathaniel Mills, w. 1838-1839. Seymour B. Wyler, *The Book of Old Silver* [New York: Crown Publishers, nineteenth printing, 1937], 198, hereinafter cited as Wyler, *The Book of Old Silver*.) Mrs. Arthur Nowell, descendant of Martha Gorman, inherited the box and gave it to Dr. Aldert S. Root, grandson of the silversmith C. B. Root. The dainty box has a hinged lid and measures 2¾ inches by 1½ inches; it is on display at the North Carolina Museum of History.

Gales of Raleigh, the bond being dated June 10.[637] In 1860 he retired from the jewelry and silversmith business and became president of the Raleigh Gas Company, a position he retained for eighteen years.[638] Captain William Harrison was mayor of Raleigh, 1858-1872, but during the early years of the Civil War Root held this office as Harrison's substitute and refused any salary for his services. Charles B. Root was a magistrate, a city alderman, and in 1884 city tax collector; and he served as chairman of the board of county commissioners. He died in Raleigh on May 7, 1903.[639]

WILLIAM E. RUFF. On November 11, 1822, William Ruff gave a bill of sale to Edward Hoell, a watchmaker and silversmith of Washington, North Carolina.[640] On January 14, 1829, he advertised watches, jewelry, and silverware for sale in Halifax. The same advertisement was being run in the *Halifax Minerva* of April 16.[641]

JOHN SARGENT bought land in Wilmington on July 4, 1820.[642] On November 17, 1821, he advertised watchmaking, repairing, and engraving and was still working in Wilmington in 1822.[643] In fact, on May 15, 1822, James Brockett, an orphan of fourteen, was apprenticed to Sargent to learn the trade of watchmaker.[644]

JACOB SASSAMAN (w. ca. 1809) was identified by profession in Rowan County Deeds, Book 20, p. 153 (November, 1809): "John Troxler conveys to Jacob Sassaman, a goldsmith & clockmaker of Rowan Co., Lot no. 9 in the East Square, Salisbury, formerly owned by Dr. Newman."[645]

JOHN Y. SAVAGE. On April 13, 1818, he announced that having resided in Raleigh for several years and having been constantly employed in the line of his profession as a silversmith, he had at length established himself.[646] He received John C. Stedman as a partner in March, 1819, and the firm was known as Savage & Stedman.[647] The partnership was dissolved on June 7, 1820, with Savage continuing the business.[648] In 1822 he advertised swords and epaulets,[649] and on January 1, 1824, he offered a reward of $25.00 for the return of a gold

Examples of J. Y. Savage's work are the six teaspoons shown above; they have pointed shoulders, oval, pointed bowls, tipped back, no drop, and are engraved *RS* in script.

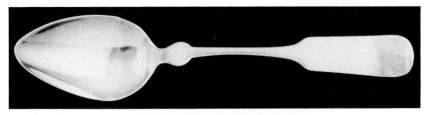

This tablespoon, one of a pair, is 8¼ inches long with flared shoulders, no drop, and tipped handle; the tablespoon not pictured has a slender handle and no shoulders. Both are marked J.Y. SAVAGE in a rectangle.

watch, five chains, a seal, and a key, which had been stolen from his shop.[650] In a deed dated April 17, 1826, of which John C. Palmer was a witness, Savage and his wife Margaret were named as citizens of Raleigh.[651] On October 22, 1829, John Y. Savage, a dentist of Richmond, Virginia, announced that he

Shown at left is a Savage teaspoon 5⅝ inches long in a fiddle style with square shoulders.

The Savage teaspoon at left is a type of fiddle with short, rounded shoulders; it is engraved *W* for the Josiah Watson family, the original owners.

Especially well proportioned is this teaspoon, 5⅝ inches long, which is still in the family of the original owners (provenance, Charlotte). It has an oval bowl, an elegant *C* engraved on the handle, tipped reverse, and chamfered shoulders. The mark J.Y. SAVAGE in a rectangle is accompanied by two pseudohallmarks.

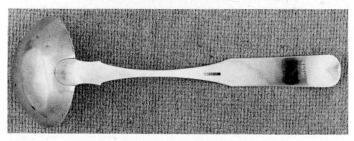

The original owner of the J. Y. Savage punch ladle pictured above was Willie Jones, who acquired it prior to 1840. The ladle has remained in the family. The engraved initials *GAJ* and the date *1913* have been added in recent years. The silversmith's mark on this piece is shown at the conclusion of the sketch.

had moved his office.[652] Among the unidentified marks given by Ensko is that of J. Y. Savage.[653] Savage had two sons, J. Y. Savage, Jr., and William M. Savage, both of Columbus, Ohio. William Savage was a silversmith, ca. 1840-1892.[654] John Y. Savage was listed in the New York City directory for 1839 and evidently was working with W. M. Savage (his son, William?).[655] If so, it may be conjectured that the Savage & Son marks found on silver in North Carolina may be the mark of these two men. A comparison of marks gives some support for this suggestion.

SAVAGE & KUNSMAN were watchmakers and jewelers of Salisbury. This firm advertised on November 24, 1823, that it had taken the shop lately occupied by Curtis Wilkinson and had a first-class workman. It also announced that there was reason to believe that some watches had not been well repaired during the past summer and that these would be repaired free of expense.[656] John Y. Savage and Henry Kunsman were independent watchmakers and jewelers in Raleigh. Whether or not these two men combined to do business in Salisbury is not known.

SAVAGE & STEDMAN (1819-1820). The partnership of John Y. Savage and John C. Stedman in Raleigh was announced on March 19, 1819,[657] and was dissolved on June 7, 1820.[658] Stedman was authorized to settle the accounts of the firm, but Savage carried on the business.

DAVID SCOTT (1797-1875). On October 18, 1826, he advertised, in Greensboro, fancy jewelry, spoons, and thimbles. He repaired watches and was grateful for past favors.[659] On August 18, 1827, Aaron Woolworth purchased Scott's jewelry and materials and took his shop.[660] Scott took back his shop on September 20, 1828[661] and in 1829 joined the firm of Scott & Anderson for a few months.[662] In 1832 he was one of five men elected to serve on the new town board, which drew up new regulations for the town. In 1840 he was a member of the firm of McAdoo & Scott, general merchants.[663] Scott evidently was a successful businessman. He died on September 11, 1875, in his seventy-eighth year, the oldest citizen of Greensboro.[664] The silversmith's wife, Jane E., and his son, David Scott, Jr., were mentioned in his will.[665]

SCOTT & ANDERSON (1829). David Scott and —— Anderson were located in Greensboro. On June 19, 1829, this firm advertised that it was prepared to do watch and clock work and had employed a first-rate workman. Jewelry and silverware were kept constantly on hand.[666] The partnership lasted only a few months.

JEHU SCOTT (d. 1819) advertised in Raleigh on December 1, 1806, that he had made and sold all kinds of jewelry and silverware.[667] In addition, over the years he had imported silverware from Philadelphia and New York. He was a frequent dealer in real estate, making his first purchase in 1807. In one transaction he acted as trustee of the Methodist church.[668] On two different occasions William Jones and Jehu Scott became securities for David Ruth when Ruth was appointed to the office of constable, and in 1814 and again in 1818 Scott served on the petit jury.[669] On February 12, 1819, he advertised that he was anxious to close his concerns and go south, that he had several lots for sale, and that his stock was cheap for cash. He also requested the settlement of all debts and the presentation of all claims.[670] Evidently he was too late, for he died in Raleigh on October 20, 1819, "an industrious and worthy citizen."[671] Scott's will was proved in November, 1819, and his executor, Thomas Cobb, was given permission to sell the perishable estate with a large quantity of jewelry, watches, and other items, "of a credit of not less than six months."[672] In 1821 guardians were appointed for his six minor children, and in 1823 his heirs sued his executor in connection with a payment he had made.[673] Scott's apprentice, George Washington Ruth, later became a silversmith in Tennessee.[674]

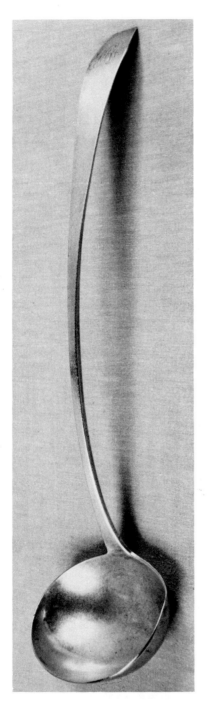

The punch ladle and four tablespoons
are graceful examples of coffin-end
silver in vogue ca. 1800. The ladle, 15¼
inches long, is on display at the North
Carolina Museum of History through
the courtesy of the owner, Mrs. Mary J.
Rogers of Raleigh. Scott's mark is
struck twice on the back of this piece.
The tablespoons, 10 inches long, are engraved with the initials of the original
owner, Richard Smith, one of the first
landowners in Raleigh. (From a private
collection.)

The Scott spoons shown in the two photographs at top are 9 inches long, with oval bowls 3 inches long and 1⅝ inches across; they are coffin-fiddle in style, with no shoulders and no engraving. (From a private collection.) Similar in style is the teaspoon pictured in the two bottom photographs. Unique and rather primitive bright-cut decoration was used to embellish the handle, which is also engraved *AT* (*AP*?) in script. The mark J·SCOTT in a serrated rectangle differs from other Scott marks. The teaspoon is on display at the North Carolina Museum of History; it was a gift from the Museum of History Associates.

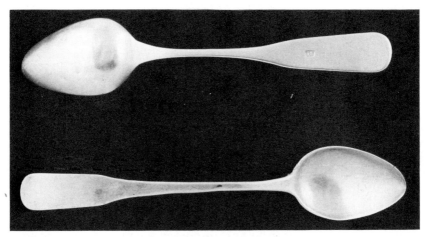

This pair of teaspoons, marked with a JS in a rectangle, a mark sometimes used by Jehu Scott, differ slightly in length, one being 5⅛, the other 5⁵⁄₁₆ inches long. Both have tapering handles, no shoulders, and no engraving. (From a private collection.)

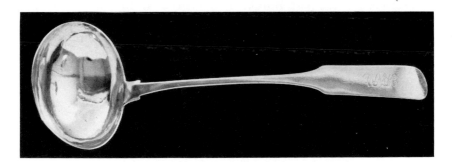

Scott made silver in the fiddle style, as evidenced by these two surviving pieces. At top is a fine ladle 12¾ inches long with squared shoulders; it is engraved *WMK* for William Kincher Kearny and Maria Alston Kearny, who lived at Hickory Grove, Warren County, and were the original owners. The spoon at bottom has short, pointed shoulders and is engraved with a *B*, although the original owner is not known. (Both pieces from private collections.)

SAMUEL SCOTT commenced the business of clockmaking and watchmaking next door to the post office, Main Street, Concord, on December 6, 1825. He made spoons to order.[675]

THOMAS SEAMAN. The bond for his marriage to Elizabeth Smith was dated December 29, 1789;[676] and on December 23, 1790, he advertised that he had imported a complete set of tools for commencing the clockmaking and watchmaking business, which he meant to carry on in Edenton.[677] A deed dated November 9, 1793, mentioned "Thomas Seaman, gentleman, and Elizabeth, his wife."[678] On January 14, 1796, he advertised the clockmaking and watchmaking business at his house nearly opposite the courthouse,[679] and in March of the following year he announced that since he had employed a silversmith and jeweler, an excellent workman, the public could be supplied at short notice with any article in this line of business.[680] The house and lots upon which he lived were offered for sale on February 20, 1799,[681] and his last recorded business transaction was in 1802.[682]

JOHN SELPH (d. 1838). John Selph and Fanny Washburn were married in Cumberland County, the bond being dated December 13, 1804.[683] In December, 1807, Selph accepted Abel Boyken (Bayken), about sixteen years of age, as an apprentice to learn the silversmith trade; and in September, 1818, John Campbell, fifteen years old, became Selph's apprentice.[684] Selph may have lost one apprentice, judging by the notice that appeared in the Fayetteville *American* of April 26, 1816:

Selph, John, clockmaker, Fayetteville, 1816

FIVE CENTS REWARD

RAN-AWAY from the Subscriber, on the 17th ult., sn [an] indented Apprentice to the Clock and Watch making business, by the name of

JAMES SNEESTON. The above reward will be given for bringing him to me, but will not defray any expenses that he may contract.

JOHN SELPH

Fayetteville, April 2, 1816

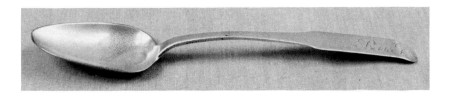

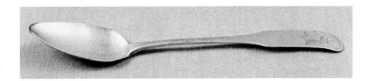

Pictured above are two spoons made by John Selph; both are on display at the North Carolina Museum of History. The tablespoon in the photograph at top is 9 inches long. It was owned by Regina De Graffenreid, which explains the *R de G* engraved on the handle. The teaspoon in the lower photograph was once the property of William Hooper. It is 5⅞ inches long and is uniquely engraved with a unicorn, shown in detail at left.

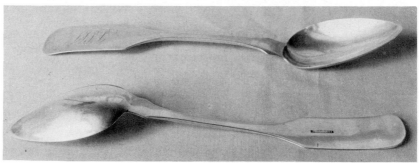

A fine collection of five Selph teaspoons (top) and a pair of tablespoons (bottom) have come to light. All have fiddle forms with pointed shoulders and no drop. A third tablespoon, not pictured, is known to exist. The teaspoons are engraved *SNP*(?), and the tablespoons, which are 9⅜ inches long, have four initials—JAST(?). The J.SELPH mark that appears at right following the sketch is from one of the tablespoons. (From private collections.)

Selph was involved in several real estate transactions in Fayetteville in 1815, 1817, and 1822.[685] He was listed in the 1820 census of manufactures as a member of the Selph & Tisdale firm. Sometime prior to December 5, 1827, he became a member of the firm of Selph & Campbell of Fayetteville. Upon the dissolution of this firm in 1829 Selph worked independently, and a Fayetteville paper carried an announcement in 1831 that the silversmith "has taken the house on the N. corner of the Courthouse square. . . ."[686]

In 1836 he advertised that he intended to enlarge his business considerably; he also advertised silver spoons and other ware of his own manufacture.[687] In 1837 he became a member of the firm of Selph & Pyle[688] and was active in business in 1838. Selph obtained a judgment against debtors in March,[689] and in May William Wynne gave him a deed of trust witnessed by J. M. Beasley.[690] When Selph died in August, 1838,[691] James Millar became administrator of his estate, giving a bond for $4,000.[692] The administrator advertised silversmith's tools among other things for sale.[693] In September, 1838, Frances Selph petitioned the court for a year's allowance from the estate,[694] and in June, 1839, she received a writ of dower.[695] In June, 1839, the Bank of Cape Fear obtained a judgment against the estate for $156.60,[696] and in June, 1840, John Campbell obtained a judgment against the estate for his claim against the firm of Selph & Pyle.[697]

SELPH & CAMPBELL (1827-1829). John Selph and John Campbell were located in Fayetteville. The partnership was probably organized early in 1827. On December 5 of the same year this firm bought the stock of William Widdifield but at first advertised the continuation of both stores, at which all kinds of gold and silver work would be done.[698] The partnership was dissolved sometime before October, 1829, with Campbell continuing the business and settling the accounts.[699]

SELPH & PYLE (1837-1838). John Selph and Benjamin Pyle II were in Fayetteville. The partnership was announced on August 29, 1837,[700] and was dissolved the following year by the death of Selph.[701]

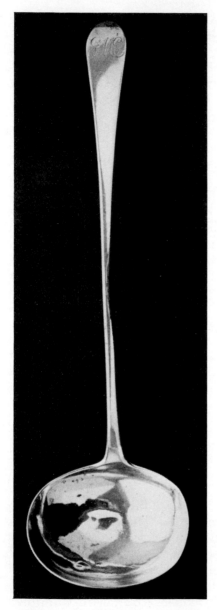 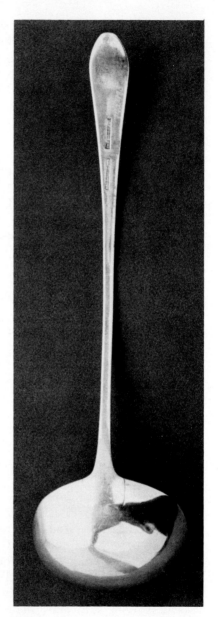

Because the mark is so rare, this was an exciting find—a graceful punch ladle struck twice on the back SELPH & PYLE in an irregular rectangle. Its overall length is 14½ inches; the bowl is 4 inches across and 3¼ inches long, with a rounded drop. The slender lines of a coffin-end style give this piece a special charm. (From a private collection.)

SELPH & TISDALE. John Selph and William Tisdale [II] were listed in the 1820 census of manufactures as being in the

business of useing about $1,000 value of gold and silver per year, employing 2 men and 1 boy, with 1 bellows, 1 plating mill, 1 watch and clock engine, all in operation, with $1,000 capital, $360 payroll and $250 other expenses per year, manufacturing "Jewelry & silverware of different descriptions, with sales value about 50% of the cost." In addition to the above about 1,000 dollars of watch repairs, the establishment is now & has been for about 12 years in about its present condition.[702]

JAMES SEVEREN was reputed to have been a silversmith in Beaufort during the period ca. 1765-1785.[703]

THOMAS SHIELD. This man apparently worked in the Halifax area in the late 1700s. The Halifax County court minutes for May 8, 1787, record that the apprentice John Champion, orphan of Benj. Champion, had been bound to Thomas Shield to learn the trade of silversmith.[704]

JOHN SHORT. On January 20, 1784, John Short deeded to William Short 110 acres of land on "Plumb Tree Island," Halifax County.[705] A certain John Short advertised in Halifax on October 17, 1792, as a clockmaker and watchmaker and announced that he had recently opened a shop in Halifax. He also said that he had served a regular apprenticeship in the city of London and had carried on business for many years in America. He wanted an apprentice.[706] On January 7, 1818, William Day deeded to John Short 24½ acres of land in Halifax County, with houses, orchards, and other property.[707] Short's will, dated January 17, 1819, was proved at the September term, 1819, of the Halifax County Court.[708]

ROBERT SINGLETON on August 5, 1839, announced that he had taken a shop east of the courthouse in Greensboro. He asserted that he repaired watches, clocks, and jewelry in a workmanlike manner.[709]

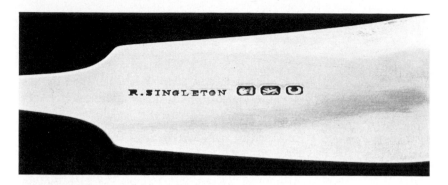

The Robert Singleton mark shown in the photograph at top was taken from one of two handcrafted fiddleback spoons (neither of which is pictured in this volume) that have survived. One of these pieces is a tablespoon 9 inches long, with *Lt. McCune* engraved on it in script; the other is a teaspoon 5½ inches long and engraved *AMB* in script. The mark shown in the photograph at bottom, which was taken from a manufactured spoon, shows the incused R.SINGLE-TON and also faint outlines of three pseudohallmarks to the left of the name. The manufacturer has not been identified, but some variation of the olive pattern was made by all the major companies. The retailed spoon (provenance, Greensboro) is one of several believed to have been in the Wiley family ca. 1845-1850. (Both pieces from private collections.)

SANFORD G. SLAYTON. There is little to support any assumption that Slayton was a working silversmith in the Concord area in the 1820s. However, a Salisbury paper carried this notice in 1824:

Clock and Watch Making. The subscriber respectfully informs the citizens of Cabarrus and the adjoining counties, that he has taken the house formerly occupied by Mr. J. H. Clark as a store, (next door to the Post Office) and solicits the patronage of all those who may want any thing done in this line, viz: clock and watch repairing, making and repairing all kinds of silver work, on the shortest notice. Sanford G. Slayton. Concord, Nov. 15, 1824.[710]

EBENEZER SLOCUM. Ebenezer Slocum advertised that he had opened an "establishment" in Elizabeth City in 1827.[711] He offered cash for gold and silver and said that "he intends carrying on the above business [clock and watch repairing], together

with Gold and Silver Smithing, Compass and Quadrant repairing and job work in general. Having had considerable experience in the above branches. . . ." The notice was repeated in
several later issues of the paper.

CHARLES CONOLLY SMITH. In a feature article entitled
"Interesting History Surrounds Silversmith" in the Fayetteville
Observer-Times (March 5, 1978), Mrs. Lucille Johnson tells the
fascinating story of Charles Conolly (Smith) as related by a
descendant, Mrs. L. N. Trammell, of Atlanta, Georgia:

> The marriage banns certificate on the church register of a fashion-
> able Episcopal Church in London, England, discloses that on "Nov.
> 23, 1827, Lady Elizabeth Ann Noble and Charles Conolly, gentle-
> man[,]" were married.
> The family writings record that "Charles Conolly was a young Irish
> silversmith from a devout Catholic family, she from as devout [an]
> Episcopal family, and both (families) vehemently opposed the mar-
> riage, but marry they did."
> "In time, several children were born, and soon they decided to come
> to New York, where they settled, making nice social contacts and lived
> in luxury with carriage and coachman and an English nurse to assist
> with the children. One day when their daughter, Sophia, was on her
> way home from dancing school, she was kidnapped. Several days later
> she was returned, unharmed. However, "they decided to leave New
> York and settled in the small village of Scottish Highlanders on the
> Cape Fear River." In order to obscure their identity, their name was
> changed to Smith. We find C. C. Smith, silversmith, publishing his
> advertisement. Some members of the family a generation later re-
> turned to the name Conolly, and some continued as Smith.

Lady Elizabeth Ann Noble Conolly Smith is buried in Cross
Creek Cemetery; there is no stone for her husband, according to
Mrs. Johnson. In her article, Mrs. Johnson used an illustration
of two spoons and two forks attributed to Smith; the four pieces
descended in the Duncan Starr family.

C. C. Smith advertised a "New Establishment" in Fayetteville on November 12, 1841. He said that he was from London
and that he would manufacture any article of jewelry and
repair watches.[712] On October 3, 1843, Edwin Glover announced
that he was at the old stand of C. C. Smith.[713] Burton tells of a
peripatetic jeweler named Charles Smith who claimed to be
from London and Paris and who operated in five different
areas in the northern part of South Carolina between 1848 and
1857.[714]

SAMUEL SPOONER (w. 1819-1823). According to an advertisement in the *Edenton Gazette* of October 26, 1819, Samuel Spooner was a silversmith in Elizabeth City, North Carolina:[715]

THE SUBSCRIBER

INFORMS his friends and the public, that he has established himself at this place, where he intends carrying on the

Gold & Silversmith Trade

in all its various branches. He will also attend to repairing and cleaning Clocks and Watches, & has now a very large assortment of Clock and Watch Materials on hand,—Orders from any part of the country will meet with immediate attention.

Samuel Spooner.

Elizabeth City, Oct. 20, 1819

The estate records of Pasquotank County include an item from the estate of Joseph Commander (d. 1823) that pertains to Spooner:

M.ʳ Joseph Commander Deceſed 1823

	To Samˡ Spooner	Dᵒ
March		
to reparing 3 finger rings		$1.25
Dᵒ making 1 Brespin Dᵒ		1.00
		$2.25
Credit by cash		1.00
	Balance	1.25

Elizabeth City   April 29.ᵗʰ 1823

The above Ballance of account of one Dollar & twenty-five Cents was placed this Day Before me according to law   May 2ⁿᵈ 1823

Mal" Jackson

JOHN C. STEDMAN (d. 1833) became a member of the firm of Savage & Stedman, Raleigh, on March 19, 1819,[716] and on the tenth of the following September married Mary E. Raboteau of Raleigh.[717] The firm was dissolved on June 7, 1820, and settled its accounts. On April 4, 1821, Stedman offered to the public his services as auctioneer and general commission merchant, advertising as such both within and outside North Carolina.[718] He was licensed as an auctioneer in May, 1821.[719] Evidently this venture was unsuccessful, and on August 14, 1822, he advertised that he had commenced the watchmaking and silversmithing business and desired an apprentice.[720] He served

Three of fourteen very fine Stedman spoons that have been identified are shown above. Those spoons thus far found are all fiddle with slight variations. At top is one given to the North Carolina Museum of History by Mr. James O. Litchford. It is 8⅞ inches long and has an oval bowl 1¾ inches across and 2¾ inches long. The feather engraving on both front and back of the pair of spoons shown in the photographs at center and bottom enhances their beauty—an *H* on the front and *ELH* on the back. They are 8½ inches long, with downturned handles and straight, rounded shoulders. Not pictured but on display at the North Carolina Museum of History are fine tablespoons given to the museum by Mrs. Nell B. Hooks and Mr. and Mrs. Charles Gignillial, Jr.

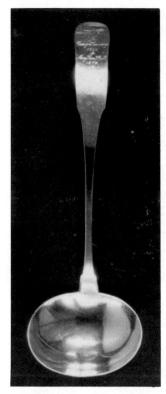

This Stedman ladle (left), in perfect condition, has descended in the same family for several generations. It is 14¾ inches in overall length, with a bowl 4½ inches across and 3¾ inches long. The handle (center) is inscribed *Mary Powell/1824/to/Carolyn Rumbaugh/1855/to Mary Lee Hill/1876/ to/Mildred Hill Izlar/1909/to/Mary Lee Smith*. (From a private collection.) The sugar tongs (right) are sturdy and well made. They are 16.2 cm long, with reinforced, scalloped arms tapering to rounded bowls. Currently on display at the North Carolina Museum of History, they are a gift from G. Wilson Douglas.

as constable of the Wake County Court in 1823 but resigned in May, 1824.[721] In February, 1829, James Gorman, an orphan nearly fifteen years of age and the son of James Gorman, was bound to Stedman to learn the silversmith business.[722] That same year Stedman served as a justice in the Wake County Court of Pleas and Quarter Sessions, and in 1830 he was appointed inspector of the polls at Raleigh for the election of members of the General Assembly.[723] In May, 1832, he was appointed guardian to his apprentice, James Gorman.[724] It appears that W. J. Ramsay and Arthur Tench also were Stedman's apprentices. On November 11, 1833, Stedman was killed in a railway accident while returning from New York, where he had been purchasing stock for his new store.[725] Hiram Lodge No. 40 passed resolutions of sympathy and appreciation, and the board of commissioners of Raleigh passed resolutions of regard and regret before appointing a new clerk of the board to fill Stedman's place. An obituary in the *Raleigh-Minerva* of September 24, 1819, described Stedman as "formerly of Chatham [County]."

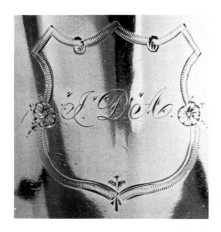

A close-up of the cartouche that so simply enhances the beauty of the Stedman cup, which is used as the frontispiece for this edition of *Silversmiths of North Carolina*, is shown at left.

THOMAS STEEL, according to the census of 1850,[726] was a silversmith in Yanceyville. The census reported his age to be twenty-five and indicated that he was a native of Philadelphia.

JOHN STEVENSON (d. ca. 1781). Some background information about this man is provided by a land deed:

Aug. 17, 1779. John Stevenson of Craven Co., N.C., goldsmith, to Waightstill Avery, attorney at law, of Jones Co., N.C., for one negro man called Stephen, deeds the one half of the land [t]he said Stevenson inherited as son of Elizabeth, the sister of Edward Franck, deceased, who died intestate since John Stevenson is only son of Elizabeth and entitled to one half of his Uncle Edward Franck's land and real estate of which 640 acres was bought by Edward Franck of Frederick Jones. . . . known as "White Rock Plantation" partly in Jones Co. and partly in Craven Co. . . .[727]

By 1779 Stevenson was a well-established craftsman. Two years earlier he had accepted at New Bern, on December 10, 1777, an apprentice, Valentine Richardson, whose mother said he would be sixteen years old on the following February 14.[728] The inventory of Stevenson's estate, taken on August 30, 1781, indicates that he was a man of considerable affluence. There are numerous items pertaining to his work as a silversmith, and he seems to have worked with other metals as well and to have done blacksmithing:

> . . . one Silver Smith Case with a Sash . . . 1 per of fier Tongs & shuvell
> . . . 6 Silversmith files one bellos one anvell one per of gin rolers one
> ring last . . . one Large black Smith's Voice [vise] 2 aprins 6 Spoon
> Stamps 2 Carving bullets & Stocks & Sement 1 lamp 2 stans for oyl
> one anvell to make hollerware 5 piercing files 25 buckel Tooles 16 Ring
> Sizes 2 laves 1 beake[r?] 2 per of Cutting Shears 3 Drawing plates for
> to make wire . . . One per of drawing pincers 2 boyling pans 2 ingrav-
> ing points for makeing buttons 3 Drills one per of Casting flasks made
> of brass one per of Round pliers 1 per of flat pliers one Small Scrue
> plate . . . 1 Spoon Gage 1 Ingravour . . . 1 per of Changing tongs one
> per of Nealing tongs one kee Saw 2 Irons to make Gold barrs . . . Ig[t] of
> old brass 4 pounds of lead pattents for buckels 108 Crucibles . . . Silver
> Buckles not finished.[729]

James Oliver bought a "Parcil of Silversmith Tools" for £19 and "2 flasks to Cast Mettle in" for £1. John Gooding bought "1 Silversmith Shop" for £15.[730] The executors were the widow and James Stevenson. At least three tablespoons made by this man are known to have survived.[731]

PETER STRONG, the son of Daniel Strong and Esther Chappell, was born July 14, 1764, in Lebanon, Connecticut. He moved to Fayetteville, North Carolina, and in 1790 married Mary McKay there.[732] On July 28, 1788, he bought a lot in Fayetteville from Samuel Fosdick;[733] and on April 25, 1789, James Patterson leased to Peter Strong, watchmaker of Fayetteville, a tract of land for ten years. Strong agreed to build thereon a one-and-one-half-story house, 14 by 28 feet, in which to carry on business as a watchmaker and clockmaker.[734] He accepted as apprentices two men who afterward worked in Fayetteville: Joseph Gale (accepted January 28, 1788)[735] and Alexander Campbell (accepted January 14, 1793).[736] In 1790 and 1791 Strong advertised for two active lads between twelve and fifteen years of age as apprentices to the watchmaking and jewelry business;[737] in 1792 he offered to pay "one hard dollar an ounce" for old silver.[738] He worked for the remainder of his life in Fayetteville and died there on June 27, 1797.

NOAH C. TAYLOR on September 7, 1844, opened a shop nearly opposite the post office in Salisbury for the purpose of repairing clocks and watches. He kept thimbles, rings, and other articles that he exchanged for gold and silver.[739]

ARTHUR (ARCHER?) TENCH (d. 1838) worked for a number of years with John C. Stedman of Raleigh; and when Stedman died, Tench opened an independent shop.[740] He made and imported silver, which he sold at his shop up to the time of his death. Tench was married in Raleigh to Elizabeth A. J. Deloach, the bond being dated July 28, 1831;[741] and he died at New Bern, April 23, 1838.[742] The *Newbern Spectator* of December 1, 1837, contained an advertisement by "Archer Tench, Clock & Watch Maker, Jeweller, Silversmith & Engraver." Tench said he would become a resident of New Bern if he had "sufficient encouragement." Since his death occurred during the following April, Tench could not have had very long to live in New Bern.

CHARLES H. THOMPSON. Five very important pieces of silver with the mark C. H. THOMPSON in a rectangle on the backs stimulated research on the Thompsons of Raleigh, since the provenance of all these pieces was found to have been in Wake County. Mrs. Elizabeth Reid Murray provided several important pieces of evidence that led to her conclusion that the silversmith was Charles, son of the cabinetmaker William Thompson, who made the desks and chairs for the North Carolina State Capitol.[743] The census of 1860 lists Charles as a jeweler and member of the William Thompson household. The age given is twenty-eight, an age Mrs. Murray questions. William Thompson had lived in Trenton, New Jersey, before moving to Raleigh. Mrs. Thompson had been Sarah Marks of Petersburg, Virginia. Their marriage was solemnized on November 24, 1819, according to the *Raleigh Register* of November 26, 1819. Mrs. William Thompson opened a millinery and mantua-making shop in 1821; her shop was "next door above her Husband's Cabinet Ware-Room on the East Side of Fayetteville Street . . . [she] having been engaged in that line for several years in Petersburg, Virginia. . . ."[744]

Charles H. Thompson placed advertisements in the *Raleigh Register* during the autumn of 1854 and for some time in 1855:

NEW JEWELRY STORE. CHARLES H. THOMPSON . . . has fitted up in splendid style the house formerly occupied by the Insurance

Company, on the west side on Fayetteville Street, and between Mr. S. H. Young's and Murray & O'Neal's Dry Good Stores . . . New Jewelry . . . Watches . . . double barrel guns brought on expressly for the hunters of Carolina . . . walking Canes . . . repairing . . . Oct. 20, 1854.[745]

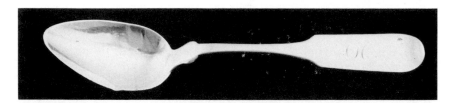

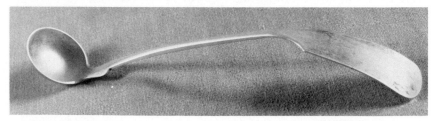

These four pieces by C. H. Thompson, all from the provenance of Wake County, have been in the same families for several generations and are well documented. The three teaspoons (top and center) are ca. 5⅞ inches long, fiddle with rounded shoulders, the two shown at center having tipped handles. Engraved on the spoon shown at top is *CH* (somewhat obliterated); those at center are clearly engraved *C.B. and Z.E.S.* (for Claudius and Zillah Elizabeth Sanders, who were married January 4, 1854). The mustard ladle (bottom), not engraved, was first owned by Mary Rosa Polk and Josiah Haughton, who were married January 15, 1859.

A story in the *Raleigh Register* of October 10, 1855, mentions a "superb silver cup" that was presented to Captain Harrison of the Oak City Guards as winner of a "target firing match." Charles H. Thompson, "the Orderly Sergeant of the Company," presented the cup. On December 22, 1858, the *Raleigh Register* reported that Charles H. Thompson had returned from New York and had new jewelry for sale.

GEORGE THOMPSON was a silversmith in Caldwell County, according to Mrs. W. E. Alexander, who, in a letter to George B. Cutten, May 19, 1953, said that silver buckles made by Thompson were still in the family.[746]

W. H. THOMPSON. During the latter part of December, 1849, and in January, 1850, the Raleigh *North Carolina Standard* carried an advertisement dated September 21, 1849. According to the announcement, W. H. Thompson had opened a "New Watch & Jewelry Store" in Raleigh. His store was located in "a part of the Store occupied by Mrs. Thompson as a Millinery establishment" and featured "a choice stock of WATCHES & JEWELRY . . . all sorts of items." Thompson offered to accept "Old Gold and Silver" in exchange.

ANDREW THOMSON (THOMPSON). The *Sampson Independent* (Clinton) of July 13, 1971, contained an article by Claude H. Moore entitled "The Thomson Family Story Reflects History." In the article, reference is made to a colonial silversmith who settled in the area of present-day Sampson County:

He [Curtis Thomson] was the son of David Thomson, a native of Stirling, Scotland, who with his brother Andrew Thomson, a silversmith, migrated to Bertie County in the 1730s, and thence to Duplin (now Sampson) around 1735 [1753?]. Curtis Thomson lived on the site where his grandfather, David Thomson, had settled and built a watermill. Andrew Thomson married two sisters, Ann Hicks and Lucretia Hicks, and he was the father of Ann Thomson who was married to Major James Moore in 1769.

Mrs. Lizzie Seay Britt also wrote about the silversmith and his family in "'Cherrydale': This Old House," a feature article in the *Warsaw-Faison News* (Warsaw), August 30, 1973. About Cherrydale she says, "This old house was built in 1832 by my mother-in-law's uncle, Lewis Moore, on land which had been granted by the crown to his great-grandfather, Andrew Thomson, around 1753. Andrew Thomson, a silversmith, had married into the Hicks Family. . . ."

Andrew Thomson was commissioned a Duplin County justice of the peace on November 29, 1769, and he was an assembly-man in 1760; David Thomson was a justice of the peace in Duplin County in 1759.[747] Curtis Thomson made a wooden secretary that has been kept in the family, according to Mrs. Britt.

WILLIAM THOMSON was born in Fifeshire, Scotland, in 1792 and died in Wilmington on December 30, 1855.[748] Presumably he learned his craft in London and by 1822 was in Jamaica, where his son, William A. Thomson, was born.[749] The elder Thomson went to North Carolina about 1827 or 1828. His earliest known advertisement in a Wilmington newspaper appeared in the *People's Press & Wilmington Advertiser* on May 8, 1833; it gives notice that gold and silver watches offered by him for sale "are warranted of a superior quality, having been made to order with the subscriber's [Thomson's] name" and also notes that Thomson's shop was located on the south side of Market Street opposite the store of Samuel Shuter, Esq. On November 6, 1834, Thomson married Theresa Simpson of Moores Creek, who became his second wife (the identity of the first wife and the date of her death are unknown). Soon afterward, he advertised the location of his shop as "On the north side of Market Street opposite the Market House" in Wilmington.[750] During the following month Thomson advertised himself as a clockmaker and watchmaker, said he sold silver, announced that he wanted to hire slaves of various ages, and thanked the public for liberal patronage.[751] By November 28, 1836, he had located in Raleigh and said he had completed his professional training in London.[752] In 1837 he became a member of the firm of Thomson & Beckwith; following dissolution of the firm in 1839 he continued the business until the firm's stock in trade was sold at auction on November 25, 1840. He then returned to Wilmington and resumed his former business at the northesast corner of the courthouse square.[753] On November 21, 1845, Thomson announced that he had been burned out by a recent fire and could be found upstairs opposite the office of the *Wilmington Chronicle*.[754] He evidently continued in business in Wilmington until his death ten years later. The name is such a common one that it is difficult to follow by court records. A William Thomson was listed as a silversmith in the New York City directories for 1810 through 1823 and 1841 through 1845.[755] This man, who was succeeded by James Thomson, made quite handsome silver, and several pieces have been found in North Carolina; but efforts to relate the North Carolina William Thomson to the New York silversmith have not been conclusive because the birth date of the North Carolina man and the dates during which the New York craftsman worked would almost certainly preclude the presumption that they could have been the same person.

THOMSON & BECKWITH (1837-1839). William Thomson and R. W. Beckwith were located at Raleigh. The partnership was announced on November 29, 1837,[756] and the dissolution on May 20, 1839.[257] Thomson carried on the business in Raleigh for a short time.

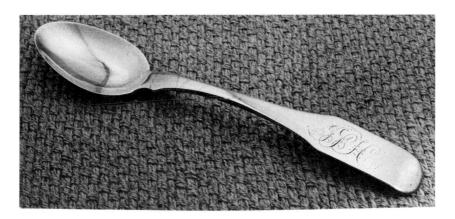

This teaspoon is the only piece of silver yet found with the Thomson & Beckwith mark. Purchased several years ago in Raleigh, it is a fiddleback, 5¾ inches long, with tipped back, oval bowl (slightly worn), and long drop. (From a private collection.)

NATHAN TISDALE (d. 1839) was a son of William Tisdale I. The date of his marriage to Mary Bryan in Craven County was May 21, 1789, and that to Polly Wade was August 2, 1804.[758] He was paid by William Attmore on January 25, 1790, for "altering a ring and mending sleeve buttons."[759] On June 13, 1795, Tisdale took Jessee Saunders as an apprentice to the silversmith's trade.[760] On October 31, 1795, John Tinley, hatmaker, stated that he "carried on the above business at the shop lately occupied by Nathan Tisdale, silversmith, at the corner of Pollock and Metcalf streets in New Bern."[761] In 1807 Nathan Tisdale and William Johnston were paid for their execution of seals (presumably silver, at $10.00 per seal) for the "several Superior Courts"—£150 authorized on July 3, 1807, another £150 on September 29, 1807; and on August 27, 1807, Tisdale wrote to Governor Nathaniel Alexander that he and Johnston had completed the seals and "We shall be happy to receive another 300 dollars by Mr. Chapman if you please."[762] A receipt for the seals was signed by an authoritative person in each of forty-one counties.[763]

Stephen F. Miller wrote that "Col. Nathan Tisdale carried on the watch repairing business, and was a gentleman of great reading and intelligence. He was a commander of the Fort at Beacon's Island, near Portsmouth, in the war of 1812-14. . . ."[764] Lieutenant Colonel Nathan Tisdale, commanding the Craven Regiment, New Bern, signed regimental orders on August 19, 1813.[765] On March 29, 1827, Tisdale announced the removal from his stand on Middle Street to a shop on Craven Street, where watches and compasses would be repaired and other work done.[766] In September, 1827, citizens of New Bern held a meeting to take appropriate action in favor of Andrew Jackson and in opposition to John Quincy Adams for the presidency. A committee of correspondence consisting of thirty-two persons was appointed, of which Colonel Nathan Tisdale was a member.[767] As a notary public he attested a declaration dated November 23, 1827,[768] and as clerk to the commissioners of the town he signed notices dated May 5 and June 28, 1828, and February 28, 1829.[769] In 1830 Tisdale moved to Mobile, Alabama, according to an obituary in the *Newbern Spectator* of October 11, 1839:

Died, At Mobile, on the 20th September last, at the venerable age of "threescore years and ten," Col. Nathan Tisdale.

The deceased was a native of this town [New Bern], and resided here (with the exception of a few years in early life, which were devoted to educational pursuits in one of the northern States) till the summer of 1830, when he removed to Mobile. The impression made here on a large circle of relatives and friends by the announcement of the death of Col. Tisdale, is in accordance with the deep affection and respect which they so long entertained for him.[770]

WILLIAM TISDALE I (1735-ca. 1796) was a prominent student who entered Harvard College with the class of 1755 but left before he had completed his first year. Dr. Louise Hall of Durham has established Tisdale's move to North Carolina as ca. 1770. In 1771 he was not only a juror and grand juror for Craven County but also a member of the assembly.[771] Representing New Bern, Tisdale was a member of the Provincial Congress that met at Hillsborough on August 21, 1775; and he

Shown above are two views of one of three tablespoons attributed to William Tisdale I. The spoons, from a private collection, have spatulate handles and elliptical bowls with drop and are engraved C·I in barred block capital letters. The maker's mark was struck twice on the back of this spoon. Although the two marks (bottom photographs) exhibit minor differences, they were no doubt made from the same die. These spoons were recently sold to a private collector after being held for many years by members of the family that originally owned them; provenance, Edenton.

was appointed to a special committee of the congress to investigate John Coulson.[772] He was also a member of the committee of safety for New Bern in 1775 and 1776.[773] On October 20, 1775, he was employed to engrave plates for bills of credit; for this he was to receive £100.[774] James Coor wrote to Colonel John Simpson on September 30, 1776: "I sent your watch for repairing. I paid Mr. Tisdale twenty shillings. . . . Mr. Tisdale contended New Bern election with Mr. Nash."[775] On March 11, 1777, Tisdale was appointed a justice of the peace, and the following April 30 Governor Richard Caswell signed Tisdale's commission as judge of the admiralty court for the Port of Beaufort.[776] On December 13 of that year Bond Vail was apprenticed to William Tisdale to learn the trade of silversmith.[777]

Among the laws of 1778 was an act that appointed Tisdale to engrave the great seal of the state, and in 1780 he was appointed one of three commissioners to superintend the printing and numbering of bills of credit in the amount of £1,240,000.[778] A petition to suspend him as judge of the court of admiralty was presented to the assembly, and in July, 1781, he was suspended until charges of bribery and corruption were refuted.[779] The committee on propositions and grievances recommended that the resolution of July, 1781, be rescinded, but the state House of Commons rejected this recommendation.[780] On April 17, 1782, he sent an address to the legislature, and on May 8, 1783, the legislature refused to appoint a judge of the admiralty court for the Port of Beaufort inasmuch as William Tisdale had not resigned but merely had been suspended for a limited time.[781] His resignation as a justice of the peace was accepted by the legislature on November 5, 1784;[782] but he was elected a member of the General Assembly, representing New Bern, in 1785 and was appointed to several committees.[783] The census of 1790 showed his household to have consisted of one white male over sixteen, one white male under sixteen, three white females, and three slaves.[784] Several deeds in which he was involved, ranging in date from 1774 to 1796, are recorded in Craven County.[785]

Nathan Tisdale was administrator of his father's estate, and during the June term of court in 1797 he filed the following inventory of the personal estate of William Tisdale:

Book debts and notes to amount of £100.0.0
Two negroe wenches & one fellow
One Horse a Cow & heifers three Tables two bedsteads mahogany
a mahogany Chest of drawers, a desk & side board
one dozen mahogany C[ha]irs with bottoms leather
bead cloths, two matresses, & three beads of feather
two Clocks, one Case of mahogany & the other of pine
House & kitchin furniture, small articles two tedious to
particularize, worth about .... £ 50
Silver Smith and watch makers tools
Materials of ditto £100
a Gun two gold watches a few books say 20 volumes

June term   1797   Nathan Tisdale Adm.[786]

William Shephard and William McClure were bondsmen with
Nathan Tisdale when he filed as administrator for the estate on
March 15, 1797.

WILLIAM TISDALE II (1791-1861), son of William Tisdale I,
was born June 30, 1791, died July 9, 1861, and was buried in
Cedar Grove Cemetery at New Bern. He opened a shop for

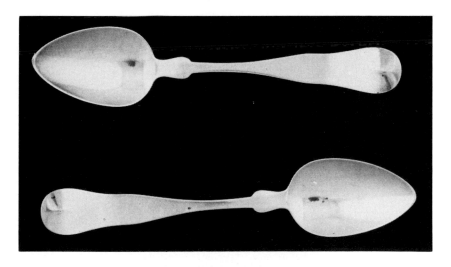

The incused mark TISDALE has been found on several pieces of silver in
North Carolina, and the owners of these pieces attribute them to North Carolina's William Tisdale II. This pair of teaspoons has such a mark. The spoons
are modified fiddle with tipped handles, rounded shoulders, and pointed, oval
bowls. (From a private collection.)

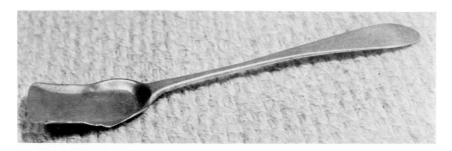

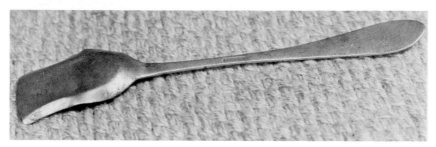

This salt shovel, ca. 3½ inches long with a spatulate, flat handle, has the mark W.T. (left) in a rectangle. It can be dated (1819) to the original owner, Elizabeth Tisdale, sister of William Tisdale II. The shovel was a gift to the North Carolina Museum of History by Mrs. Mary Carter Whitehurst Guion in memory of her mother, Mrs. Maria Forbes Gooding Whitehurst. A punch ladle and a memorial spoon with this mark are also known to have survived. The mark can be compared to that attributed to William Tisdale I.

clockmaking and watchmaking in Washington, North Carolina, on September 6, 1816.[781] He was listed in the 1820 census of manufactures as a silversmith in Fayetteville who employed two men and one boy in the manufacture of silverware and jewelry. On December 19, 1821, he took the shop in New Bern lately occupied by John Gill; there he repaired watches, clocks, and jewelry of all kinds.[788] In 1857 he sold land in New Bern,[789] and in 1858 he was involved in the security of a note.[790]

NATHANIEL (NATHANIELL, NATHANILL) TOMES. Tomes was living in the county of Albemarle in 1697/8 and on February 15 was paid for making spoons:

Paid to the said Nathanill Tomes for makin 14 spoons   0:03:3
Per Jno. Hawkins

(Mattie Erma Edwards Parker [ed.], *North Carolina Higher-Court Records, 1697-1701*, Volume III of *The Colonial Records of North Carolina, Second Series*, edited by Mattie Erma Edwards Parker and others [Raleigh: Division of Archives and History, Department of Cultural Resources (projected multivolume series, 1963—), 1971], 353.)

Although the metal used in making the spoons is not mentioned, this entry suggests that Tomes may have been a seventeenth-century North Carolina silversmith.

JAMES TOWNSLEY was a silversmith in Salisbury from 1772 to 1790. The only available knowledge of him comes from the Rowan County records, principally from the deed books. His name first appears on May 7, 1772, when he purchased a lot on Main Street, Salisbury, from W. T. Coles. On May 6, 1775, James Townsley of Rowan County, silversmith, conveyed to William McBride two lots in South Square, Salisbury.[791] On November 4, 1784, Townsley bought one half of lots Nos. 8 and 16 from James Brandon, these being the other half of lots purchased from Coles in 1772.[792] On February 20, 1790, Townsley is again referred to as a silversmith.[793] In the tax list of 1778 he is credited with property to the extent of £1,082, which was a considerable amount at that time. The Rowan County court minutes of February 9, 1791, indicate that James Townsley II was appointed administrator of the estate of James Townsley I and was granted letters testamentary.[794] It therefore appears that James Townsley, Sr., died sometime between November 1, 1790, and the date of that record, inasmuch as the court met quarterly. There is no indication that his son was a silversmith.

PINCKNEY TROTTER (b. ca. 1832) evidently was the son of Thomas Trotter, who was advertising in 1856 as Thomas Trotter & Son (*Western Democrat*, October 7, 1856). In the census of 1850 (Mecklenburg County, Population Schedule, 199) he was listed as a member of Thomas Trotter's household as a young man of eighteen. Thomas Trotter had listed his own occupation as silversmith, and the son had indicated "Ditto"; thus it can be inferred that he, along with another young man, James G. Wilkinson, was learning the craft from his father at that time.

THOMAS TROTTER (1800-1865) was born in Nansemond County, Virginia, on December 7, 1800, the son of William Trotter. When eighteen years of age he went to Salisbury, North Carolina, where he was apprenticed to a silversmith, perhaps Hugh Horah. They did not get along well, and Trotter left in 1820 before finishing his apprenticeship; but he paid his master for his unexpired time.[795] Just where he finished his training is not known, but he later opened a shop in Greensboro, where on July 22, 1824, he notified the public that he was leaving their town, requested the payment of all bills to John M. Logan, and asked persons who had left watches to come and take them away.[796] Soon after this, Trotter settled in Charlotte and was well established there in 1827.[797] On November 18, 1828, he married Margaret Graham of Charlotte.[798]

He became successively a member of the firms of Thomas Trotter & Co. (1828),[799] Trotter & Huntington (1828-1832), and Trotter & Alexander (1837-1838).[800] In an advertisement in May, 1833,[801] Trotter announced that "he [Trotter] still con-

This handsome pitcher made by Thomas Trotter and still in the hands of a descendant has a pear-shaped body embellished on the side with a spray of grapes and foliage, a molded upper rim and base, and a scrolled handle. The grape and leaf motif is comparable to that on an unmarked communion set presented in 1857 to the First Presbyterian Church in Charlotte— the church Trotter attended and to which he was extremely loyal.

This collection of eleven pieces by Trotter contains four forks—unusual in North Carolina. The style of the service is, of course, fiddle, with rounded shoulders and tipped handles. (From a private collection.)

tinues to manufacture SILVER SPOONS and other articles of Gold and Silver, and he would here inform the public, that this is the only shop in town where such articles are repaired." Trotter also suggested that he would "flux gold" and do "gilding and engraving" on order. In 1838 he purchased the stock of Trotter & Alexander,[802] but on October 21 of the following year he sold the entire establishment to S. P. Alexander.[803] In June, 1841, Trotter advertised that he continued to repair clocks and watches if requested by the owner to do so and that he had a shop in the jewelry store of S. P. Alexander.[804] In 1842 he advertised watch repairing, "cash system," and published his scale of prices. On July 8, 1843, he purchased the stock of S. P. Alexander and advertised that he would then give this business his personal and exclusive attention.[805]

On December 31, 1850, he was again married, this time to Jane Elizabeth Brown of Steele Creek Church community. He continued as a silversmith and watchmaker, becoming a member of the firm of Thomas Trotter & Son in 1856[806] and of J. G. Wilkinson & Co. in 1858.[807] Between 1828 and 1863 there were

At left is a Trotter punch ladle purchased by the Museum Associates for the North Carolina Museum of History. Once owned by the Lyon family, it is 13½ inches long with a bowl 4⅛ inches wide; it is fiddle in style with flared, rounded shoulders and is engraved *1855-1902* on the back. Shown below (top to bottom) are three small pieces: a tablespoon 8½ inches long, handle with tipped end, engraved *S*; a teaspoon 6½ inches long with oval, pointed bowl 1⅞ inches long and 1¹/₁₆ inches wide, pointed shoulders, and handle engraved *SG* in script, crosshatched; a fiddleback mustard ladle with tipped handle and rounded shoulders.

numerous real estate transactions to which he was a party. He accumulated considerable property in Charlotte; but after his four sons enlisted in the Confederate army, Trotter sold most of his property and invested the proceeds in Confederate bonds. He died in Charlotte on March 31, 1865. S. P. Alexander was the executor of his estate. For nearly forty years Trotter dominated the jewelry and silver business of Charlotte. Osmond Barringer, a longtime resident of Charlotte, remembered that the silversmith was known as "honest Tom Trotter."[808]

THOMAS TROTTER & CO. (1827-1828). "Trotter & Huntington of the late firm of Thomas Trotter & Co." seems to indicate that these two men previously were members of a larger partnership known as Thomas Trotter & Co. This firm announced on March 6, 1827, that it had opened a shop in Charlotte;[809] the partnership was dissolved on January 15, 1828.[810]

TROTTER & ALEXANDER (1837-1838). Thomas Trotter and Samuel P. Alexander were located in Charlotte. The new firm was announced on November 24, 1837,[811] and dissolved on November 26, 1838, with Trotter continuing the business.[812]

TROTTER & HUNTINGTON (1828-1832). Thomas Trotter and John Huntington, in Charlotte, succeeded Thomas Trotter & Company early in 1828.[813] The firm bought land in Charlotte in March and April, 1829,[814] and announced on December 1, 1829, that it would dissolve inasmuch as one of the members intended leaving the state.[815] In an advertisement dated December, 1830, and which was still appearing in the *Miners' and Farmers' Journal* (Charlotte) as late as February 17, 1831, Trotter and Huntington announced the establishment of their shop in the former building of R. Gillespie, "100 yards north-east from the Court-House." The firm advertised military goods, watch repairing, and "the manufacture of silver Table and Tea Spoons and North Carolina gold worked into any articles that may be ordered." Dissolution took place on February 22, 1832.[816]

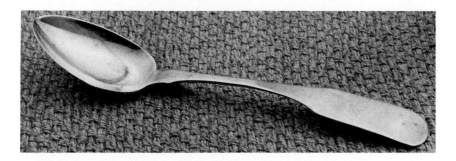

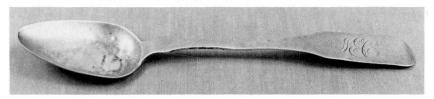

Shown in the photographs at top and center is a small Trotter & Huntington teaspoon 5½ inches long, one of several in a set dispersed by auction in Davie County. It is fiddle with pointed shoulders, and the handle is tipped on the reverse; there is no engraving. Pictured at bottom is a dessertspoon measuring 7¾ inches in length, with the initials *JEC* elegantly engraved on the handle; the T&H mark pictured at the conclusion of the sketch is taken from the dessertspoon.

FRANKLIN TURNER. Burton lists him as a native of Connecticut who went to Cheraw, South Carolina, about 1812, after residing briefly in Wadesboro. He still had ties in Wadesboro as late as 1822 as a member of the firm of Clark & Turner.[817] Turner apparently spent his last years in Cheraw as a silversmith and jeweler, advertising in 1823; he died there at the age of seventy-nine.[818]

RICHARD VEALE,[819] of Northampton County, died between March 18 and December 13, 1781. His will, dated March 18, 1781, makes these provisions:

. . . to my son JOHN VEAL plantation where my mother [not named] formerly lived, part of my other plantation which joins my Spring and SIMON JEFFERS and 50 acres in Holly Pocoson to my son WILLIAM BRIDGES VEAL plantation whereon I now live and all the rest of my land, also my still to my Sister PATIENCE [illegible] 5 pounds in gold and silver and her maintenance out of my estate during her life or widowhood provided she live on one of my plantations and take care of my Children; if not, I leave her only the 5 pounds my negroes to work on plantation until my son JOHN VEAL comes to age 21, then negroes and remainder of my Estate to be equally divided between my two sons

Extrs: JOHN KNOX and THOMAS WHITE
Wits: JOHN PEELE [?], Josiah OUTLAND[820]

An inventory of Veale's estate, recorded on December 13, 1781, and affirmed by John Knox and Thomas White, included items that suggest Veale had been engaged in silversmithing:

. . . 22 Negroes . . . 12 Silver Dollars . . . [extensive household items] . . . 4 Augers, 2 Gouges, 4 Chisells, 1 Shingle Jointer, 2 Hand Saws, 1 Tenent Ditto . . . A Parcell of Old Iron, 20½ lbs of Copper a small Parcell of Brass, . . . A Sett of Black and Silver Smiths Tools, To wit 1 Anvil and Bellows, 1 Vice & Hedge . . . 3 pair of Tongs, 3 Screw Plantes 46 Files 40 Carving and Engraving tools, 1 Small hand Vice & Bench 2 Small Hammers, 1 Scraper & 1 Burnisher . . . 2 pair of Nippers, 2 Drill Stocks, 1 Blow Pipe, 1 pair of Compasses, 26 Buckle Patterns a pair of Brass Plyers, . . . 1½ Doz.^{ns} Silver Buttons Suitable for a Coat, & 2½ Doz.^{ns} D.^{o} Waistcoat D.^{o} 2 pairs D.^{o} Shoe Buckles & 13 Ditto Unfinished 2 pair Ditto Knee Buckles & 2 D.^{o} Unfinished, 2 Ditto Stock Buckles & 1 D.^{o} Unfinished 8 pair Ditto Sleeve Buttons Unfinished 3 Ounces of Filings & Rough Silver & 4 Pw.^{ts}—Cl [?] Gold and Filings.[821]

No total value is given, although separate parts of the estate were valued at £741 12s. 0d., £879 16s. 0d., and £900. In June, 1783, an audit of the Veale estate in account with the executors included various amounts paid for taxes for 1780, 1781, 1782; £6 13s. 4d. paid to Latimer Jolliff [Veale's brother-in-law?]; and a variety of other expenses.[822]

ELIAS ALEXANDER VOGLER (1825-1876), the son of John Vogler and Christina Spach, was born October 31, 1825, in Salem, North Carolina. He was apprenticed to his father and went into partnership with him in 1846. On October 21, 1847, he married Emma Antoinette Reich in Salem. On March 24, 1866, the Salem *People's Press* carried this advertisement:

Jeweler Shop Re-opened.

I HAVE RE-OPENED MY SHOP, WHERE Clocks, Watches and Jewelry will again be repaired with fidelity and despatch, by a competent workman.

E. A. Vogler

Salem, N.C., March 10th, 1866.

Vogler carried on a silversmith and jewelry business in Salem for many years and died there on November 17, 1876.[823] In 1873 H. W. Fries, assignee of Vogler's estate, advertised that he would "sell at the Court-house door . . . the balance of a stock of Jewelry, Silver Ware, all of which is new, and some very desirable" (*People's Press*, August 14, 1873).

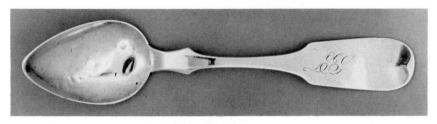

This teaspoon, signed E.A.VOGLER and measuring 5¼ inches in length, is in the Old Salem Collection. Photograph courtesy MESDA.

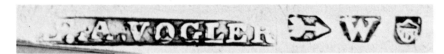

Photograph courtesy MESDA.

JOHN VOGLER (1783-1881) was born in Friedland, North Carolina, November 20, 1783, the son of George Michael Vogler and Anna Maria Kunzel. He moved to Salem in 1802, where he learned the gunsmith trade with his uncle. Where and when he learned the silversmith trade is not known, but he probably transferred his gunsmith skill to silver, perhaps through the influence of his visits to Bethlehem, Pennsylvania. In 1805 he was listed as a gunsmith and in 1806 as a silversmith, at which craft he worked for the rest of his life—although he was also skillful with wood and various metals. Minutes of the *Aufseher Collegium*, Salem, July 15, 1806, reveal the rivalry between Johann Eberhardt (Eberhard, Eberhart) and John Vogler. The minutes record that the board found no cause to prohibit Vogler's pursuing his desire to be a watchmaker and silver-

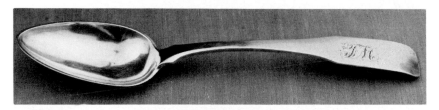

Four representative tablespoons made by John Vogler are these. In the topmost photograph is a fiddleback 8½ inches long with flared shoulders, downturned handle, and oval bowl 1⅝ inches across; the spoon is engraved *TEF* in feathered script and marked I.VOGLER in a rectangle. Second from the top is a variation of fiddle with pointed shoulders that is engraved *FM* in feathered script and marked I.VOGLER in a rectangle. In the third photograph is a tablespoon 8½ inches long with tipped handle and chamfered shoulders; it is engraved *WMC* and marked J.VOGLER in a rectangle. In the photograph at bottom is a spoon 9 inches long with no shoulders and a downturned handle; it is engraved *ML/KEG* in script and marked I.VOGLER in a rectangle. (All from private collections.)

smith, "mainly since he promised not to deal with wall clocks, which is Br. Eberhardt's business alone."[824]

Among other things, Vogler made a silhouette machine. He was very active in the Moravian Church and was an early promoter of Sunday school work. His election in 1808 to the *Aufseher Collegium*, one of the two chief boards of the church, was a great honor for one so young. In 1816 he refused an invitation to go to Bethlehem as the master silversmith. Vogler's house, planned by him and built in 1819, is considered an architectural triumph. On March, 7, 1820, Vogler married Christina Spach.

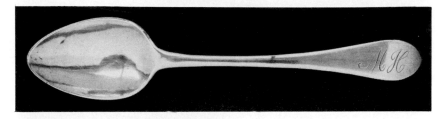

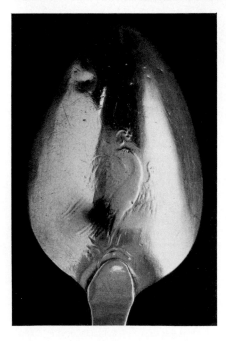

Especially charming are these memorial spoons descended through two families. The spoon shown at top is 5 inches long, fiddle with pointed shoulders, and engraved *JLM* (for James Lafayette McClelland). The spoon in the bottom photograph is 5 inches long and has a pointed-end handle and a slender stem with drop but no shoulders; its special feature is the Vogler eagle stamped on the back of the bowl (shown in detail at left), a die mark that may have been purchased from Johann Ludwig Eberhardt (Albright, *Johann Ludwig Eberhardt*, 44). The I.VOGLER mark that appears at right at the conclusion of the sketch is taken from this spoon, which was originally made for Maria Elizabeth Hauser before her marriage to John Jacob Shore—hence the initials *MH* engraved on the spoon.

He became the leading citizen of Salem at that time, and the chicf room in the Wachovia Museum, named for him, contains his tools and possessions. He died in Salem, June 15, 1881.[825]

These four pieces made by John Vogler are typical of the elegant simplicity of his work. The ladle pictured at top is 13 inches long; the final three of six initials engraved on the handle are *GBR* (for Gotthold Benjamin Reichel of Salem). Just below the ladle is a dainty memorial spoon ca. 5 inches long with *GS* engraved on the pointed-end handle. The tablespoon (third from top), one of three, is 9½ inches long and is engraved *DS* (for Dawdy Stockton of Salem). The Vogler mark that appears at left following the sketch is taken from this spoon. The ladle shown at bottom differs from the other three pieces. A fiddleback, it is ca. 12⅛ inches long, has a slender but sturdy handle, and is engraved *EH* in feathered script. Photographs courtesy MESDA.

Pictured above is a snuffbox attributed to John Vogler, although it is unsigned. The box, silver with gilt interior, was made to commemorate the fiftieth
birthday of Elisabeth Pfohl of Salem. It measures 1¾ inches by 2¾ inches and
is 1 inch deep. Photograph courtesy MESDA.

It seems probable that more silver made by John Vogler is
preserved in North Carolina than that credited to any other silversmith. The question may arise whether this is attributable
to the fact that his Moravian friends and descendants were
more careful of their possessions and suffered less in the Civil
War, or that Vogler made more silver. He was very industrious
and worked many years during his long life. So far as is
known, after he took his son Elias into partnership in 1846 he
still used his own mark. John Vogler made no pieces of great
importance, but he made all varieties of spoons from salt
spoons to soup ladles. Some spoons of his manufacture were of
the pattern common twenty years before his first venture into
silversmithing, and he fashioned some with a bird on the back
of the bowl—so characteristic of Philadelphia makers. This
showed the Bethlehem influence in his design. His die for
stamping these birds is exhibited in the museum room on the
second floor of the John Vogler House in Old Salem.

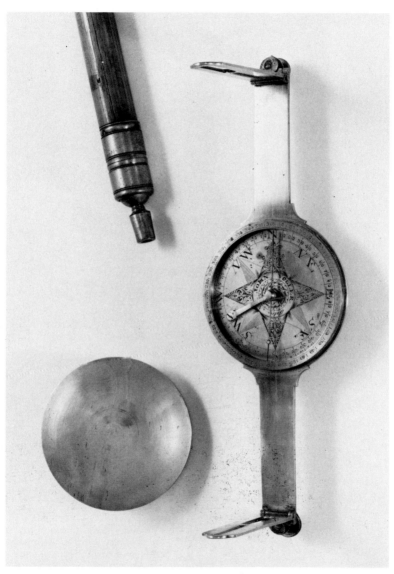

John Vogler fashioned the surveyor's compass, cover, and staff depicted above. The compass, brass with silvered face, is 15 inches long. Photograph courtesy MESDA.

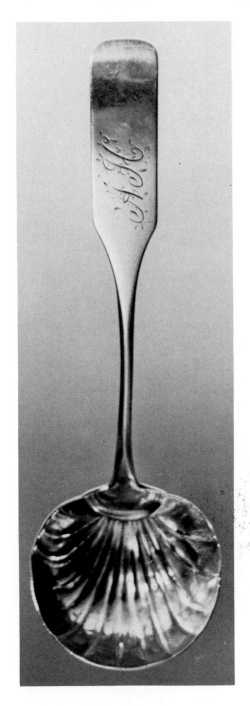

Pictured at left is a John Vogler ladle measuring $6^{11}/_{16}$ inches in length; the bowl is repoussé rather than die-punched. The teaspoon shown above is $5^{3}/_{16}$ inches long, with the initials of Gottlieb Schober of Salem engraved in an oval wreath. Photographs courtesy MESDA.

Pictured above are sugar tongs and a salt spoon stamped I.VOGLER and struck with the shell punch shown to the right of the tongs. The tongs, 5⅞ inches long, are distinguished by a unique serpentine design on the outer edge. The spoon, 3⅝ inches long, is engraved with the initials of John and Christina Vogler. These items are on display at Old Salem. (Photograph courtesy MESDA.) Quite different in style is the simple salt spoon pictured below. It is 4¼ inches long with *1806* engraved on the front. (From a private collection.)

An unusual item attributed to John Vogler, albeit unsigned, is this cape clasp, which has a *J* engraved on the left half and a *V* on the right; each half is ½ inch by ¹³⁄₁₆ inch. This item is on display at Old Salem. Photograph courtesy MESDA.

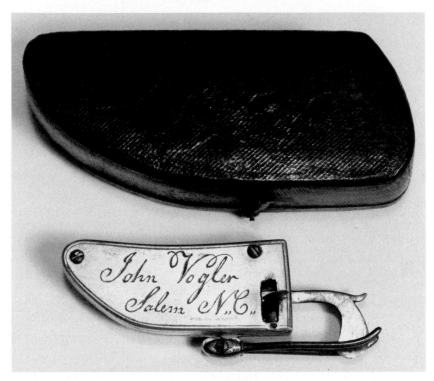

This trigger lancet was made by John Vogler of steel and gilt brass; it measures 2⅞ inches in length. Photograph courtesy MESDA.

Part of the tools made and used by John Vogler are pictured here; the Vogler tools are in the Old Salem Collection. Shown here are spoon and ladle punches. Vogler's name die is in the center. Photograph courtesy MESDA.

Versatile John Vogler produced silhouettes in addition to silverware. The silhouette of himself pictured here is reprinted from Cutten's first edition; the original belonged to Mrs. A. H. Patterson of Chapel Hill.

Shown at right is "a copper plate for printing watch papers," according to Mr. John F. Bivins, Jr., curator of the Old Salem Collection. The inscription around the outer rim reads: "IN THIS TIME PRE-PARED BE: FOR ON EACH MOMENT HANGS ETERNI-TY." Original photograph from a print owned by Mrs. A. H. Patterson, Chapel Hill.

JOHN UTZMANN VOGLER (1812-1856) was born in Salisbury, June 7, 1812, the son of Johann George Vogler and Christina Utzmann. He learned his trade in Salem with his uncle, John Vogler. On June 25, 1835, he married Maria Louise Reich in Salem.[826] On April 16, 1841, he advertised that he had commenced business in Salisbury and mentioned his long experience.[827] In January, 1845, he advertised that he had opened a shop on Main Street, where he made to order jewelry, rings, and breastpins.[828] He died in Salisbury on April 30, 1856. The obituary refers to him as Captain John U. Vogler.[829] The census of 1850 lists him as a silversmith.

An exceptional find recently made by a private collector was a tablespoon made by John Utzmann Vogler. The spoon is in very bad condition, but the mark, shown above, is quite clear.

A. J. WALKER is listed as a silversmith of Locust Hill in Caswell County in the census of 1850. Nothing else has been learned about him.

NATHAN B. WALKER. One researcher notes that an entry in the Franklin County indentures for June 10, 1846, certifies that Nathan B. Walker bound George W. Hayes as an apprentice to learn the silversmith's and watchmaker's trades.[830] The indenture notice is also in the June 10 minutes of the Franklin County Court of Pleas and Quarter Sessions, but this notice does not include the word "silversmith."[831]

JAMES WALLACE, JUNIOR, was probably born in Edenton, the son of James Wallace. Until recent research revealed that there were earlier silversmiths, Wallace was considered North Carolina's first. On April 11, 1739, a bill for £7 was presented to John Taylor for making a ring, and the following day Wallace, referred to as a silversmith, gave a bond for £14 to cover costs in instituting a suit against Taylor for the collection of this bill.[832] On August 23 of the same year, he signed Thomas Kinsay's bond for £100, guaranteeing that Kindsay would abide by regulations governing innkeepers.[833] A bond for his marriage to Elizabeth Slaughter, widow, was filed September 4, 1741.[834] On December 1, 1742, a warrant for the arrest of Laws Predy and Mary Richards was issued "for assault[ing] and violently beat[ing] James Wallace and Elizabeth his wife."[835] This seems to have been but an incident along a romantic trail, for Predy and Mrs. Richards were afterward married.

Wallace served on a grand jury in 1744,[836] and in July of that year he made application to keep an ordinary in his own dwelling, Solomon King going on his bond for £30.[837] Every year after that until the time of his death he made a successful application for a license, and after his death his wife Elizabeth continued to receive a license.[838] Whether or not this meant that he had given up silversmithing is not known. In 1746 he was a witness to a bond to enable James Trotter to keep an ordinary.[839] He was on a list of tithables in 1749[840] and on a list of patents signed in Edenton in 1751.[841] In October, 1755, John Craven brought suit against Elizabeth Wallace, administratrix of the estate of James Wallace. In the bill of particulars it was stated that James Wallace was alive on February 27, 1754.[842] In an undated petition Robert Wallace asserted that he was the son of James Wallace, Sr., whose son James Wallace was the administrator of his estate but had made no distribution. James Wallace, Junior, died intestate, and his effects were in the possession of Elizabeth Wallace. Robert asked that the justices see that he had his due.[843]

JAMES WAY (w. 1773; d. ca. 1807) was described as a silversmith in a land deed dated October 10, 1773, in which Thomas Polk granted him property of an unspecified acreage on both sides of Four-Mile Creek for the sum of £102 10s. 0d. proclamation money.[844] A receipt for a purchase of silversmith's tools dated June 28, 1793, and signed by Spruce Macay indicates a partial payment of £2 by James Way as Robert Mur's executor (from Rowan County Miscellaneous Records, State Archives, arranged and described by archivist Caroline Banks). In his will of January 9, 1807, Way left his property to his wife and stepson, Aaron Griffith:

. . . I do order this my last will & testament that the half of my Estate be put out at intrest [sic] and that my wife Catorine receive the income yearly & every year for her support during her natural life & at her death to Descend as hereafter directed;
I give and bequeath to my wife's son Aaron Griffith all the rest of my Estate to him and his heirs & assigns forever & all that part I left to his Mother to be his at her death. . . .[845]

In the inventory of Way's estate made by the executor, Aaron Griffith, his silversmithing tools are mentioned:

600^{wt} of Brown Sugar at 20^d [per lb wt] $120
20 Gallons of Molasses @ 10 p gill 20
1 Lot of Old Smiths Tools 12
1 Gross Small Watch Crystals 7
1 Old bed & Blanket 6

                                                                    $165.00
Articles Appraised by Jm^s Wilson & T. Jo Haynes   17.40
                                                                    $182.40

There is due to the Estate of James Way deceased a sum of money due by John Valentine of South Carolina and the obligations were lodged in the hands of a man by the name of Chertre of South Carolina to the amount of between four and five hundred Dollars, which it is expected will never be recovered.

due from David Griffith twenty-Seven Dollars [for] a dome bottle lent him and not returned ....

Also thirty three Dollars sent to redeem a mare from execution—this is also an Insolvent Debt. . . .[846]

DAVID WELSH settled in Lincolnton in the early days of 1848. On April 10, 1849, he advertised as a watchmaker and clockmaker and respectfully thanked the public of Lincoln and adjoining counties for the patronage he had received during the fifteen months he had been in business.[847] He was still there in April, 1851. According to the Lincolnton *Carolina Republican* of January 27, 1853, one David Welch, "of Scotland," married Miss Rose Wesson of Lincolnton on January 24, 1853.

JOSEPH WHEDBEE. For Whedbee's marriage to Thomazen Garrett in Edenton, the bond for which was filed on July 27, 1771, Everard Garrett was a bondsman.[848] Later that year Whedbee bought a "looking glass" and a parcel of books at the sale of the estate of Robert Gibson.[849] In 1773 he signed two petitions, one to change the course of a road, the other to have a line run between Chowan and Pasquotank counties.[850] In 1774 he was included in a list of insolvents.[851] He attended another sale in 1777 and bought dishes from the estate of Charles Burbury.[852] On March 23, 1778, he accepted Joseph Leming as an apprentice to be taught the trade and art of silversmith,[853] and on June 23 of that year he signed an oath of allegiance to the state.[854] His assessment for tax purposes in Edenton for the year 1779 was listed as £8,370.[855] The account of "Mr. Joseph Whidby" to James Hayes during the years 1785-1787 has been preserved in the Chowan County Record of Accounts, 1707-1912, State Archives:

```
1785
   July 29     To Supper Grog ............................................ £0—3—0
   Aug.ᵗ 2ⁿᵈ   To Sling ........................................................        1
   Dec.ʳ 31    To 1 Bowl of Tody ......................................        2
   January 1   To julep .......................................................        1


1786           To dᵒ ............................................................        1
               To bowl of Tody .........................................        2
   Feb. 28     To supper 2 ..................................................        2
   March 5     To apper 2 the 9ᵗʰ T Grog .............................        3


1787           ommitted d/o Sling ....................................        1

   May 5       To supper grog ...........................................        1
   1786        To omit sling ..............................................        1
```
                              Carryed Over [to back]

Items were listed on the back in similar form through September, 1786.

In October, 1787, Joseph Whedbee sued William Righton, executor of the estate of Francis Hardy, for £3 8s. 7d.; the bill submitted by Whedbee and approved for payment by the Chowan County Court of Pleas and Quarter Sessions itemized payment owed to Whedbee by the deceased Hardy for having made in 1782 and 1783 gold buttons and shoe buckles and for repairing a watch. Payment was made in December, 1793. (Estate of Francis Hardy, Chowan County Estate Records, State Archives.)

WHEELER & CARPENTER. In the *Wilmington Gazette* for December 4, 1800, a notice declared that the firm of "Wheeler & Carpenter, Watch & Silversmiths, beg leave to inform the public that they have commenced business in Front-street. . . ." The two men have not been identified further, and there is no clue as to how long they were in business.

DAVID H. WHIPPLE may have been a working silversmith in Caswell County ca. 1780. The Caswell County apprentice indentures for December 20, 1780, note that Whipple bound Solomon Seal, orphan, aged fifteen and a half, and John Brown, aged eleven, as apprentices to the silversmith's trade. These apprenticeships are also recorded in the Caswell County court minutes for December 19, 1780. By 1811 Whipple was a silversmith, watchmaker, and clockmaker in the town of Gallatin, Sumner County, Tennessee, according to Caldwell, "Tennessee Silversmiths" (p. 913).

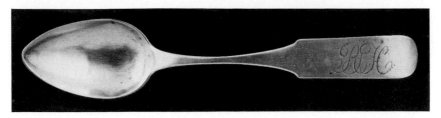

The mark DW, attributed to David Whipple, is on the back of this modified fiddle teaspoon; *RSH* is engraved in feathered script on the handle. (From a private collection.)

WILLIAM WIDDEFIELD, JUNIOR, is listed as a watchmaker in the Philadelphia directories of 1820-1822,[856] but he came to Fayetteville, North Carolina, in 1820 and took charge of the store of Charles Clark. In 1823 he acquired the stock[857] and worked as a watchmaker and jeweler until December 5, 1827, when he sold his stock to Selph & Campbell and appointed George R. Ferguson as his agent and attorney to settle his business affairs.[858] On May 8, 1832, he advertised that he had returned to Fayetteville as a clockmaker and watchmaker,[859] and judgments were obtained against him in 1834 and 1839.[860] He is reported as a resident of Fayetteville in the census of 1840. Widdefield married Mary Campbell, the bond being dated July 30, 1823, with Charles Clark one of the bondsmen.[861]

ALVAN WILCOX (WILLCOX; 1783-1870) was born in Berlin, Connecticut, in 1783, the oldest son of Jacob Wilcox and Rachel Porter.[862] From 1805 to 1807 he was a member of the firm of Hart & Wilcox of Norwich, Connecticut, and later lived in New Jersey.[863] In March, 1819, Wilcox bought land in Fayetteville,[864] although he must have had a silversmith's shop in the town as early as July, 1818, inasmuch as a newspaper advertised "Silver Plate, Clocks, Watches & Jewelry. . . . All kinds of Gold & Silver work made at the shortest notice. . . ."[865]

On May 31, 1823, he leased a house and lot in Fayetteville to John Peabody,[866] and on July 17 Peabody advertised that he had purchased the stock in trade of Alvan Wilcox.[867] Wilcox mortgaged land on April 1, 1823, to Nathaniel Cornwell of Berlin, Connecticut, to secure a note for $730.[868] Cornwell was a

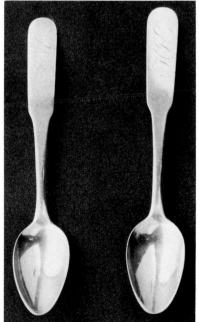 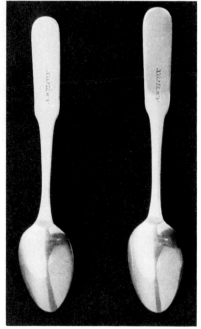

These three pieces have the mark A.WILCOX in italic capital letters. The punch ladle (top), on loan by Mrs. C. G. McIver, Jr., to the North Carolina Museum of History, is 38.5 cm. long, has a bowl 8.7 cm. long and 10.7 cm. wide, and is engraved with the initial *S* in script. The teaspoons, from a private collection, are 5¾ inches long and are engraved *HJE*.

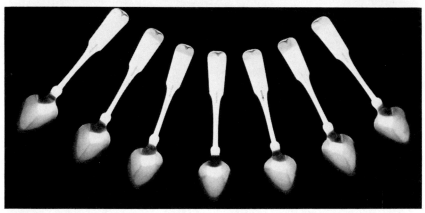

These fiddle dessertspoons exemplify the superb craftsmanship of Alvan Wilcox. They are marked by the maker A.WILCOX in roman capital letters in a rectangle. The spoons measure 6⅛ inches in length and have rounded shoulders, handles tipped on the reverse, and oval bowls with crescent drop; they are engraved *HAP* on the front of the handles.

silversmith who worked at one time in Danbury, Connecticut; from him Wilcox may have learned his trade. Wilcox located in New Haven, Connecticut, in 1824 and evidently spent the remainder of his life there. The first New Haven directory, issued in 1841, lists him as a silver worker; the 1850 directory lists him as a gold and silver thimble and spectacle maker; and in 1857 he is described as a "silver-plater."[869] His younger brother, Cyprian, was a silversmith in New Haven in 1827,[870] and his son, Wallace, was the headmaster of a boy's school in Stamford. Alvan Wilcox died on August 17, 1870. His name was sometimes spelled Willcox.

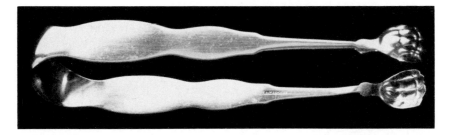

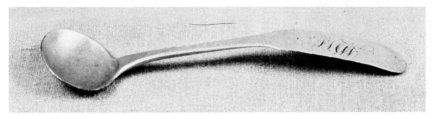

These tongs (top) by Alvan Wilcox have scalloped arms tapering to claw grips. They are 17.5 cm. in length and are engraved *SLM* in script. The Wilcox salt spoon (bottom), depicted in its actual size, has a fiddle handle; the handle is engraved *SICW*. Both of these pieces are in the collection of the North Carolina Museum of History.

WILLIAM WILKINGS (WILKINS; d. ca. 1761), who was located in Charleston, South Carolina, by 1749, represented himself to be a goldsmith from London who "makes, and sells at reasonable rates, all sorts of gold and silver work . . . in the newest fashion" and added that he "has a wet nurse to hire."[871] In 1751 he advertised a number of articles to be sold by lot at 40s. per lot; "among the sixty-two lots were a silver tankard valued at one hundred pounds, a pint mug, a silver watch, and a silver hilted sword."[872]

Wilkings apparently moved from Charleston to Wilmington, North Carolina, before or around 1750. His name appears in the minutes of the Wilmington town book kept from 1743 through 1778[873] and in various county records between 1750 and 1761.[874] He was operating an ordinary by 1759 and served as coroner for New Hanover County, according to these records. "In 1760 an advertisement appeared in the *South Carolina Gazette* [August 8] stating that a porringer stamped W.W. in one [meaning not clear] had been stolen. Possibly this was the mark of William Wilkings, for we know that his contemporary, William Wright, . . . stamped his silver W. Wright."[875]

CURTIS WILKINSON was a member of the firm of Wilkinson & Horah[876] of Salisbury, 1820-1821. After the dissolution of this firm he worked independently in Salisbury for a time.[877] On November 24, 1823, Savage & Kunsman advertised that they had taken the shop lately occupied by Curtis Wilkinson.[878]

WILKINSON & HORAH (1820-1821). Curtis Wilkinson and Hugh Horah were located at Salisbury. The partnership was announced on July 25, 1820,[879] and its dissolution occurred on February 5, 1821. Horah settled the accounts, and Wilkinson carried on the business.[880]

JAMES G. WILKINSON was listed in the census of 1850 (Mecklenburg County, Population Schedule, 199) as a member of Thomas Trotter's household. He was at that time twenty-five years of age and was either working as a silversmith or was learning the trade with Trotter, inasmuch as he had listed his occupation as "Ditto" under Trotter's own designation of himself as a silversmith. A firm known as J. G. Wilkinson & Co. (Trotter and Wilkinson) advertised in the Charlotte *North Carolina Whig* of November 2, 1858.

On a very handsome punch ladle in an early pattern produced by an unidentified manufacturer is the retailer's mark used by J. G. Wilkinson & Co. No handcrafted silver with Wilkinson's mark has been located.

WILLIAM ROWAN WILSON (1821-1866), the son of John Wilson, was born in Allentown, Pennsylvania, January 29, 1821.[881] He moved from Philadelphia to Salisbury, North Carolina, and became a member of the firm of Boger & Wilson in 1846.[882] On March 25, 1852, he married Sarah Alice Slater in Salisbury. Following the dissolution of the firm of Boger & Wilson in 1853, Wilson bought Boger's interest[883] and worked independently until the time of his death in Salisbury on January 14, 1866.[884] The census of 1850 lists him as silversmith.

JOHN WINCKLER (1730-1803)[885] was the son of Johann Nikolaus Winckler, a goldsmith, and his first wife. He was born in Essling, near Stuttgart, Germany, on April 18, 1730. When twenty-one years of age he left home and went to London where, presumably, he worked at his trade and learned to speak English. In 1761 he moved to Charleston, South Carolina, and in July of that year advertised as a silversmith and chaser from London, stating that he carried on the business of silversmithing in all its branches at his shop near the State House. In May, 1763, he announced that he had removed from Queen Street to the Bay, at the corner of Unity-Alley, where he continued the same business as formerly. Shortly after this he moved from there and, according to family history, went to North Carolina, near where the city of Raleigh now stands.

This John Winckler teaspoon (top) is 6 inches long, with an oval, pointed bowl 1¹⁵⁄₁₆ long, chamfered shoulders, and handle engraved *MLK* in script. The mark that appears at the conclusion of the sketch is taken from this spoon. Winckler's tools are depicted in the bottom photograph. Photographs courtesy MESDA.

Little is known of him during his years of residence in North Carolina. Only one reference to him has been found, and that is political rather than occupational—he was a Regulator. On May 31, 1771, Governor William Tryon issued a proclamation of pardon to all those who had been involved in

Treasons, Insurrections and Rebellions done or committed on or before the 16th Inst., provided they make their submission beforesaid on or before the 10th of June next. The following persons are however excepted from the benefits of the Proclamation, Viz. All the outlaws, the prisoners in Camp, and the undernamed persons. . . .

Then follows a list of fourteen names, included in which is "John Winkler." In a long and comprehensive list of the names of Regulators, with county residence and political affiliations, is that of John Winkler; but no residence is given for him, and his party affiliation is also missing.

On May 11, 1778, he bought 95 acres of land in Mecklenburg County, Virginia, from John Hatchell and James Toone for £40. There, just south of the town of Boydton, he lived until his death in 1803.

JAMES WOOD. This man may have been a silversmith working in the Washington, North Carolina, area in 1808. However, there is nothing to prove that he was, except for an announcement in the *Washington Gazette*[886] which stated that "he intends carrying on the Watch Repairing, Silver Smith, & Jewelry business, in all its various branches." He also offered cash for old gold and silver.

FREEMAN WOODS (ca. 1766-1834). Freeman Woods first worked in New York prior to his move into North Carolina; his name appears in the New York City directories from 1791 to 1794.[887] On December 27, 1794, he advertised in New Bern, North Carolina, stating that he had commenced business two doors above William Lawrence's store, where anything in the "above branch" might be had, particularly waiters, tankards, teapots, sugar dishes, milk pots, tablespoons, teaspoons, sugar tongs, and the like, in the newest fashions and at the shortest notice.[888] He took David Murdock as an apprentice on June 10, 1805. The *Newbern Herald*, November 27, 1809, contained an

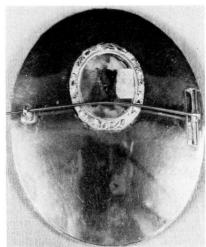

Reputed to be a likeness of Freeman Woods is this miniature on ivory encased in a frame of 18k gold; the work is attributed to Ezra Ames. The brooch was once the property of Zephra Woods Ames (Mrs. Ezra Ames). Now in a private collection, it was located in the provenance of New Bern. In the back of the brooch (right) is a small compartment containing a braid of light brown hair (Woods's?).

advertisement that boasted "Silver Spoons particularly of every description, he warrants lower than they can be bought anywhere to the northward—and of superior workmanship."

Few facts about Woods's family have been determined, but the Raleigh newspapers reported the death of "Mrs. Hannah Woods, wife of Mr. Freeman Woods," which occurred in October, 1811, in New Bern.[889] In 1818 Woods advertised for an apprentice to the goldsmithing and silversmithing business;[890] in 1822, silver tablespoons and teaspoons and soup ladles;[891] in 1824, gold and silver work;[892] and in 1826, superb silver tablespoons and teaspoons.[893] In August, 1827, as one of the executors of the estate of Benjamin C. Good, he gave notice that notes were due.[894] In September, 1827, citizens of New Bern held a meeting to take appropriate action in favor of Andrew Jackson and in opposition to John Quincy Adams for the presidency. A committee of correspondence, consisting of thirty-two persons, was appointed; Freeman Woods was among them.[895] The *Newbern Spectator* for November 20, 1834, contained a notice of Woods's death at age sixty-eight and an invitation to attend his funeral on November 21. This would establish his birth date at ca. 1766. The obituary stated that "Mr. Woods was a native of New Jersey, and for the last forty years a resident of this town." An inventory of his property contained many items relative to his profession:

"An Inventory Account. Sales of the Property of Freeman Woods Taken and Sold by Elijah Clark Adm. 11th March 1835."

3 pr. silver sugar tongs	1.30	3.90
1 pr. ditto		.85
3 pr. ditto	.50	1.50
½ dz. teaspoons		4.50
½ dz. ditto		4.25
½ dz. ditto		4.85
½ dz. ditto		4.80
1 dessert spoon		1.00
2 salt ditto	.32	.64
2 mustard ditto	.40	.80
1 mustard ditto		.50
2 salt ditto	.40	.80
2 salt ditto		.84
2 salt ditto		.85
2 salt ditto		.90
2 salt ditto		.90
2 salt ditto		.86
2 salt ditto		.80
2 salt ditto		.92
2 salt ditto		.95
2 salt ditto		.80
2 salt ditto		1.02
2 mustard spoons	.46	.92
1 silver punch ladle		1.05
½ doz. table spoons		15.25
½ doz. ditto		15.25
½ doz. ditto		15.25
1 oil cream pot and ladle		15.25
88 Oz 17 dwt. old silver		89.73 ¾	1.01 oz. [i.e., per oz.]
169 ½ dwt. old gold		50.85	.30 dwt. [i.e., per dwt.]
1 pr. crucible tongs		.25
1 show box		1.70
1 ditto		1.80
1 ditto		2.45
1 ditto large		3.50
2 guards for ditto		1.00
1 shew [sic] box		1.65
1 ditto		2.05
1 pr. globes		5.00
1 shader		5.41
10 lot tools [no further description; sold to various buyers]		
1 plating mill [sold to A. Fitch]		1.50

1 grindstone	
[sold to S. S. Smith]	.80
1 small anvil	
[sold to Wm. Hindles]	.80
1 large ditto	
[sold to John J. Pasteur]	1.60
1 lathe [sold to H. Whitford]	4.25
Dwelling House	
[sold to A. Hutchins]	100.25
Total value of estate —	$910.09 ¾[896]

A large stock of jewelry was also itemized, as well as sixty-six volumes in his library. The titles and authors of many reveal that Woods was a scholar of discriminating taste.

Reproduced from Cutten's first edition is this handsome sugar bowl and creamer made by Woods and in 1948 a part of the Robert Ensko Collection. Note the pineapple finial of the sugar bowl, the beading used at the upper rim of the body and at the base of the foot, and the bright-cut shield cartouche with *HC* engraved within. The creamer has the neoclassic helmet shape with strap handle and trumpet foot.

Much admired by visitors to the North Carolina Museum of History is this sophisticated Woods creamer presently on loan from Mr. Steve Harvey. The original owner has not been identified. Like its counterpart in the Ensko set, this creamer, 19.1 cm. in height, has the neoclassic helmet shape, trumpet foot, bead trim, and strap handle. *PH* is boldly engraved in a free, feathered script on the front, rather than the side, of the body.

A third cream pitcher made by Freeman Woods was recently acquired for the North Carolina Museum of History by the Museum of History Associates. The pitcher is not engraved but is almost identical in its neoclassic style and proportions to the pitcher the museum presently holds on loan.

This pair of Freeman Woods spoons 5¾ inches long are elegantly fashioned with coffin-end handles and bright-cut engraving. Engraved in block lettering and enclosed within an oval wreath are three initials—$_M W_A$—for Mary Ann Wright (Mrs. Moses Ernull II), the original owner. The spoons were given to the North Carolina Museum of History by Mrs. Mary Carter Whitehurst Guion. A third spoon, in the same style but engraved $_S K_H$, is also on display at the museum.

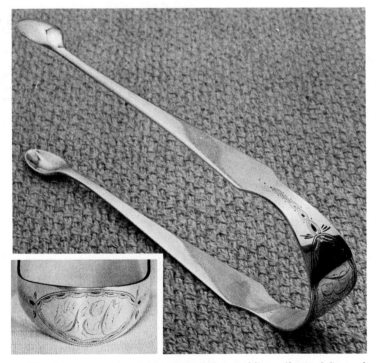

These Woods sugar tongs were part of the wedding silver of Samuel and Elizabeth Gitting Oliver of New Bern. The couple were married in Craven County in 1805. The bright-cut cartouche is shown inset at left.

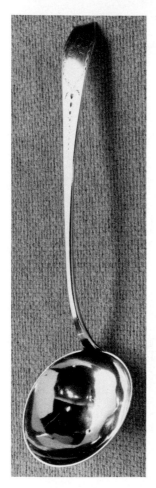

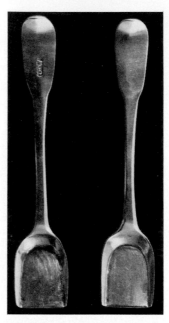

Entirely different in style are this handsome
Woods punch ladle (left) and the salt shovels
(above) of a later period. The coffin-end ladle,
from a private collection, is 13¹³/₁₆ inches long,
with a bowl 3½ inches long and 3¾ inches
across. Woods used bright-cut decoration with
RC engraved inside a wreath to conform to the
shape of the handle. The salt shovels are not
characteristic of other pieces of work by Woods
found in North Carolina. Both of them are 4 inches
long; one has a shovel width of 1 inch, the other
¹³/₁₆ inch. In somewhat strange fashion, Woods
placed his mark—an FW in an outlined
rectangle—on the front of one shovel and on the
back of the other. The shovels have been acquired
for the North Carolina Museum of History by
the Museum Associates.

JAMES WOODS (w. ca. 1804?). It is suggested in one newspaper item that this man may have "at times worked at the
silversmith's trade":

A Proclamation.

BY authority of the President of the United States, a reward of 500
dollars is hereby offered to any person or persons, who shall appre-

hend and secure in some jail within the United States, or deliver to the community officer of any military post within the United States, or its territories, JAMES WOODS, charged with the murder of a Cherokee Indian, in Buncomb county, in the state of North Carolina, on or about the 14th day of January last—Said Woods is about thirty two or thirty three years of age, five feet nine or ten inches in height, is stout and well made, has thick sandy hair and beard, and a fair complexion, has at times worked at the silversmith's trade, and has left a wife at Pigeon settlement, near where the murder was committed.

Given at the War-Office, City of Washington,
the last day of March, 1804.

II. DEARBORN, *Sec'r of War*[897]

DAVID WOODSON was born in Prince Edward County, Virginia, about 1735, the oldest son of Captain Obadiah Woodson and Constance Watkins.[898] His younger brother Richard, also a silversmith, settled in Petersburg, Virginia. On April 18, 1766, the following advertisement appeared: "Richard Woodson, late silversmith of Petersburg, being dead, those who have work in his hands call as soon as possible at the shop kept by him, attended by his brother, David Woodson."[899]

Just when David went to Salisbury with his wife Sarah is not known, but from 1774 to 1807 he was very active in real estate transactions[900] and was probably the largest landowner in Rowan County; he had land in several of the western counties of North Carolina, particularly Burke and Buncombe, and even in the state of Tennessee. It was in a transaction dated March 29, 1783, in which William McBride sold him Lot No. 19 in the Great West Square, Salisbury, that he was first designated as a silversmith.[901] Woodson was a very important man in the community, serving as county treasurer before the Revolution. He held other prominent offices, among which was that of justice of the Rowan County Court of Pleas and Quarter Sessions in 1816; this office he continued to hold for several years. In the tax list for 1778 he is credited with property valued at £1,727, which represented exceptional wealth in those days.

AARON WOOLWORTH (1801-1856) was born at Longmeadow, Massachusetts, January 28, 1801. On February 16, 1825, he announced that he had opened a shop on Main Street, Salisbury, North Carolina, and placed emphasis on gold and silver work.[902] In 1827 he moved to Greensboro and advertised on August 18 that he had purchased David Scott's jewelry and materials and had taken his shop.[903] A year later he moved to a house opposite Scott's.[904] On November 21, 1829, the firm of

Woolworth & Anderson was announced in Greensboro.[905] Just when Woolworth returned to Salisbury is uncertain, but it was probably in 1830; there he lived the remainder of his life. The census of 1850 lists him as a silversmith. On November 5, 1827, he married Mary Hampton in Salisbury.[906] (She should not be confused with Mary Anne Hampton, who married John C. Palmer, the silversmith, three weeks earlier.) Woolworth died in Salisbury on September 14, 1856.[907]

WOOLWORTH & ANDERSON (1829-1830). Aaron Woolworth and ——— Anderson were located in Greensboro. They advertised in November, 1829,[908] but the partnership was of short duration.

ROBERT WYNNE first appeared as a member of the firm of Huntington & Wynne in Salisbury in 1827.[909] The partnership was dissolved in 1828,[910] and Wynne continued independently— but evidently not very successfully. On February 1, 1830, to satisfy the conveyance and execution of a deed of trust, John A. Merony advertised the sale of the property of Robert Wynne, consisting of one set of silversmith's tools, one set of watchmaker's tools, and various articles and materials.[911] On November 1, 1832, Robert Wynne advertised in Halifax, North Carolina, for an apprentice to the silversmithing business.[912]

NOTES

[1]Pleasants and Sill, *Maryland Silversmiths*, 283.

[2]*Petersburg* (Virginia) *Intelligencer*, October 16, 1807.

[3]*Edenton Gazette*, December 15, 1809.

[4]*Edenton Gazette*, June 15, 1810.

[5]All citations to manuscript materials except deeds and wills refer to the collections of the Archives, Division of Archives and History, Department of Cultural Resources, Raleigh. The deeds and wills maintained in the various county seats were used by Dr. Cutten when he compiled his material for the original edition of this book; all county records of wills and deeds hereinafter cited in this volume are also available on microfilm in the State Archives.

[6]Adelaide L. Fries, Douglas LeTell Rights, Minnie J. Smith, and Kenneth G. Hamilton (eds.), *Records of the Moravians in North Carolina* (Raleigh: North Carolina Historical Commission, 11 volumes, 1922-1969), VIII, 3740, 3741, hereinafter cited as Fries and others, *Records of the Moravians*.

[7]An obituary in the *Charlotte Daily Observer* of March 20, 1900, cited Sharon Township as the place of Alexander's birth. However, an obituary in the evening paper (*Charlotte News*) of the same date listed Sugar Creek Township as his birthplace, a correction substantiated by the research of Mrs. Mary Boyer. Mrs. Boyer also concluded that Oswald and his first wife, Sarah, had three children—James, Mary, and William; children of Oswald and his second wife, Hannah, were Sarah, John, Thomas, Samuel, Charles, and Mark. Oswald owned and occupied the Hezekiah Alexander Rock House after 1805. Mary Boyer to Memory F. Mitchell, March 2, 1974.

[8]J[ohn] B[revard] Alexander, *History of Mecklenburg County from 1740 to 1900* (Charlotte: Observer Printing House, 1902), 188ff.

[9]*Charlotte Journal*, November 24, 1837, December 7, 1838.

[10]*Charlotte Journal*, October 24, 1839.

[11]*Charlotte Journal*, July 11, 1843.

[12]*Charlotte Journal*, October 13, 1848.

[13]Obituary in *Charlotte Daily Observer*, March 20, 1900.

[14]Obituary in *Charlotte Daily Observer*, March 20, 1900.

[15]Estate Papers of Zebulon Alexander, Office of the Register of Deeds, Mecklenburg County Courthouse, Charlotte. Mary Boyer to Mary Reynolds Peacock, October 25, 1976.

[16]Mary Boyer to Mary Reynolds Peacock, October 25, 1976.

[17]Minutes of the Mecklenburg County Court of Pleas and Quarter Sessions, January 29, 1805, State Archives, hereinafter cited as Mecklenburg County Court Minutes. All further references to minutes of the courts of pleas and quarter sessions will be cited as Court Minutes, with the appropriate county noted, and can be found in the State Archives.

[18]Estate of James Harris, Mecklenburg County Estate Papers, State Archives. Mary Boyer to Mary Reynolds Peacock, October 25, 1976.

[19]Mecklenburg County Court Minutes, April and July terms, 1810.

[20]Mecklenburg County Court Minutes, January term, 1810.

[21]Mecklenburg County Deeds, Office of the Register of Deeds, Mecklenburg County Courthouse, Charlotte, Book 17, p. 695, to Book 21, p. 237, hereinafter cited as Mecklenburg County Deeds.

[22]Mecklenburg County Wills, Office of the Clerk of Court, Mecklenburg County Courthouse, Charlotte, Book I, p. 31, hereinafter cited as Mecklenburg County Wills; or Record of Wills, Office of the Clerk of Court, Mecklenburg County Courthouse, Charlotte, Book A, p. 71, hereinafter cited as Mecklenburg Record of Wills.

[23]Notes of George Barton Cutten, Southern Historical Collection, University of North Carolina Library, Chapel Hill, hereinafter cited as Cutten Notes. Following publication of the original book, Dr. Cutten obviously continued his research; these findings have been incorporated into this edition.

[24]New Hanover County Deeds, Office of the Register of Deeds, New Hanover County Courthouse, Wilmington, Book AA, p. 850, hereinafter cited as New Hanover County Deeds.

[25]New Hanover County Deeds, Book W, p. 351.

[26]*Morning Star* (Wilmington), June 16, 1871, hereinafter cited as *Morning Star.*

[27]Will of Elizabeth Peacock, New Hanover County Wills, Office of the Clerk of Court, New Hanover County Courthouse, Wilmington, Book E, p. 1, hereinafter cited as New Hanover County Wills.

[28]Will of Thomas William Brown, New Hanover County Wills, Book E, p. 251.

[29]*Greensborough Patriot*, June 13, 1829.

[30]*Greensborough Patriot*, November 21, 1829.

[31]*Greensborough Patriot*, July 4, 1829.

[32]*North Carolina Journal* (Halifax), July 27, 1798, hereinafter cited as *North Carolina Journal* (Halifax) [not to be confused with the *North Carolina Journal* of Fayetteville].

[33]Walter Clark (ed.), *The State Records of North Carolina* (Winston and Goldsboro: State of North Carolina, 16 volumes, numbered XI-XXVI, 1895-1914), XXVI, 600, hereinafter cited as Clark, *State Records.*

[34]Halifax County Deeds, Office of the Register of Deeds, Halifax County Courthouse, Halifax, Book 15, p. 206, and Book 17, p. 362, hereinafter cited as Halifax County Deeds.

[35]Halifax County Deeds, Book 23, p. 275.

[36]James H. Craig, *The Arts and Crafts of North Carolina* (Winston-Salem: Museum of Early Southern Decorative Arts, Old Salem, Inc., 1965), 29, hereinafter cited as Craig, *The Arts and Crafts of North Carolina.*

[37]Louis H. Manarin and Weymouth T. Jordan, Jr. (eds.), *North Carolina Troops, 1861-1865: A Roster* (Raleigh: Division of Archives and History, Department of Cultural Resources [projected multivolume series, 1966—]), V, 310, hereinafter cited as Manarin and Jordan, *North Carolina Troops.*

[38]William S. Powell, *When the Past Refused to Die: Caswell County History, 1777-1977* (Durham: Moore Publishing Co., 1977), 130.

[39]Palmer to Dudley, December 21, 1839, Governors Letter Books, Edward B. Dudley, State Archives. Information provided by George Stevenson, researcher.

[40]Caswell County Marriage Bonds, State Archives. Information provided by George Stevenson. All references to marriage bonds hereinafter cited in this volume will denote records available in the State Archives.

[41]Rockingham County Marriage Bonds. Information provided by George Stevenson.

[42]Cutten Notes. Dr. Cutten also wrote of a spoon marked "ATKINSON Milton, N.C.," incised in unusually large letters. The present whereabouts of this spoon are not known.

[43]Information from the files of the Museum of Early Southern Decorative Arts, Old Salem, Inc., Winston-Salem, North Carolina, hereinafter cited as MESDA.

[44]Mrs. Mary Hardin McCown to Mary Reynolds Peacock, February 1, 1975. See also Benjamin H. Caldwell, Jr., "Tennessee Silversmiths Prior to 1860: A Check List," *Antiques*, C (December, 1971), 909-913, hereinafter cited as Caldwell, "Tennessee Silversmiths."

[45]*Raleigh Register*, February 4, 1805.

[46]Wake County Marriage Bonds.

[47]Cutten Notes, citing Henry Wyckoff Belknap, *Artists and Craftsmen of Essex County, Massachusetts* (Salem, Mass: Essex Institute, 1927), 85, hereinafter cited as Belknap, *Artists and Craftsmen of Essex County.*

[48]*Cape Fear Recorder* (Wilmington), April 5, 1817, hereinafter cited as *Cape Fear Recorder.*

[49]*Cape Fear Recorder*, May 9, 1818.

[50]Cutten Notes, citing Belknap, *Artists and Craftsmen of Essex County*, 85.

[51]*North Carolina Journal* (Halifax), August 22, 1792.

[52]*Free Press* (Tarboro), November 28, 1826, hereinafter cited as *Free Press.*

[53]*North-Carolina Free Press*, August 21, 1832.

[54]*Tarboro' Press*, April 8, 1837.

[55]*Tarboro' Press*, May 18, 1839.

[56]*Tarboro' Press*, August 31, 1839.

[57]Rowan County Court Minutes, 1768-1772, p. 13.

[58]Cutten Notes, quoting W. D. Kizziah to George B. Cutten, September 13, 1950. The deed can be found in Rowan County Deeds, Office of the Register of Deeds, Rowan County Courthouse, Salisbury, Book VIII, p. 210, hereinafter cited as Rowan County Deeds.

[59]Cutten Notes.

[60]*Fayetteville Observer*, October 17, 1838.

[61]Cumberland County Marriage Bonds.

[62]Cumberland County Deeds, Office of the Register of Deeds, Cumberland County Courthouse, Fayetteville, Book 43, p. 372, hereinafter cited as Cumberland County Deeds.

[63]Cumberland County Deeds, Book 50, p. 503.

[64]Statements made to Dr. George B. Cutten by H. M. Pemberton and John A. Oates, Fayetteville.

[65]William Davis Miller, *The Silversmiths of Little Rest, Rhode Island* (Boston: Merrymount Press, 1928), 39.

[66]George B. Cutten, "Ten Silversmith Families of New York State," Part I, *New York History*, 27 (January, 1946), 88-95.

[67]Letter to George B. Cutten from Louis S. Gaines, Fayetteville.

[68]Letter to George B. Cutten from John A. Oates, Fayetteville.

[69]*Fayetteville Observer*, June 27, 1889.

[70]*Fayetteville Observer*, August 15, 22, 1889.

[71]Clarence Griffin, *The Bechtlers and Bechtler Coinage, and Gold Mining in North Carolina, 1814-1830* (Forest City: Forest City Courier, 1929), 4ff., hereinafter cited as Griffin, *The Bechtlers and Bechtler Coinage.*

[72]Griffin, *The Bechtlers and Bechtler Coinage*, 4f.

[73]*Western North Carolina Republican* (Rutherfordton), July 29, 1847.

[74]Burton, *South Carolina Silversmiths*, 253f.

[75]Maurice Brix, *List of Philadelphia Silversmiths and Allied Artificers, 1682-1850* (Philadelphia: Privately printed, 1920), 2, hereinafter cited as Brix, *Philadelphia Silversmiths.*

[76]*North Carolina Spectator and Western Advertiser* (Rutherfordton), August 6, 1830, hereinafter cited as *North Carolina Spectator and Western Advertiser.*

[77]*North Carolina Spectator and Western Advertiser*, August 27, 1831.

[78]*Carolina Gazette* (Rutherfordton), August 11, 1836.

[79]Griffin, *The Bechtlers and Bechtler Coinage*, 4f.

[80]*Raleigh Register*, December 4, 1837.

[81]*Newbern Spectator*, May 16, 1840.

[82]*Tarboro' Press*, May 27, 1843.

[83]*Hornet's Nest* (Charlotte), June 1, 1850.

[84]*North Carolina Whig* (Charlotte), April 12, 1859, hereinafter cited as *North Carolina Whig.*

[85]*Western Democrat* (Charlotte), June 4, 1866, hereinafter cited as *Western Democrat.*

[86]Information provided by Mrs. Anna Sherman.

[87]*American Recorder* (Washington), September 18, 1816, hereinafter cited as *American Recorder.*

[88]*Cape Fear Recorder*, April 5, 1817.

[89]*Cape Fear Recorder*, May 9, 1818.

[90]*Cape Fear Recorder*, March 20, 1819.

[91]New Hanover County Court Minutes, August 13, 1821.

[92]New Hanover County Court Minutes, November 17, 1821.

[93]New Hanover County Court Minutes, August 12, 1822.

[94]New Hanover County Court Minutes, August 12, 1823.

[95]Brix, *Philadelphia Silversmiths*, 10.

[96]*Miners' and Farmers' Journal* (Charlotte), March 10, 1831, hereinafter cited as *Miners' and Farmers' Journal.*

[97]*Miners' and Farmers' Journal*, March 2, 1833.

[98]*Miners' and Farmers' Journal*, February 8, 1834.

[99]Information for Blyth sketch researched by George Stevenson.

[100]From Hillsborough District Superior Court Records: Civil Action Papers, 1772, State Archives.

[101]New Hanover County Deeds, Book E, p. 281, Book F, p. 317, Book R, p. 251; Alexander McD. Walker (comp.), *New Hanover County Court Minutes* (Bethesda, Md.: By the author [projected multivolume series of abstracts, 1958—]), II, 63, 81, hereinafter cited as Walker, *New Hanover County Court Minutes* [abstracts]; William L. Saunders (ed.), *The Colonial Records of North Carolina* (Raleigh: State of North Carolina, 10 volumes, 1886-1890), VII, 178, IX, 1143, X, 161, hereinafter cited as Saunders, *Colonial Records*; Clark, *State Records*, XV, 191, XXII, 383.

[102]*Carolina Watchman* (Salisbury), February 8, 1845, hereinafter cited as *Carolina Watchman.*

[103]*Carolina Watchman*, March 20, 1846.

[104]*Carolina Watchman*, December 7, 1848.

[105]Cutten Notes.

[106]*Carolina Watchman*, April 14, 1853.

[107]*Carolina Watchman* March 20, 1846.

[108]*Carolina Watchman* April 14, 1853.

[109]Information provided by George Stevenson.

[110]*North Carolina Journal* (Fayetteville), March 5, 1828, hereinafter cited as *North Carolina Journal* (Fayetteville).

[111]*Mecklenburg Jeffersonian* (Charlotte), January 18, 1842, hereinafter cited as *Mecklenburg Jeffersonian.*

[112]Mecklenburg County Marriage Bonds.

[113]*Mecklenburg Jeffersonian*, September 4, 1843.

[114]Burton, *South Carolina Silversmiths*, 8.

[115]Information provided by Mr. Weymouth T. Jordan, Jr., from records being compiled for Manarin and Jordan, *North Carolina Troops.*.

[116]Rowan County Court Minutes, February, 1793-February, 1800, p. 129.

[117]Mrs. A. M. McKoy, whose husband was a descendant of Thomas W. Brown, provided to Dr. Cutten information about Brown from family records.

[118]Photocopies of Brown's obituary from the *Wilmington Post*, October [16?], 1872, and a feature story on Mrs. Mary Baker G. Eddy from the *Sunday American* (Boston, Massachusetts[?]), May 22, 1904, enclosed in a letter from Mrs. Charles P. Graham, a Brown descendant, to Mary Reynolds Peacock, February 12, 1982.

[119]*Morning Star*, June 16, 1871.

[120]*Western Carolinian* (Salisbury), January 2, 1821, March 12, 1822, hereinafter cited as *Western Carolinian.*

[121]*Raleigh Minerva*, September 13, 1810.

[122]*Heads of Families at the First Census of the United States Taken in the Year 1790: North Carolina* (Washington: Government Printing Office, 1908), 463.

[123]Cumberland County Court Minutes, January 14, 1793.

[124]*North Carolina Minerva* (Fayetteville), May 12, 1798, hereinafter cited as *North Carolina Minerva.*

[125]*North Carolina Minerva*, June 30, 1798.

[126]*Raleigh Register*, February 27, 1818.

[127]Burton, *South Carolina Silversmiths*, 211.

[128]Cumberland County Court Minutes, September term, 1818.

[129]*North Carolina Journal* (Fayetteville), December 12, 1827.

[130]*Carolina Observer* (Fayetteville), June 7, 1831, hereinafter cited as *Carolina Observer.*

[131]Cumberland County Deeds, Book 40, p. 297.

[132]*Fayetteville Observer*, June 3, 1834, April 14, 1836.

[133]Burton, *South Carolina Silversmiths*, 211. Burton based his conclusion on information from the *Cheraw* (South Carolina) *Gazette* and from silver spoons in the collection of Mrs. W. R. Godfrey dating ca. 1835 and marked on the back "Made by J. Campbell, Cheraw, S.C."

[134]*Fayetteville Observer*, September 15, 1836.

[135]Cumberland County Deeds, Book 42, p. 273.

[136]Cumberland County Deeds, Book 45, p. 140.

[137]Caldwell, "Tennessee Silversmiths," 908.

[138]*Fayetteville Observer*, June 3, 1834.

[139]*Fayetteville Observer*, April 14, 1836.

[140]The advertisement was dated April 18, 1809, and was still being used in the *North Carolina Star* (Raleigh), hereinafter cited as *North Carolina Star*, on May 4, 1809.

[141]*Raleigh Minerva*, March 1, 1810; *Raleigh Register*, March 1, 1810; *North Carolina Star*, March 8, 1810.

[142]*Fayetteville Gazette*, February 14, 1821.

[143]*Fayetteville Gazette*, May 9, 1822.

[144]*Carolina Observer*, August 7, 1823.

[145]Cumberland County Marriage Bonds.

[146]*United States Directory*, 1822.

[147]*Carolina Observer*, August 7, 1823.

[148]Chowan County Miscellaneous Papers, III, 64, 156, V, 84, VIII, 13, State Archives, hereinafter cited as Chowan County Papers.

[149]Chowan County Papers, VII, 15.

[150]Chowan County Papers, IV, 98, V, 4.

[151]Chowan County Papers, V, 69, VII, 92.

[152]Chowan County Marriage Bonds.

[153]Chowan County Papers, VI, 21.

[154]Chowan County Papers, VI, 44, 77, 120.

[155]Chowan County Papers, VII, 63.

[156]Chowan County Papers, VII, 86.

[157]Chowan County Papers, IX, 111, 123.

[158]Chowan County Papers, XI, 83.

[159]Chowan County Papers, XIII, 120.

[160]Chowan County Papers, XVI, 95.

[161]George Barton Cutten,*The Silversmiths of Virginia* (Richmond: Dietz Press, 1952), 89, hereinafter cited as Cutten, *Silversmiths of Virginia*.

[162]Cutten, *Silversmiths of Virginia*, 90.

[163]Cutten, *Silversmiths of Virginia*, 91.

[164]Cutten, *Silversmiths of Virginia*, 91.

[165]Cameron Family Papers, Vol. 2, Southern Historical Collection.

[166]Information found on Coleman in Cutten Notes: Hugh Johnston to George B. Cutten, May 31, 1951; researched in Edgecombe County Records , 1758-1830, Vol. III, p. 15, and Edgecombe County Wills, Book D, p. 294.

[167]Chowan County Papers, XIII, 105

[168]Chowan County Papers, XIX, 54

[169]Chowan County Wills, Office of the Clerk of Court, Chowan County Courthouse, Edenton, Book A, p. 128, hereinafter cited as Chowan County Wills.

[170]Noted by Mrs. Rosemary Estes in "Silversmiths in North Carolina Prior to 1820" (unpublished master's thesis, University of North Carolina at Greensboro, 1977).

[171]Information found by Mrs. Helen Watson, researcher, Rocky Mount.

[172]First noted by Gale J. Farlow in "Black Craftsmen in North Carolina before 1850" (unpublished master's thesis, University of North Carolina at Greensboro, 1979).

[173]*Elizabeth City Star*, March 11, 1829; *Roanoke Advocate* (Halifax), February 24, 1831, hereinafter cited as *Roanoke Advocate*.

[174]Information about Daughtery was supplied by Mrs. Rosemary Estes from research done at MESDA.

[175]*Raleigh Minerva*, February 10, 1815; *Lynchburg* (Virginia) *Press*, March 9, 1815; *Nashville* (Tennessee) *Whig*, March 14, 1815.

[176]Northampton County Record of Estates, 1807-1810, p. 272, State Archives, hereinafter cited as Northampton County Estates.

[177]Northampton County Guardians and Other Fiduciary Accounts, Volume 3 (1781-1802), p. 12, State Archives.

[178]George Stevenson to Mary Reynolds Peacock, February 25, 1980; Estate of Alexander Lewis, 1785 (original), Mecklenburg County Estate Records, 1762-1929, State Archives (Mrs. Mary Boyer, researcher).

[179]Tucker Littleton to Mary Reynolds Peacock, October 30, 1977. See also Will of Ann Winwright, Secretary of State Records, North Carolina Wills, 1663-1789, State Archives.

[180]*Newbernian* (New Bern), August 27, 1850, hereinafter cited as *Newbernian*.

[181]Zae Hargett Gwynn, *Abstracts of the Records of Onslow County, North Carolina* (N.p.: n.p., 2 volumes, 1961), I, 445; Onslow County Deeds, Book S, p. 24 (Tucker Littleton, researcher).

[182]*North Carolina Star*, June 1, 1809.

[183]*North-Carolina Gazette* (New Bern), April 15, 1790, hereinafter cited as *North-Carolina Gazette*.

[184]Saunders, *Colonial Records*, X, 309, 310, 432, 592, XXI, 975, 978.

[185]*Miners' and Farmers' Journal*, June 21, 29, July 6, 1831.

[186]Edgecombe County Court Minutes, 1772-1784 (unpaged).

[187]Observation made by researcher Hugh Johnston to Mrs. Lee Albright, June 20, 1979.

[188]Fries and others, *Records of the Moravians*, IV, 1847.

[189]*Newbernian*, July 28, 1846.

[190]*Newbernian*, May 23, 1848.

[191]Craven County Court Minutes, June, 1786-August, 1787, p. 15.

[192]*North Carolina Star*, December 4, 1828.

[193]*Star and North Carolina Gazette* (Raleigh), June 28, 1833, hereinafter cited as *Star and North Carolina Gazette*.

[194]*North Carolina Standard* (Raleigh), December 15, 1835, hereinafter cited as *North Carolina Standard*.

[195]*Star and North Carolina Gazette*, November 17, 1836.

[196]*Raleigh Register*, November 17, 1843.

[197]Wake County Deeds, Office of the Register of Deeds, Wake County Courthouse, Raleigh, Book 16, p. 290, hereinafter cited as Wake County Deeds.

[198]Wake County Deeds, Book 17, p. 294.

[199]Jerry L. Cross to Mary Reynolds Peacock, August 1, 1977. Dr. Cross based his conclusions upon information found in documents from the State Archives and from Polk family records in the Genealogical Reference Section, North Carolina State Library, Raleigh.

[200]*Raleigh Daily Sentinel*, September 3, 1874.

[201]Clark, *State Records*, XVI, 1052.

[202]Pasquotank County Deeds, Office of the Register of Deeds, Pasquotank County Courthouse, Elizabeth City, Book J, p. 164, hereinafter cited as Pasquotank County Deeds.

[203]Pasquotank County Apprenticeship Papers, State Archives, hereinafter cited as Pasquotank County Apprenticeship Papers.

[204]Clark, *State Records*, XXVI, 875.

[205]Frank P. Albright, *Johann Ludwig Eberhardt and His Salem Clocks* (Chapel Hill: University of North Carolina Press for Old Salem, Inc., 1978), 10, hereinafter cited as Albright, *Johann Ludwig Eberhardt*.

[206]Albright, *Johann Ludwig Eberhardt*, 11.

[207]Albright, *Johann Ludwig Eberhardt*, 11.

[208]Albright, *Johann Ludwig Eberhardt*, 12.

[209]Albright, *Johann Ludwig Eberhardt*, 13.

[210]Albright, *Johann Ludwig Eberhardt*, 60.

[211]Fries and others, *Records of the Moravians*, VI, 2622, 2808, 2862.

[212]*Greensboro Daily News*, January 17, 1943.

[213]*Greensborough Patriot*, April 12, 1845.

[214]*Greensboro Daily News*, January 17, 1943.

[215]Bessie Alford Ballance, unpublished typescript, Greensboro Public Library.

[216]*Western Carolinian*, January 2, 1821.

[217]*Western Carolinian*, January 2, 1821.

[218]Cutten Notes: Mrs. W. E. Alexander to George Barton Cutten, May 19, 1953.

[219]Scott, *Annals of Caldwell County* (Lenoir: News-Topic Print, [1930]), 91, hereinafter cited as Scott, *Annals of Caldwell County*.

[220]Scott, *Annals of Caldwell County*, 93-94.

[221]Seventh Census of the United States, 1850: Caldwell County, North Carolina, Population Schedule, 2, microfilm of National Archives manuscript copy, State Archives, hereinafter cited as Seventh Census, 1850, with appropriate county, schedule, and page number.

[222]Inventory of Property of Isaac Emmons, Caldwell County Estate Records, 1841-1934, State Archives; George Stevenson, researcher.

[223]*Minerva* (Raleigh), September 15, 1806, hereinafter cited as *Minerva* (Raleigh) [not to be confused with the Fayetteville *North Carolina Minerva*]; *Raleigh Register,* September 10, 1806.

[224]Moses N. Amis, *Historical Raleigh* (Raleigh: Edwards and Broughton, 1902), 89, hereinafter cited as Amis, *Historical Raleigh*.

[225]Hope Summerell Chamberlain, *History of Wake County, North Carolina* (Raleigh: Edwards and Broughton, 1922), 103.

[226]*Star* (Raleigh), December 18, 1812, hereinafter cited as *Star*.

[227]*Minerva* (Raleigh), February 19, 1813.

[228]Wake County Court Minutes, August term, 1816.

[229]Wake County Court Minutes, August term, 1816.

[230]Wake County Court Minutes, November term, 1816, May term, 1817, August and November terms, 1819.

[231]*Raleigh Register*, January 31, 1817.

[232]Wake County Deeds, Book 5, p. 149.

[233]Wake County Court Minutes, November term, 1821.

[234]Pleasants and Sill, *Maryland Silversmiths*, 51, 269.

[235]Chowan County Marriage Bonds.

[236]Chowan County Deeds, Office of the Register of Deeds, Chowan County Courthouse, Edenton, Book B-2, p. 323, hereinafter cited as Chowan County Deeds.

[237]Craven County Marriage Bonds.

[238]*Newbernian*, June 17, 1845.

[239]*Newbernian*, May 23, 1848.

[240]*Goldsboro Telegraph*, February 28, 1850.

[241]Photocopy enclosed in a letter from John Kalmar to Mary Reynolds Peacock, July 23, 1975.

[242]George Munson Curtis, *Early Silver of Connecticut and Its Makers* (Meriden, Conn.: International Silver Company, 1913), 86, hereinafter cited as Curtis, *Early Silver of Connecticut*; Stephen G. C. Ensko, *American Silversmiths and Their Marks* (New York: Privately printed, 5 volumes, 1927), I, 14f., hereinafter cited as Ensko, *American Silversmiths and Their Marks*.

[243]*Federal Republican*, January 25, 1817.

[244]Craven County Marriage Bonds.

[245]*Carolina Centinel* (New Bern), October 17, 1818, hereinafter cited as *Carolina Centinel* or *Carolina Sentinel.*

[246]*Carolina Centinel*, October 5, 1821.

[247]*Carolina Sentinel*, October 21, 1826.

[248]Craven County Deeds, Office of the Register of Deeds, Craven County Courthouse, New Bern, Book 45, p. 350, hereinafter cited as Craven County Deeds.

[249]Cutten Notes.

[250]Fries and others, *Records of the Moravians*, VII, 3479.

[251]Fries and others, *Records of the Moravians*, VIII, 3870.

[252]Cutten Notes.

[253]Manarin and Jordan, *North Carolina Troops*, V, 485.

[254]Cumberland County Court Minutes, January 28, 1788.

[255]*Fayetteville Gazette*, November 6, 1792.

[256]*North Carolina Minerva*, November 3, 1798.

[257]Cumberland County Court Minutes, April 15, 1797.

[258]Cumberland County Court Minutes, April term, 1799.

[259]William Wade Hinshaw (ed.), *Encyclopedia of American Quaker Genealogy* (Ann Arbor, Mich.: Edwards Brothers, Inc., 6 volumes, 1936), I, 498, 540, hereinafter cited as Hinshaw, *Encyclopedia of American Quaker Genealogy.*

[260]Hinshaw, *Encyclopedia of American Quaker Genealogy*, I, 541.

[261]Hinshaw, *Encyclopedia of American Quaker Genealogy*, I, 389.

[262]*Minerva* (Raleigh), April 21, 1807.

[263]Mecklenburg County Court Minutes, April 24, 1810.

[264]Mecklenburg County Deeds, Book 19, pp. 744, 759, 761, 762.

[265]Hinshaw, *Encyclopedia of American Quaker Genealogy*, I, 252.

[266]Burton, *South Carolina Silversmiths*, 241-242, citing *Greenville* (South Carolina) *Republican*, July 14, 1826, July 20, August 4, 11, 1827.

[267]Ralph M. Kovel and Terry H. Kovel, *A Directory of American Silver, Pewter and Silver Plate* (New York: Crown Publishers, eleventh printing, 1978), 108, hereinafter cited as Kovel and Kovel, *Directory of American Silver.*

[268]Caldwell, "Tennessee Silversmiths," 910.

[269]*Greensborough Patriot*, January 14, 1843.

[270]*Greensboro' Patriot*, October 28, 1843.

[271]*Greensborough Patriot*, May 11, 1844.

[272]*Greensborough Patriot*, June 28, 1845.

[273]*Greensborough Patriot*, July 5, 1845.

[274]*Charlotte Journal*, December 19, 1845.

[245]*Charlotte Journal*, July 24, 1846.

[276]Chowan County Marriage Bonds.

[277]Chowan County Papers, X, 81.

[278]Chowan County Papers, X, 150.

[279]Chowan County Papers, XI, 12.

[280]Chowan County Papers, XI, 110, 125.

[281]Chowan County Papers, XI, 41.

[282]Chowan County Papers, XV, 117.

[283]In a letter to Mary Reynolds Peacock dated May 11, 1979, Hugh B. Johnston writes, "I suspect that he [Gatlin] worked for Josiah Solomon Pender, artist, who apparently ran a jewelry store in Tarboro before moving to Beaufort." Mr. Johnston prepared a sketch of Josiah Solomon Pender to be used in a forthcoming volume of William S. Powell's *Dictionary of North Carolina Biography.*

[284] *Western Carolinian*, May 15, 1827.

[285] *Yadkin and Catawba Journal* (Salisbury), February 24, 1829, hereinafter cited as *Yadkin and Catawba Journal*.

[286] Undoubtedly John Geddy was erroneously listed as Joseph Gaddy in Dr. Cutten's original *Silversmiths of North Carolina* and in the first revised edition. Dr. Claiborne T. Smith, Jr., has done extensive research on John Geddy and has provided the genealogical information used in this sketch. Additional research was done by George Stevenson, and his findings have been used here. Mrs. Alice Cotten checked material in the Raymond Shute Collection at the Southern Historical Collection. See also Ivor Noel Hume, *James Geddy and Sons, Colonial Craftsmen*, Colonial Williamsburg Archaeological Series, No. 5 (Williamsburg: Colonial Williamsburg Foundation, 1970). There are still some unresolved questions about the Geddys.

[287] J. Raymond Shute Collection, Item L889, Folder 20, Southern Historical Collection.

[288] Inventory of the Estate of Samuel Yeargin, Warren County Estate Records, State Archives.

[289] Inventory of the Estate of John Geddy, Franklin County Estate Records, State Archives.

[290] Geddy, Inventory of Estate.

[291] Information provided by Dr. Claiborne T. Smith.

[292] Craven County Wills, Office of the Clerk of Court, Craven County Courthouse, New Bern, Book B, p. 209.

[293] Craven County Apprenticeship Papers, State Archives, hereinafter cited as Craven County Apprenticeship Papers.

[294] *Carolina Centinel*, July 11, 1818.

[295] *Carolina Centinel*, April 10, 1819.

[296] *Carolina Centinel*, May 8, 1819.

[297] Craven County Marriage Bonds.

[298] *Carolina Centinel*, December 22, 1821.

[299] *Carolina Sentinel*, June 2, 1827.

[300] Craven County Apprenticeship Papers.

[301] Letter to George B. Cutten from Gertrude Sprague Carraway.

[302] *Newbern Spectator*, November 20, 1830.

[303] *Newbern Spectator*, March 22, 1839.

[304] Craven County Deeds, Book 55, p. 514.

[305] Craven County Deeds, Book 56, p. 268.

[306] *Raleigh Register*, November 7, 1803.

[307] Presbyterian Cemetery Records, Morganton, North Carolina.

[308] *Raleigh Register*, October 6, 1801.

[309] *Raleigh Register*, January 4, 1803.

[310] *Virginia Gazette* (Williamsburg), April 11, 1771, hereinafter cited as *Virginia Gazette*.

[311] *Virginia Gazette*, February 4, 1773.

[312] Clark, *State Records*, XXII, 173.

[313] *Raleigh Register*, February 4, 1805.

[314] *Fayetteville Observer*, October 3, 1843.

[315] *Fayetteville Observer*, July 16, 1845.

[316] Cumberland County Marriage Bonds.

[317] Cumberland County Deeds, Book, 58, p. 311.

[318] Cumberland County Deeds, Book, 59, p. 323.

[319] See "Greenewalt & Cover" spoon and mark in Appendix A.

[320] *Free Press*, November 14, 1826.

[321]Lyman Chalkley (comp.), *Chronicles of the Scotch-Irish Settlement in Virginia, Extracted from the Original Court Records of Augusta County, 1745-1800* (Rosslyn, Va.: Privately printed for Mary S. Lockwood by the Commonwealth Printing Company, 3 volumes, 1912-1913), I, 423, hereinafter cited as Chalkley, *Court Records of Augusta County.* This work was reprinted in 1965 by the Genealogical Publishing Company, Baltimore.

[322]Chalkley, *Court Records of Augusta County,* II, 278.

[323]Chalkley, *Court Records of Augusta County,* II, 27.

[324]Chalkley, *Court Records of Augusta County,* III, 530.

[325]Chalkley, *Court Records of Augusta County,* III, 539.

[326]Chalkley, *Court Records of Augusta County,* I, 189.

[327]Chalkley, *Court Records of Augusta County,* I, 207.

[328]Chalkley, *Court Records of Augusta County,* II, 431

[329]Chalkley, *Court Records of Augusta County,* I, 509.

[330]Chalkley, *Court Records of Augusta County,* III, 171.

[331]Chalkley, *Court Records of Augusta County,* III, 134.

[332]Chalkley, *Court Records of Augusta County,* II, 307.

[333]Chalkley, *Court Records of Augusta County,* I, 423.

[334]Manarin and Jordan, *North Carolina Troops,* V, 359, 378.

[335]Jethro Rumple, *A History of Rowan County,* with an appendix (Salisbury: J. J. Bruner, 1881; republished by Elizabeth Maxwell Steele Chapter, Daughters of the American Revolution [1929]), 205, hereinafter cited as Rumple, *A History of Rowan County.*

[336]*Western Carolinian,* August 13, 1822.

[337]*Western Carolinian,* October 14, 1828.

[338]*Western Carolinian,* April 20, 1830.

[339]Rowan County Marriage Bonds.

[340]*Western Carolinian,* September 3, 1832.

[341]Rowan County Wills, Office of the Clerk of Court, Rowan County Courthouse, Salisbury, Book H, p. 687, hereinafter cited as Rowan County Wills.

[342]*Raleigh Minerva,* March 10, 1815.

[343]*Western Carolinian,* April 20, 1830.

[344]*Western Carolinian,* March 19, 1832.

[345]Lee B. Weathers, *The Living Past of Cleveland County* (Shelby: Star Publishing Co., 1956), 41-42; Cutten Notes.

[346]Fries and others, *Records of the Moravians,* VIII, 3758.

[347]Information provided in a note from Carlos Smith to Mary Reynolds Peacock, January 1, 1979.

[348]*Carolina Observer,* April 24 1823.

[349]Cumberland County Marriage Bonds.

[350]Cumberland County Court Minutes, April term, 1801.

[351]*Minerva* (Raleigh), January 6, 1806.

[352]*Star,* February 22, 1810.

[353]Cumberland County Deeds, Book 27, p. 19.

[354]Cumberland County Deeds, Book 27, p. 387.

[355]*American* (Fayetteville), October 13, 1814, hereinafter cited as *American.*

[356]Caldwell, "Tennessee Silversmiths," 910.

[357]Beaufort County Wills, Office of the Clerk of Court, Beaufort County Courthouse, Washington, Book A, p. 291.

[358]*North-Carolina Gazette,* September 2, 1774.

[359]*American Recorder,* March 26, 1819.

[360]Beaufort County Deeds, Office of the Register of Deeds, Beaufort County Courthouse, Washington, fifteen entries from Book 11, p. 245, to Book 26, p. 131, hereinafter cited as Beaufort County Deeds.

[361]Information provided by the late J. G. de Roulhac Hamilton, longtime professor in the Department of History at the University of North Carolina in Chapel Hill. For several years prior to his death in 1961, Dr. Hamilton was director of the Southern Historical Collection.

[362]Beaufort County Deeds, Book 38, p. 138.

[363]Information provided by Tucker Littleton.

[364]*American Recorder*, August 22, 29, 1823.

[365]Information provided by Tucker Littleton.

[366]Warren County Court Minutes, February, 1780-May, 1783, p. 119.

[367]Rowan County Wills, 1743-1900, State Archives.

[368]Rowan County Court Minutes, 1773-1786, p. 361.

[369]*Cyclopedia of Eminent and Representative Men of the Carolinas of the Nineteenth Century* (Madison, Wis.: Brant & Fuller, 2 volumes, 1892), II, 365, hereinafter cited as *Cyclopedia of Eminent and Representative Men of the Carolinas*.

[370]William Montgomery Clemens (ed.), *North and South Carolina Marriage Records from the Earliest Colonial Days to the Civil War* (New York: E. P. Dutton [c. 1927]), 133.

[371]Rumple, *A History of Rowan County*, 267.

[372]*Western Carolinian*, July 25, 1820.

[373]Rumple, *A History of Rowan County*, 179.

[374]*Western Carolinian*, October 1, 1822.

[375]Rowan County Court Minutes, February, 1793-February, 1800, p. 243.

[376]Rowan County Court Minutes, 1800-1807, p. 23.

[377]Rowan County Court Minutes, 1807-1813, p. 140.

[378]*Cyclopedia of Eminent and Representative Men of the Carolinas*, II, 365.

[379]*Carolina Watchman*, May 17, 1849.

[380]*Cyclopedia of Eminent and Representative Men of the Carolinas*, II, 365.

[381]Information provided by Mrs. Martha Haney and Mrs. Gertrude Caldwell Nicholson.

[382]Cabarrus County Marriage Bonds.

[383]Kovel and Kovel, *Directory of American Silver*, 142.

[384]Chowan County Wills, Book C, p. 86.

[385]Chowan County Wills, Book C, p. 150.

[386]Chowan County Marriage Bonds.

[387]*Edenton Gazette*, January 13, 1827.

[388]*Edenton Gazette*, January 9, 1830.

[391]Brix, *Philadelphia Silversmiths*, 53.

[392]*North Carolina Journal* (Halifax), May 21, 1798.

[393]*Hall's Wilmington Gazette*, October 11, 1798.

[394]*North Carolina Minerva*, November 3, 1798.

[395]Cutten Notes: from *Tarboro' Press*, November 26, 1836, February 11, 18, 1837.

[396]For more complete biographical information about the Huntington family, see William Johnston Hogan, *Huntington Silversmiths, 1763-1885* (Durham: Sir Walter Press, 1977), hereinafter cited as Hogan, *Huntington Silversmiths*.

[397]*Hillsborough Recorder*, December 16, 1824.

[398]*Western Carolinian*, July 3, 1827.

[399]*Western Carolinian*, August 5, 1826.

[400]*Hillsborough Recorder,* October 29, 1834; the notice was dated October 22, 1834.

[401]E. B. Huntington, *A Genealogical Memoir of the Huntington Family in This County* . . . (Stamford, Conn.: Privately printed [by the author], 1863), 853, 858, hereinafter cited as Huntington, *A Genealogical Memoir.*

[402]*Hillsborough Recorder,* October 22, 1834.

[403]Orange County Deeds, Office of the Register of Deeds, Orange County Courthouse, Hillsborough, Book 13, p. 262, hereinafter cited as Orange County Deeds.

[404]*Milton Intelligencer,* April 2, May 6, 1819.

[405]Orange County Deeds, Book 25, p. 191.

[406]*Milton Intelligencer,* May 6, 1819.

[407]Huntington, *A Genealogical Memoir,* 290, 853.

[408]*Milton Spectator,* September 27, 1836.

[409]Ensko, *American Silversmiths and Their Marks,* I, 21.

[410]Orange County Wills, Office of the Clerk of Court, Orange County Courthouse, Hillsborough, Book A, p. 341; Orange County Deeds, Book 3, p. 30.

[411]Jean Anderson, Hillsborough Historical Society *Newsletter,* XV (January, 1976), citing George Washington Bruce in a letter to the editor, *Hillsborough Recorder,* June 9, 1875.

[412]Treasurer and Comptroller Papers: Miscellaneous Group, 1738-1930, State Archives.

[413]*Proceedings of Grand Lodge,* 36, 38.

[414]Orange County Marriage Bonds.

[415]Clark, *State Records,* XXI, 219, 221.

[416]Orange County Deeds, Book 8, p. 54.

[417]*Raleigh Register,* March 31, 1802.

[418]*Milton Spectator,* September 27, 1836.

[419]Huntington, *A Genealogical Memoir,* 853f.

[420]*Star,* December 15, 1815.

[421]*Raleigh Register,* September 27, 1816.

[422]*Hillsborough Recorder,* June 14, 1820.

[423]*Hillsborough Recorder,* September 19, 1821.

[424]*Hillsborough Recorder,* May 27, 1822.

[425]*Hillsborough Recorder,* January 29, 1823.

[426]*Hillsborough Recorder,* May 28, September 10, 1828.

[427]*Hillsborough Recorder,* December 16, 1824.

[428]*Hillsborough Recorder,* July 30, 1828.

[429]*Hillsborough Recorder,* August 19, 1829.

[430]*Hillsborough Recorder,* January 8, 1833.

[431]*Raleigh Register,* September 27, 1816.

[432]*Hillsborough Recorder,* June 14, 1820.

[433]*Hillsborough Recorder,* December 16, 1824.

[434]*Western Carolinian,* January 16, July 3, 1827.

[435]*Western Carolinian,* January 29, 1828.

[436]*Western Carolinian,* August 12, 1828.

[437]Information provided by Tucker Littleton.

[438]*Greensborough Patriot,* July 30, 1842.

[439]Craven County Court Minutes, September 19, 1778.

[440]Stephen N. Dennis, quoting a letter from Miss Gertrude Carraway to Stephen N. Dennis, November 17, 1974, hereinafter cited as Carraway letter. Miss Carraway had researched the minutes of St. John's Lodge.

[441]Carraway letter.

[442]Photocopy, Robert B. Studebaker, *History of Eagle Lodge, 1791-1937* (Hillsborough: Privately published for Eagle Lodge, 1937), 11-12.

[443]Studebaker, *History of Eagle Lodge*, 28.

[444]Nathan Tisdale to Nathaniel Alexander, March 19, 1807, Governors Letter Books, Nathaniel Alexander, State Archives, hereinafter cited as Governors Letter Books, Alexander.

[445]Craven County Estate Records, 1745-1945, State Archives, hereinafter cited as Craven County Estate Records.

[446]Manarin and Jordan, *North Carolina Troops*, VI, 87.

[447]Robeson County Record of Deeds, 1792-1793, pp. 4-6, 12-15, State Archives, hereinafter cited as Robeson County Deeds.

[448]Robeson County Deeds, 1792-1793, pp. 161-163.

[449]Robeson County Wills, 1783-1851, Office of the Clerk of Court, Robeson County Courthouse, Lumberton, Book II, p. 50.

[450]Inventory, Estate of John Kirkland, Craven County Estate Records, State Archives, hereinafter cited as Kirkland, inventory of estate; George Stevenson, researcher.

[451]Kirkland, inventory of estate.

[452]*Star and North Carolina Gazette*, January 2, 1824.

[453]*Wilmington Chronicle*, October 27, 1795.

[454]*Hall's Wilmington Gazette*, February 16, 1797.

[455]*Hall's Wilmington Gazette,* May 31, 1798.

[456]*Wilmington Gazette*, June 13, 1799.

[457]Cutten Notes.

[458]Cutten Notes.

[459]Cutten Notes. Dr. Cutten suggested that Lambertoz's first name was Desiré.

[460]Pasquotank County Wills, Office of the Clerk of Court, Pasquotank County Courthouse, Elizabeth City, Book H, p. 18.

[461]Pasquotank County Marriage Bonds.

[462]Clark, *State Records*, XVI, 2, XIX, 246.

[463]Pasquotank County Apprenticeship Papers.

[464]Pasquotank County Deeds, Book K, p. 158.

[465]Pasquotank County Deeds, Book J, p. 248.

[466]Pasquotank County Deeds, Book M, p. 63.

[467]Clark, *State Records*, XXVI, 880.

[468]Clark, *State Records*, XXI, 1069.

[469]Pasquotank County Deeds, Book P, p. 257.

[470]*Wilmington Chronicle*, July 10, 1795.

[471]*Wilmington Chronicle*, April 14, 1796.

[472]*Miners' and Farmers' Journal*, October 4, 1834.

[473]*Mecklenburg Jeffersonian*, June 8, 1841.

[474]Mecklenburg County Wills, Book I, p. 64.

[475]Paw Creek Cemetery Records.

[476]*Mecklenburg Jeffersonian*, January 18, 1842.

[477]*Mecklenburg Jeffersonian*, September 4, 1843.

[478]Mary Boyer to Mary Reynolds Peacock, January 21, 1977, citing Mecklenburg County Deeds, Book 3, p. 332. The word "silversmith" is reasonably legible.

[479]Information provided to George B. Cutten by Adelaide L. Fries, Winston-Salem. See also Fries and others, *Records of the Moravians*, VII, 3150, 3153, 3210, 3468, 3469, 3476, VIII, 3636, 3639, 3647-4135 passim, IX, 4377, 4390; *Old Salem Gleaner*, XVII (July, 1973).

[480]Bertie County Court Minutes, 1778-1792, p. 140.

[481]*Fayetteville Gazette*, November 6, 1792.

[482]Carteret County Court Minutes, September, 1789-May, 1799, p. 689.

[483]Information provided to George B. Cutten by E. M. Lynch, Hillsborough.

[484]*Hillsborough Recorder*, July 30, 1828.

[485]Orange County Marriage Bonds.

[486]*Greensborough Patriot*, June 30, 1830.

[487]*Greensborough Patriot*, September 29, 1830.

[488]*Western Carolinian*, April 23, 1832.

[489]*Hillsborough Recorder*, June 4, 1834.

[490]*Hillsborough Recorder*, October 4, 1834.

[491]Mary Claire Engstrom, "The Clock Goes on a Journey," Historic Hillsborough Commission Bicentennial Series, No. 5, *News of Orange County*, May 16, 1975, p. 10.

[492]Stephen N. Dennis to Mary R. Peacock, November 18, 1974, hereinafter cited as Dennis to Peacock.

[493]Dennis to Peacock.

[494]*Cape Fear Recorder*, January 30, 1819.

[495]Burton, *South Carolina Silversmiths*, 63.

[496]*Minerva* (Raleigh), April 21, 1807.

[497]Mecklenburg County Deeds, Book 18, p. 191-Book 21, p. 107 passim.

[498]Mecklenburg County Court Minutes, 1810.

[499]Mecklenburg County Court Minutes, April term, 1810.

[500]Mecklenburg County Court Minutes, May term, 1813, November term, 1814.

[501]Mecklenburg County Deeds, Book 20, p. 248, Book 21, p. 410.

[502]Mecklenburg County Deeds, Book 19, p. 151.

[503]Death notice in *Western Carolinian*, September 26, 1826.

[504]*Minerva* (Raleigh), April 21, 1807.

[505]The material on McClenehan was provided by George Stevenson.

[506]Inventory, Estate of John McClenehan, 1827, Granville County Estate Papers, 1746-1919, State Archives, hereinafter cited as McClenehan, inventory of estate.

[507]McClenehan, inventory of estate.

[508]Iredell County Court Minutes, March, 1789-November, 1805, p. 596.

[509]*Raleigh Minerva*, February 5, 1813, noted in MESDA files.

[510]*Raleigh Minerva*, March 22, 1810; *North Carolina Star*, March 22, 1810.

[511]Cutten Notes: Albert S. McLean to George B. Cutten, March 4, 1956.

[512]Cutten Notes.

[513]*Carolina Federal Republican* (New Bern), January 25, 1812, hereinafter cited as *Carolina Federal Republican*.

[514]*Carolina Federal Republican*, July 3, 1813.

[515]*Carolina Sentinel*, November 17, 1821.

[516]*Carolina Sentinel*, May 22, 1824.

[517]*Carolina Sentinel*, April 7, 1827.

[518]*Newbern Spectator*, January 9, 1830.

[519]Craven County Marriage Bonds.

[520]Ensko, *American Silversmiths and Their Marks*, I, 97.

[521]*State Gazette of North Carolina* (New Bern), November 11, 1791, hereinafter cited as *State Gazette of North Carolina*.

[522]*State Gazette of North Carolina*, November 16, 1792.

[523]Chowan County Deeds, Book U, p. 310.

[524]Chowan County Deeds, Book S, p. 268.

[525]*State Gazette of North Carolina*, March 3, 1796.

[526]New York City directories; *United States Directory*, 1822.

[527]Ensko, *American Silversmiths and Their Marks*, I, 97.

[528]*New York Evening Post*, November 27, 1838.

[529]Ensko, *American Silversmiths and Their Marks*, I, 97.

[530]Wake County Court Minutes, 1823-1827, p. 386, 1831-1837, p. 42.

[531]Craven County Court Minutes, 1810-1813, p. 43.

[532]Craven County Court Minutes, December 8, 1800.

[533]*Hall's Wilmington Gazette*, May 31, 1798.

[534]New Hanover County Marriage Bonds.

[535]*Hall's Wilmington Gazette*, July 19, 1798.

[536]Cumberland County Marriage Bonds.

[537]*North Carolina Journal* (Fayetteville), January 1, 1830.

[538]*North Carolina Journal* (Fayetteville), August 3, 1831.

[539]*Semi-Weekly News* (Warrenton), February 5, 1856.

[540]Cameron Moore has been a subject of extensive research by Mr. Fred Hughes, who provided valuable information for this sketch. Mr. Hughes's findings about Moore and his compass were published by Abe D. Jones, Jr., in "New Found Value of Compass May Enlighten History," in the *Greensboro Record*, January 1, 1981, hereinafter cited as Jones, "New Found Value." A letter of June 16, 1981, to Mr. Hughes from Mr. Jay Worrell, hereinafter cited as Worrell to Hughes, provided much additional information about Moore's family from Hinshaw's *Encyclopedia of American Quaker Genealogy*, VI, 260, 266-267, 289.

[541]Worrell to Hughes.

[542]Worrell to Hughes.

[543]Fred Hughes to Mary Reynolds Peacock, August, 1981, hereinafter cited as Hughes to Peacock.

[544]Hughes to Peacock.

[545]Death notice in *Raleigh Register*, July 4, 1845; Hughes to Peacock.

[546]Hughes to Peacock.

[547]Hughes to Peacock.

[548]*Carolina Federal Republican*, April 25, 1812.

[549]Craven County Marriage Bonds.

[550]Craven County Court Minutes, 1814-1816, p. 6.

[551]*Carolina Centinel*, April 10, 1819.

[552]Craven County Court Minutes, 1801-1807 [unpaged].

[553]*Edenton Gazette*, August 27, 1811.

[554]Chowan County Wills, Book B, p. 302.

[555]Cutten Notes.

[556]*Western Whig Banner* (Lincolnton), June 27, 1840.

[557]Chowan County Marriage Bonds.

[558]Chowan County Deeds, Book D, pp. 287, 288, 290.

[559]*Edenton Gazette*, June 8, 1810.

[560]*Edenton Gazette*, February 8, 1811.

[561]Chowan County Deeds, Book H2, p. 459.

[562]*Miners' and Farmers' Journal*, September 24, 1832.

[563]*Fayetteville Gazette*, October 9, 1792.

[564]*Fayetteville Gazette*, October 16, 1792.

[565]*Fayetteville Gazette*, June 4, 1793.

[566]Cumberland County Court Minutes, October 15, 1793.

[567]William D. Palmer and Sherwin McRae (eds.), *Calendar of Virginia State Papers and Other Manuscripts, from January 1, 1785, to July 2, 1789, Preserved in the Capitol at Richmond* (Richmond: R. U. Derr, Superintendent of Public Printing, 1884), IV, 171.

[568]Rowan County Deeds, Book 24, p. 322. The late James S. Brawley of Salisbury provided valuable information from his research on the Palmer family.

[569]Rowan County Deeds, Books 23, 24, 32, 35.

[570]*News and Observer* (Raleigh), November 17, 1893, hereinafter cited as *News and Observer*.

[571]Clement Dowd, *Life of Zebulon B. Vance* (Charlotte: Observer Printing and Publishing House, 1897), 8.

[572]Rowan County Marriage Bonds.

[573]Rowan County Wills, Book H, p. 687.

[574]*Carolina Watchman*, August 23, 1834.

[575]*North Carolina Standard*, November 25, 1840.

[576]*North Carolina Standard*, September 24, 1845.

[577]Mrs. Elizabeth Reid Murray to Mary Reynolds Peacock, November, 1979.

[578]*News and Observer*, November 17, 1893.

[579]Miss Elizabeth Norris and Mrs. Elizabeth Reid Murray to Mary Reynolds Peacock, 1979.

[580]Miss Elizabeth Norris to Mary Reynolds Peacock, 1979.

[581]*North Carolina Standard*, November 24, 1847.

[582]*Star*, June 6, 1855.

[583]Caswell County Deeds, Office of the Register of Deeds, Caswell County Courthouse, Yanceyville, Book EE, p. 401, hereinafter cited as Caswell County Deeds.

[584]Caswell County Deeds, Book II, p. 259.

[585]Caswell County Deeds, Book JJ, p. 392.

[586]Caswell County Court Minutes, June, 1777-September, 1781, p. 123.

[587]*Cape Fear Recorder*, February 2, 1822.

[588]New Hanover County Court Minutes, February 12, 1823.

[589]*Carolina Observer*, July 17, 1823.

[590]*Fayetteville Observer*, October 6, 1825.

[591]Cumberland County Marriage Bonds.

[592]Vital Statistics of Norwich, Connecticut.

[593]Curtis, *Early Silver of Connecticut and Its Makers*, 106.

[594]New Hanover County Deeds, Book H, p. 454.

[595]*Hall's Wilmington Gazette*, November 15, 1798.

[596]*True Republican or American Whig* (Wilmington), May 2, 1809.

[597]*Yadkin and Catawba Journal*, November 26, 1832.

[598]*Carolina Watchman*, November 20, 1840.

[599]*Yadkin and Catawba Journal*, November 26, 1832.

[600]Rowan County Marriage Bonds.

[601]*North State Whig* (Washington), July 26, 1846, hereinafter cited as *North State Whig*.

[602]*North State Whig*, February 24, 1847.

[603]Beaufort County Deeds, Book 29, p. 274.

[604]Beaufort County Deeds, Book 18, p. 83.

[605]Beaufort County Deeds, Book 20, p. 225.

[606]*North State Whig*, April 27, 1843.

[607]Beaufort County Deeds, Book 22, p. 152.

[608]See Kovel and Kovel, *Directory of American Silver*, 222.

[609]*Fayetteville Daily Observer*, January 6, 1909.

[610]*Fayetteville Observer*, June 3, 1834.

[611]Cumberland County Marriage Bonds.

[612]*Fayetteville Observer*, October 3, 1838.

[613]Cumberland County Deeds, Book 42, p. 272.

[614]Cumberland County Deeds, Book 43, p. 372.

[615]*Fayetteville Observer*, June 27, 1889.

[616]Information provided to George B. Cutten by Mrs. Charles Rankin, Fayetteville, North Carolina.

[617]*Federal Republican*, February 6, 1813.

[618]*Federal Republican*, January 30, 1813.

[619]*Fayetteville Observer*, August 30, 1837.

[620]*Fayetteville Observer*, September 19, 1838.

[621]*Fayetteville Observer*, October 17, 1838.

[622]Caldwell, "Tennessee Silversmiths," 912.

[623]*Fayetteville Observer*, November 10, 1841.

[624]Wake County Marriage Bonds.

[625]*North Carolina Standard*, November 15, 1833.

[626]*Newbern Spectator*, May 16, 1840.

[627]*North Carolina Standard*, November 24, 1847.

[628]*North Carolina Standard*, February 27, 1856.

[629]*North Carolina Standard*, November 15, 1833.

[630]*Star and North Carolina Gazette*, September 22, 1836.

[631]*Newbern Spectator*, May 16, 1840.

[632]Cutten Notes.

[633]Information concerning Robertson was provided by George Stevenson from Edenton District Superior Court Records, Estates: John Robertson (Robinson), State Archives.

[634]The Robinson mark is still being studied.

[635]*Cyclopedia of Eminent and Representative Men of the Carolinas*, II, 364f.

[636]*Raleigh Register*, November 17, 1843.

[637]Wake County Marriage Bonds.

[638]Amis, *Historical Raleigh*, 79.

[639]*News and Observer*, May 8, 1903.

[640]Beaufort County Deeds, Book 13, p. 379.

[641]*Halifax Minerva*, March 5, April 16, 1829.

[642]New Hanover County Deeds, Book S, p. 536.

[643]*Cape Fear Recorder*, February 2, 1822.

[644]New Hanover County Court Minutes, May 15, 1822.

[645]Cutten Notes; James S. Brawley to Mary Reynolds Peacock.

[646]*Raleigh Register*, May 29, 1818.

[647]*Raleigh Register*, March 19, 1819.

[648]*Star and North Carolina Gazette*, June 9, 1830.

[649]*Raleigh Register*, February 8, 1822.

[650]*Star and North Carolina Gazette*, January 2, 1824.

[651]Wake County Deeds, Book 7, p. 134.

[652]*Enquirer* (Richmond, Virginia), October 27, 1829.

[653]See Ensko, *American Silversmiths and Their Marks*, II, 81.

[654]*New York Silversmiths* (Eggertsville, N.Y.: Darling Foundation of New York State Early American Silversmiths and Silver, 1964), 155, hereinafter cited as *New York Silversmiths*.

[655]The mark of William M. Savage appears in Belden, *Marks of American Silversmiths in the Ineson-Bissell Collection*, 373.

[656]*Western Carolinian*, December 2, 1823.

[657]*Raleigh Register*, March 19, 1819.

[658]*Star and North Carolina Gazette*, June 9, 1820.

[659]*Greensborough Patriot*, October 18, 1826.

[660]*Patriot, and Greensborough Palladium*, October 20, 1827.

[661]*Patriot, and Greensborough Palladium*, October 25, 1828.

[662]*Greensborough Patriot*, June 13, 1829.

[663]James W. Albright, *Greensboro, 1808-1904* (Greensboro: Jos. J. Stone, 1904), 35.

[664]*Greensboro Patriot*, September 15, 1875.

[665]Guilford County Deeds, Office of the Register of Deeds, Guilford County Courthouse, Greensboro, Book E, p. 155.

[666]*Greensborough Patriot*, June 13, 1829.

[667]*Raleigh Register*, December 1, 1806.

[668]Wake County Deeds, Book 2, p. 156.

[669]Wake County Court Minutes, February term, 1812, February term, 1814, May term, 1818.

[670]*Raleigh Register*, February 12, 1819.

[671]*Raleigh Register*, October 22, 1819.

[672]Wake County Court Minutes, November term, 1819.

[673]Wake County Court Minutes, November term, 1821, August term, 1823.

[674]Caldwell, "Tennessee Silversmiths," 912.

[675]*Western Carolinian*, December 15, 1825.

[676]Chowan County Marriage Bonds.

[677]*State Gazette of North Carolina*, December 31, 1790.

[678]Chowan County Deeds, Book S, p. 315.

[679]*State Gazette of North Carolina*, January 14, 1796.

[680]*State Gazette of North Carolina*, March 23, 1797.

[681]*State Gazette of North Carolina*, February 20, 1799.

[682]Chowan County Deeds, Book W1, p. 535.

[683]Cumberland County Marriage Bonds.

[684]Cumberland County Court Minutes, December term, 1807, September term, 1818.

[685]Cumberland County Deeds, Book 28, p. 234.

[686]*North Carolina Journal* (Fayetteville), June 7, 1831.

[687]*Fayetteville Observer*, September 29, 1836.

[688]*Fayetteville Observer*, August 30, 1837.

[689]Cumberland County Court Minutes, March term, 1838.

[690]Cumberland County Court Minutes, May 29, 1838.

[691]*Fayetteville Observer*, August 29, 1838.

[692]Cumberland County Court Minutes, September term, 1838.

[693]*Fayetteville Observer*, September 4, 1838.

[694]Cumberland County Court Minutes, September term, 1838.

[695]Cumberland County Court Minutes, June term, 1839.

[696]Cumberland County Court Minutes, June term, 1839.

[697]Cumberland County Court Minutes, June term, 1840.

[698]*North Carolina Journal* (Fayetteville), December 12, 1827.

[699]*North Carolina Journal* (Fayetteville), October 21, 1829.

[700]*Fayetteville Observer*, August 30, 1837.

[701]*Fayetteville Observer*, August 29, 1838.

[702]Records of the 1820 Census of Manufactures, Roll 19: Schedules for North Carolina, South Carolina, and Georgia, National Archives Microfilm Publications, Microcopy No. 279 (Washington: National Archives and Records Service, 1965), document 68, microfilm copy in State Archives.

[703]Jean Bruyere Kell and Thomas A. Williams (eds.), *North Carolina's Coastal Carteret County during the American Revolution, 1765-1785* (Greenville: Era Press, 1976), 143.

[704]Halifax County Court Minutes, 1784-1787, p. 215.

[705]Halifax County Deeds, Book 15, p. 140.

[706]*North Carolina Journal* (Halifax), October 17, 1792.

[707]Halifax County Deeds, Book 25, p. 24.

[708]Halifax County Wills, Office of the Clerk of Court, Halifax County Courthouse, Halifax, Book 3, p. 645, hereinafter cited as Halifax County Wills.

[709]*Greensborough Patriot*, August 13, 1839.

[710]*Western Carolinian*, November 23, 1824.

[711]*Elizabeth City Star*, August 18, 1827.

[712]*Fayetteville Observer*, November 17, 1841.

[713]*Fayetteville Observer*, October 3, 1843.

[714]Burton, *South Carolina Silversmiths*, 245-246.

[715]The material used for this sketch was compiled by Mr. John Bivens for MESDA.

[716]*Raleigh Register*, March 19, 1819.

[717]Wake County Marriage Bonds.

[718]*Raleigh Register*, April 6, 1821; *Norfolk and Portsmouth Herald* (Virginia), April 18, 1821.

[719]Wake County Court Minutes, May term, 1821.

[720]*Raleigh Register*, August 27, 1822.

[721]Wake County Court Minutes, May term, 1823, May term, 1824.

[722]Wake County Court Minutes, February term, 1829.

[723]Wake County Court Minutes, May term, 1829, May term, 1830.

[724]Wake County Court Minutes, May term, 1832.

[725]*Raleigh Register*, November 19, 1833.

[726]Seventh Census, 1850: Caswell County, North Carolina, Population Schedule, 193.

[727]John Stevenson to Waightstill Avery, Jones County Deeds, Book B, pp. 90-91, State Archives; George Stevenson, researcher.

[728]Craven County Apprenticeship Papers, State Archives.

[729]Inventory of Estate of John Stevenson, Craven County Estate Records, State Archives.

[730]Sale of Estate of John Stevenson, January 1, 1783, Craven County Estate Records, State Archives.

[731]John Kalmar to Mary Reynolds Peacock, July 12, 1975.

[732]Benjamin Woodbridge Dwight, *The Descendants of Elder John Strong, of Northampton, Mass.* (Albany, N.Y.: J. Munsell, 1861), 796.

[733]Cumberland County Deeds, Book 9, p. 97.

[734]Cumberland County Deeds, Book 9, p. 265.

[735]Cumberland County Court Minutes, January 28, 1788.

736Cumberland County Court Minutes, January 14, 1793.

737*North Carolina Chronicle and Fayetteville Gazette*, October 25, 1790, January 17, 1791.

738*Fayetteville Gazette*, August 7, 1792.

739*Carolina Watchman*, September 7, 1844.

740*Raleigh Register*, December 17, 1833.

741Wake County Marriage Bonds.

742*Raleigh Register*, April 30, 1838.

743Elizabeth Reid Murray to Mary Reynolds Peacock, November 21, 1979; this letter provided information used in this sketch.

744*Raleigh Register*, November 16, 1821, November 18, 1830.

745*Raleigh Register*, August 11, 1855.

746Cutten Notes.

747John L. Cheney, Jr. (ed.), *North Carolina Government, 1585-1974: A Narrative and Statistical History* . . . (Raleigh: North Carolina Department of the Secretary of State, 1975), 46; Clark, *State Records*, XXIII, 779; Saunders, *Colonial Records*, IV, 522, VI, 351, 362, 377, 427, 470, 514.

748Death notice in *Wilmington Journal*, January 4, 1856.

749Seventh Census, 1850: New Hanover County, North Carolina, Population Schedule.

750*People's Press & Wilmington Advertiser*, November 12, 19, 26, 1834.

751*People's Press & Wilmington Advertiser*, December 24, 1834.

752*Star and North Carolina Gazette*, December 1, 1836.

753*Raleigh Register*, December 4, 1837; *North Carolina Standard*, November 25, 1840.

754*Wilmington Journal*, November 21, 1845.

755Belden, *Marks of American Silversmiths*, 408. George Stevenson contributed many invaluable items of information concerning this sketch.

756*Raleigh Register*, December 4, 1837.

757*Star and North Carolina Gazette*, May 22, 1839.

758Craven County Marriage Bonds.

759Cutten Notes. Carolina Constable to George B. Cutten, July 8, 1948.

760Craven County Court Minutes, 1795-1801, p. 23.

761*North Carolina Gazette*, October 31, 1795.

762Governors Letter Books, Alexander, State Archives.

763Governor's Office Papers, Warrant Books, 1799-1809, State Archives.

764Stephen F. Miller, "Recollections of Newbern Fifty Years Ago," in *Our Living and Our Dead*, I (December, 1874), 345.

765*Federal Republican*, August 21, 1813.

766*Carolina Sentinel*, March 31, 1827.

767*Carolina Sentinel*, September 24, 1827.

768*Carolina Sentinel*, November 24, 1827.

769*Carolina Sentinel*, May 10, July 5, 1828, February 28, 1829.

770Cited by Craig, *The Arts and Crafts of North Carolina*, 84.

771Clifford K. Shipton, *New England Life in the 18th Century: Representative Biographies from Sibley's Harvard Graduates* (Cambridge: Belknap Press of Harvard University Press, 1964), 648; Saunders, *Colonial Records*, VIII, 508f, IX, 223.

772Saunders, *Colonial Records*, X, 166, 168.

773Saunders, *Colonial Records*, X, 215, 414, 444.

774Saunders, *Colonial Records*, X, 285.

775Saunders, *Colonial Records*, X, 826.

776Clark, *State Records*, XI, 710, XIII, 108.

777Craven County Apprenticeship Papers.

778Clark, *State Records*, XXIV, 166.

779Clark, *State Records*, XVI, 22, 24, XVII, 60.

780Clark, *State Records*, XVI, 106, 108.

781Clark, *State Records*, XIX, 5f, 197f, 325.

782Clark, *State Records*, XIX, 483.

783Clark, *State Records*, XVII, 265.

784Clark, *State Records*, XXVI, 414.

785Craven County Deeds, Book 21, p. 104, Book 32, p. 651.

786Inventory of Estate of William Tisdale, Craven County Estate Records.

787*American Recorder*, September 18, 1816.

788*Carolina Centinel*, December 22, 1821.

789Craven County Deeds, Book 63, p. 471.

790Craven County Deeds, Book 66, p. 138.

791Rowan County Deeds, Book 8, p. 313.

792Rowan County Deeds, Book 10, p. 498.

793Rowan County Deeds, Book 12, p. 62.

794Rowan County Court Minutes, V, p. 342.

795Personal information given to George B. Cutten by Miss Ann E. Trotter of Charlotte.

796*Star and North Carolina Gazette*, July 23, 1824.

797*Catawba Journal* (Charlotte), October 2, 1827, hereinafter cited as *Catawba Journal*.

798Mecklenburg County Marriage Bonds.

799*Yadkin and Catawba Journal*, April 29, 1828.

800*Charlotte Journal*, November 24, 1837.

801*Miners' and Farmers' Journal*, May 23, 1833.

802*Catawba Journal*, November 26, 1838.

803*Catawba Journal*, October 24, 1839.

804*Catawba Journal*, June 3, 1841.

805*Catawba Journal*, July 11, 1843.

806*Western Democrat*, October 7, 1856.

807*North Carolina Whig*, November 2, 1858.

808Miss Hallie E. Trotter to Mary R. Peacock, June 5, 1980.

809*Catawba Journal*, March 6, 1827.

810*Catawba Journal*, March 18, 1828.

811*Charlotte Journal*, November 24, 1837.

812*Charlotte Journal*, December 7, 1838.

813*Yadkin and Catawba Journal*, April 29, 1828.

814Mecklenburg County Deeds, Book 21, p. 666.

815*Yadkin and Catawba Journal*, January 26, 1830.

816*Miners' and Farmers' Journal*, February 22, 1832.

817*United States Directory*, 1822.

818Burton, *South Carolina Silversmiths*, 211-212.

819Information for this sketch provided by researcher Rosemary Estes from MESDA documentary research files.

820Northampton County Wills, 1759-1792, Will 166, Book I, p. 245. This extract is from Margaret M. Hofmann, *Genealogical Abstracts of Wills, Northampton County, North Carolina, 1759-1808* (Weldon: Roanoke News Co., 1975), 38-39.

821Northampton County Estates, 1781-1791, p. 1, State Archives.

822Northampton County Estates, 1781-1791, p. 33, State Archives.

[823]Information furnished to George B. Cutten by Adelaide L. Fries, Cutten Notes.

[824]Fries and others, *Records of the Moravians*, VI, 2862; information supplied by Old Salem, Inc., and quoted in Craig, *The Arts and Crafts of North Carolina*, 36.

[825]Information furnished to George B. Cutten by Adelaide L. Fries, Cutten Notes.

[826]Information furnished to George B. Cutten by Adelaide L. Fries, Cutten Notes.

[827]*Western Carolinian*, April 16, 1841.

[828]*Carolina Watchman*, January 18, 1845.

[829]*Republican Banner* (Salisbury), May 6, 1856, hereinafter cited as *Republican Banner*.

[830]Craig, *The Arts and Crafts of North Carolina*, 86.

[831]Franklin County Court Minutes, 1846 [unpaged].

[832]Chowan County Papers, II, 44.

[833]Chowan County Papers, II, 83.

[834]Chowan County Marriage Bonds.

[835]Chowan County Papers, III, 33.

[836]Chowan County Papers, III, 95.

[837]Chowan County Papers, III, 118.

[838]Chowan County Papers, IX, 8.

[839]Chowan County Papers, IV, 53.

[840]Chowan County Papers, V, 70.

[841]Chowan County Papers, VI, 15.

[842]Chowan County Papers, VIII, 80.

[843]Chowan County Papers, XIX, 12.

[844]Mrs. Mary Boyer to Mary Reynolds Peacock, January 21, 1977, citing Mecklenburg County Deeds, Book 9, p. 253.

[845]Will of James Way, Mecklenburg County (Original) Wills, 1749-1904, State Archives; George Stevenson, researcher.

[846]Estate of James Way, 1807, Mecklenburg County Estate Records, 1762-1929, State Archives; George Stevenson, researcher.

[847]*Carolina Republican* (Lincolnton), April 10, 1849.

[848]Chowan County Marriage Bonds.

[849]Chowan County Papers, XIV, 140.

[850]Chowan County Papers, XV, 19; Clark, *State Records*, IX, 633f.

[851]Chowan County Papers, XV, 69.

[852]Chowan County Papers, XV, 141.

[853]Chowan County Papers, XVI, 17.

[854]Chowan County Papers, XVI, 31. Whedbee's religious affiliation is not known, but when the North Carolina General Assembly met in January, 1779, one measure proposed as a means of dealing with dissenting religious sects was to require all Quakers, Moravians, Mennonites, and Dunkards to take an oath of allegiance to the state. It is thus possible that Whedbee's loyalty to the state was in question.

[855]Chowan County Papers, XVI, 57.

[856]Brix, *Philadelphia Silversmiths*, 109.

[857]*Carolina Observer*, July 31, 1823.

[858]*North Carolina Journal* (Fayetteville), December 12, 1827.

[859]*Carolina Observer*, May 8, 1832.

[860]Cumberland County Court Minutes, March and June terms, 1834, December term, 1839.

[861]Cumberland County Marriage Bonds.

[862]C. M. North, *History of Berlin, Connecticut* [complete bibliographical data not available].

[863]Curtis, *Early Silver of Connecticut and Its Makers*, 115.

[864]Cumberland County Deeds, Book 32, p. 46.

[865]*American*, July 23, 1818.

[866]Cumberland County Deeds, Book 35, p. 12.

[867]*Carolina Observer*, July 17, 1823.

[868]Cumberland County Deeds, Book 35, p. 6.

[869]Curtis, *Early Silver of Connecticut and Its Makers*, 115.

[870]Curtis, *Early Silver of Connecticut and Its Makers*, 115.

[871]Quoted from the *South Carolina Gazette* (Charleston), August 21-28, 1749, in Burton, *South Carolina Silversmiths*, 193.

[872]Burton, *South Carolina Silversmiths*, 193.

[873]Lennon and Kellam, *The Wilmington Town Book*, 65, n. 83.

[874]New Hanover County Deeds, Book C, pp. 347-349, Book D, p. 8; Saunders, *Colonial Records*, VI, 211; Walker, *New Hanover County Court Minutes*, I, 38, 48.

[875]Burton, *South Carolina Silversmiths*, 194.

[876]*Western Carolinian*, July 25, 1820.

[877]*Western Carolinian*, November 12, 1822.

[878]*Western Carolinian*, December 2, 1823.

[879]*Western Carolinian*, July 25, 1820.

[880]*Western Carolinian*, February 13, 1821.

[881]Information copied from family Bible by Mrs. J. S. Callaway, Greensboro, Georgia.

[882]*Carolina Watchman*, March 20, 1846.

[883]*Carolina Watchman*, April 14, 1853.

[884]*Carolina Watchman*, January 22, 1866.

[885]Winckler is listed in Cutten's *Silversmiths of Virginia*, 78-80, and in Burton's *South Carolina Silversmiths*, 194-195, but he is not listed in Cutten's *Silversmiths of North Carolina*, first edition. However, Winckler, a productive silversmith in both South Carolina and Virginia, lived in North Carolina from ca. 1763 until 1778; and although evidence of his activity as a silversmith in North Carolina is lacking, it seems appropriate to quote from *Silversmiths of Virginia* (pages 78-79) that part of Winckler's biographical sketch pertaining to his life in North Carolina.

[886]*Washington Gazette*, November 22, 1808.

[887]Ernest M. Currier, *Marks of Early American Silversmiths . . .*, *List of New York Silversmiths, 1815-1841*, edited by Kathryn C. Buhler (Portland, Me.: Southworth-Anthoesen Press, 1938), 154.

[888]*North-Carolina Gazette*, February 21, 1795.

[889]*Raleigh Register*, November 1, 1811. Notice of Mrs. Woods's death also appeared in the *Raleigh Minerva*, November 1, 1811, and the *North Carolina Star*, November 1, 1811.

[890]*Carolina Centinel*, July 18, 1818.

[891]*Carolina Centinel*, September 7, 1822.

[892]*Carolina Centinel*, October 2, 1824.

[893]*Carolina Centinel*, October 14, 1826.

[894]*Carolina Centinel*, August 25, 1827.

[895]*Carolina Centinel*, September 24, 1827.

[896]Craven County Inventories of Estates and Accounts of Sales, V: 1833-1838, 87-95, State Archives; Mr. William M. Biggers, researcher.

[897]Information provided by Mrs. Rosemary Estes from the files of MESDA, citing the *Virginia Argus* (Richmond), March 7, 1804.

[898]Henry Morton Woodson, *Genealogy of the Woodsons and Their Connnections* (Memphis: Privately published by the author, 1915), 55.

[899]*Virginia Gazette*, April 18, 1766.

[900]Rowan County Deeds, Book 8, p. 475.

[901]Rowan County Deeds, Book 9, p. 265.

[902]*Western Carolinian*, March 1, 1825.

[903]*Patriot, and Greensborough Palladium*, October 20, 1827.

[904]*Patriot, and Greensborough Palladium*, October 25, 1828.

[905]*Greensborough Patriot*, November 21, 1829.

[906]Rowan County Marriage Bonds.

[907]*Republican Banner*, September 23, 1856.

[908]*Greensborough Patriot*, November 21, 1829.

[909]*Western Carolinian*, July 3, 1827.

[910]*Western Carolinian*, January 29, 1828.

[911]*Western Carolinian*, February 11, 1830.

[912]*Roanoke Advocate*, November 15, 1832.

Geographical Distribution of Silversmiths in North Carolina

Albemarle County
Tomes, Nathaniel

Anson County (Wadesboro)
Clark & Turner
Turner, Franklin

Bath County (Pamtecough Precinct; later, Beaufort County)
Mellyne, Robert

Beaufort County (Washington)
Berson & Roberts
Hoell, Edward
Holland, John
Pool, James M.
Pratt, William T.
Pyle, Benjamin, I
Tisdale, William, II
Wood, James

Bertie County (Windsor)
Daniel (a slave)
Leming, John

Bladen County
Benbow, John

Buncombe County
Woods, James

Burke County
Brookshire, William
Emmons, Isaac

Cabarrus County (Concord)
Atkinson, William
Houlton, David
Lynch, Lemuel
Palmer, John C.
Scott, Samuel

Caldwell County (Lenoir?)
Thompson, George

Carteret County (Beaufort)
Davis, John
Holland, John
Lukeman, John A.
Severin, James

Caswell County (Locust; Milton; Yanceyville)
Atkinson, _____
Atkinson, Adolphus
Huntington, M. P. & Co.
Paxton, John W.
Paxton, William C.
Payne, Robert (?)
Steel, Thomas
Walker, A. J.
Whipple, David

Chowan County (Edenton)
Adams, Thomas F.
Agnis, Thomas
Castile, Anthony
Cleland, John
Copeland, John
Debruhl, Edward
Faris, William, Jr.
Garrett, Everard
Howcott, Nathaniel
Marquand, Isaac
Niel, Henry
Noxon, Martin
Seaman, Thomas
Wallace, James, Jr.
Whedbee, Joseph

Cleveland County
Harry, John Bishop

Craven County (New Bern)
Beckwith, Robert W.
Carsan (Carson), Robert
Davis, Riley A.
De St. Leger
Duff, George C.
Dunn, Stephen
Ferguson, Elijah
Fitch, Allen
Gill, John
Johnston, William
Kirkland, John
Machen, Thomas W.
Masters, Christopher M.
Murdock, David A.
Perret, Lewis
Ramsay & Beckwith
Stevenson, John
Tench, Arthur
Tisdale, Nathan
Tisdale, William, I
Tisdale, William, II
Woods, Freeman

**Cumberland County
(Fayetteville)**
Beasley, John M.
Brennan, P. N.
Campbell, Alexander
Campbell, John
Campbell & Prior
Clark, Charles
Clark & Turner
Gale, Joseph
Glover, Edwin
Hilliard, George W.
Hilliard, William
Lord & Gale
Mills, John B.
Ott, Philip
Peabody, John
Perret, Lewis
Prior, Warren
Pyle, Benjamin, II
Selph, John
Selph & Campbell
Selph & Pyle
Selph & Tisdale
Smith, C. C.
Strong, Peter
Widdefield, William, Jr.
Wilcox, Alvan

Currituck County
Robertson (Robinson), John

Duplin County
Debruhl, Edward

**Edgecombe County
(Tarboro)**
Archer, William
Barrington, Joseph
Beckwith, Robert W.
Braswell, Benjamin B.
Coleman, Aaron
Cravey, James
Drake, William
Gatlin, Thomas
Holland, John
Moore, Joseph

Forsyth County (Salem)
Albrecht, William
Dresen, Immanuel
Eberhardt, Johann Ludwig
Fockel, Johann Jacob
Hauser, Simon Peter
Leinbach, Nathaniel A.
Leinbach, Traugott
Vogler, Elias A.
Vogler, John

Franklin County (Louisburg)
Geddy, John
Walker, Nathan B.

Granville County (Oxford)
Huntington, John
Huntington, William
Lynch, Thomas M.
McClenahan, John
Palmer, John C.

Guilford County (Greensboro)
Anderson, _____
Eckel, Alexander P.
Flere, Thomas
Garland, John R.
Johnson, Elisha
Lynch, Lemuel
Martin, Pleasant Henderson
Moore, Cameron
Scott, David
Scott & Anderson

Singleton, Robert
Trotter, Thomas
Woolworth, Aaron
Woolworth & Anderson

Halifax County (Halifax)
Archer, John
Daniel, George C.
Geddy, John
Greenawalt, William
Ruff, William E.
Shield, Thomas
Short, John
Wynne, Robert

Henderson County
Justus, Meridy D.

Hyde County
Griffen, John (Germantown)
Highe, Thomas (Plymouth)

Iredell County (Statesville)
McKay, Neil
McLean, John

Johnston County (Smithfield)
Killingsworth, John

Lincoln County (Lincolnton)
Norman, James S.
Welsh, David

Mecklenburg County (Charlotte)
Alexander, Samuel P.
Alexander, Zenas
Beckwith, Robert W.
Blandin, Victor G.
Brewer, N. Alexander F.
Davis, John
Doret, A. M.
Gardner, Barzillai
Garland, John R.
Huntington, John
Hyams, ___
Lawing, Samuel
Lawing & Brewer
Lee, Joseph
McBride, Andrew
McBride & Gardner
McRae, James

Olmstead, Gideon
Trotter, Pinckney
Trotter, Thomas
Trotter, Thomas & Co.
Trotter & Alexander
Trotter & Huntington
Way, James
Wilkinson, James G.

New Hanover County (Wilmington)
Anderson, William S.
Baker, Stephen
Bishop, Joseph
Blyth, George
Blythe, James
Brown, Thomas W.
Brown & Anderson
Burr, Turner
Dana, Nathaniel
Davenport, John
Flere, Thomas
Hughes, James
Kirkwood, John
Lambertoz, D.
LaPlace, Charles
Lyon, George
Melville, Henry
Peabody, Asa
Peabody, John T.
Sargent, John
Thomson, William
Wheeler & Carpenter
Wilkings (Wilkins), William

Northampton County
Daughtery, John
Veale, Richard

Orange County (Hillsborough)
Cocke, ___
Huntington, John
Huntington, Roswell
Huntington, William
Huntington, William & Co.
Huntington & Lynch
Lynch, L. George
Lynch, Lemuel
Lynch, Seaborn

**Pasquotank County
(Elizabeth City; Nixonton)**
Cluff, Matthew
Daniel, George C.
Eastman, Benjamin
Lane, William (Nixonton)
Slocum, Ebenezer
Spooner, Samuel

Pitt County (Greenville)
Hoell, Edward

Randolph County
Johnston, John

Robeson County
Kelly, Patrick
McLean, Angus

Rockingham County
Guerrant, John C.

Rowan County (Salisbury)
Barrington, J.
Baxter, German
Boger, John E.
Boger & Wilson
Brown, Daniel
Burnham, E. B.
Dickey, John
Elliott, Zebulon
Elliott & Burnham
Gay, Joshua
Hampton, James B.
Hampton, William
Hampton & Palmer
Horah, Henry
Horah, Hugh
Horah, James
Horah, William H.
Huntington, John
Huntington & Wynne
Kunsman, Henry
Palmer, John C.
Pool, David L.
Read, Andrew
Sassaman, Jacob
Savage & Kunsman
Slayton, Sanford G.
Taylor, Noah C.
Townsley, James
Trotter, Thomas

Vogler, John U.
Wilkinson, Curtis
Wilkinson & Horah
Wilson, William R.
Woodson, David
Woolworth, Aaron
Wynne, Robert

**Rutherford County
(Rutherfordton)**
Bechtler, Augustus
Bechtler, Christopher, Jr.
Bechtler, Christopher, Sr.

Sampson County (Clinton)
Thomson, Andrew

Surry County
McGee, Drewery

Wake County (Raleigh)
Baird, _____
Beckwith, Robert W.
Campbell, Thomas L.
Decosta, Caton
Dumoutet, John B. (?)
Dupuy, Bernard
Emond, Thomas
Fowler, Thomas H.
Glass, David
Glass, Thomas
Glass & Baird
Kunsman, Henry
Mahler, Henry
Mason, John M.
Palmer, John C.
Palmer & Ramsay
Ramsay, Walter J.
Ramsay, W. J. & Co.
Ramsay & Beckwith
Root, Charles B.
Savage, John Y.
Savage & Stedman
Scott, Jehu
Stedman, John C.
Tench, Arthur
Thompson, C. H.
Thompson, W. H.
Thomson, William
Thomson & Beckwith
Winckler, John

Warren County (Warrenton)
Holliman, William
Montcastle, William R.

Location undetermined
Dumoutet, John Baptiste
Hanna, J. C.
Harry, John B.
Huguenin, Charles F.

List of Apprentices (or Understudies)

Apprentice or Understudy	Silversmith	Beginning Date of Indenture or Approximate Date of Association	County
Adams, William	Mason, John M.	1832	Wake
—, Albrecht	Vogler, John	1825	Forsyth
Alexander, Samuel P.	Trotter, Thomas	ca. 1820-1825	Mecklenburg
Allen, Bonaparte	Noxon, Martin	1812	Chowan
Anderson, William S.	Brown, T. W.	ca. 1830-1836	New Hanover
Andrews, Brice	Horah, Hugh	1809	Rowan
Ball, Henry	Marquand, Isaac		Chowan
Ball, Joseph	Lambertoz, Dain	1798	New Hanover
Bechtler, Augustus	Bechtler, Christopher	1829?	Rutherford
Black, William	Marquand, Isaac	1807	Chowan
Boyken (Bayken), Abel	Selph, John	1807	Cumberland
Brockett, James	Sargent, John	1822	New Hanover
Brown, John	Payne (Paine), Robert	1782	Caswell
Brown, John	Whipple, David	1780	Caswell
Bruce, George	Masters, Christopher	1810	Craven
Cahoon, Carney	Gill, John	1828	Craven
Campbell, Alexander	Strong, Peter	1793	Cumberland
Campbell, John	Selph, John	1818	Cumberland
Champion, John	Shield, Thomas	1812	Halifax
Collier, Charles Henry	Emond, Thomas	1787	Orange
Cullifer, Jeremiah	Leming, John	1785	Bertie
Darnell, James	Drake, William	1783	Edgecombe
Duncan, John	Holliman, William	1783	Warren
Duncan, Willie	Holliman, William	1783	Warren

Dunn, George	Dunn, Stephen	1786	Craven
Dye, William	Hilliard (Hillard), William	1801	Cumberland
Fisher, Samuel	Murdock, David A.	1814	Craven
Fockel, Jacob	Vogler, John	1818	Forsyth
Gale, Joseph	Strong, Peter	1788	Cumberland
Garret, Everard	Agnis, Thomas [possibly]		Chowan
Gill, John	Murdock, David	1814	Craven
Gorman, James	Stedman, John C.	1829	Wake
Hayes, George B.	Walker, Nathan B.	1846	Franklin
Horah, William H.	Horah, Hugh	ca. 1800?	Rowan
Huntington, Roswell	Carpenter, Joseph	ca. 1780?	Norwich, Conn.
Huntington, William	Huntington, Roswell	ca. 1805?	Orange
Johnston, William	Tisdale, William, I	1778	Craven
Jones, Horatio	Horah, Hugh	1796	Rowan
Kitschelt, Samuel	Leinbach, Samuel	1826	Forsyth
Leinbach, Traugott	Vogler, John	1811	Forsyth
Leming, Joseph	Whedbee, Joseph	1778	Chowan
Lynch, Lemuel	Huntington, William	ca. 1820	Orange
McBride, Henry	Alexander, Zenas	1810	Mecklenburg
McKay, Alexander	McKay, Neil	1804	Iredell
McRea (McRae), James	Alexander, Zenas	1810	Mecklenburg
Masters, Christopher	Woods, Freeman	1800	Craven
Miller, George	Brown, Daniel	1795	Rowan
Miller, John	Horah, Henry	1783	Rowan
Murdock, David A.	Woods, Freeman	1805	Craven
Nash, Francis	Huntington, Roswell	1785	Orange
Palmer, John C.	Savage, John Y.	ca. 1821?	Wake
Pilly, Stephen	Emond, Thomas	1816	Wake
Ramsay, W. J.	Stedman, John C. [possibly]	ca. 1826	Wake [?]
Richardson, Valentine	Stevenson, John	1778	Craven
Ruth, George Washington	Scott, Jehu		Wake (?)

Apprentice or Understudy	Silversmith	Beginning Date of Indenture or Approximate Date of Association	County
Saunders, Jessee	Tisdale, Nathan	1795	Craven
Seal, Solomon	Whipple, David	1780	Caswell
Short, Samuel	Moore, Camm	1787	Guilford
Smart, Elisha	Alexander, Zenas	1810	Mecklenburg
Smith, Willis	Lukeman, John A.	1791	Carteret
Sneed, Johnston	[_____ Atkinson?]	ca. 1839	Caswell
Sneeston, James	Selph, John	ca. 1816	Cumberland
Sylvestre, William	Lane, William	1785	Pasquotank
Taylor, William	Payne (Paine), Robert	1782	Caswell
Tench, Arthur (Archer)	Stedman, John C. [possibly]	___	Wake
Thomason, James	Payne (Paine), Robert	1779	Caswell
Todd, Joseph	Baxter, Germon	1768	Rowan
Trotter, Pinckney	Trotter, Thomas	ca. 1850	Mecklenburg
Trotter, Thomas	Horah, Hugh [possibly]	1818	Rowan
Vail (Veal), Bond	Tisdale, William, I	1777	Craven
Vogler, Elias Alexander	Vogler, John	ca. 1840	Forsyth
Vogler, John Utzmann	Vogler, John	1827	Forsyth
Ward, Benjamin	Eastman (Easman), Benjamin	1787	Pasquotank
Wellwood, John	Cleland, John	ca. 1751	Chowan
Whitehouse, John	Archer, William	1791	Edgecombe
Wilkinson, James G.	Trotter, Thomas	ca. 1850	Mecklenburg
Williams, Anderson B.	Mason, John M.	1826	Wake
Williams, Nathan	Horah, Hugh	1800	Rowan

Appendix A
Makers' Marks Not Identified

The silver items pictured in this appendix bear various types of marks that have not been positively identified as those of known North Carolina silversmiths. The photographs are included nonetheless in the hope that they might provide information useful in identifying the makers of the respective pieces.

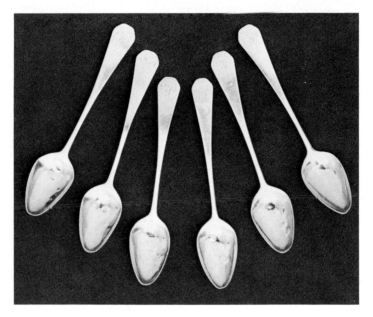

Family tradition endows with a romantic history the six unidentified teaspoons pictured above. Mrs. Thad S. Page, a descendant of the original owner, John Hinton, tells the story in a letter to the editor. During the Revolutionary War, Major John Hinton, a patriot, was attacked at his home, Clay Hill, by Edmund Fanning's men, who unwittingly gave their victim an opportunity to escape. "During that tense interval Major Hinton, unnoticed, managed to untie himself, slipped from the house, and sent a messenger to his brother Col. James Hinton. . . . Thinking of some unhidden silver spoons, his little daughter Mary snatched them—escaping through the darkness into the garden and hid them in the bed of pinks. They were ever after called the 'pink bed spoons' and are still in the possession of the family. . . ."

The graceful spoons are coffin-end, 5½ inches long, with slender stems and pointed oval bowls that measure 1¾ inches long and 1⅛ inches wide. The single initial *H* is engraved in feathered script on the handle.

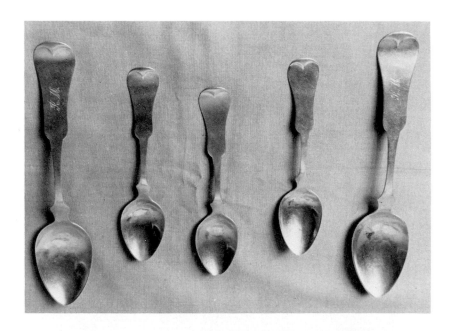

The flared fiddleback, tipped handles of the spoons shown above are the work of craftsmen whose location has not been determined; the incused mark could quite possibly indicate the retailers rather than the makers. William Albrecht's mark has not been unquestionably verified, nor has the mark of the Philadelphian, Henry Huber, Jr. (1818-1824), listed in Kovel and Kovel, *A Directory of American Silver*, p. 144. The collection, presently owned by a North Carolina collector, consists of two serving spoons 7⅞ inches long and three teaspoons 5¾ inches long. They were acquired by purchase.

 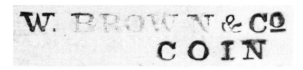

The chevron and horse's head depicted on this mustard spoon, a manufactured piece, have also been found on pieces of handcrafted silver in North Carolina. Was W. Brown related to T. W. Brown of Wilmington? The chevron and horse's head used by T. W. Brown are similar but not identical.

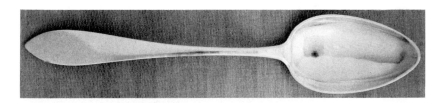

This fine tablespoon 9½ inches long with the maker's mark BURMEISTER flanked by a griffon and the number 12 is in a private collection (provenance, the piedmont) that also includes Vogler silver and the Albrecht spoon depicted in this book. Nothing has been learned about the origin of this mark, but there is a remarkable similarity in the workmanship of Vogler, Burmeister, and Albrecht that suggests the influence of Vogler upon the other two. The back of the bowl has a very nicely executed foliate decoration. The handle is engraved *F. Schuldt 1851.*

Was this teaspoon (6 inches long) made by John Church and a partner? Was the John Campbell whose mark is on this spoon the John Campbell who was a working craftsman in North Carolina and Tennessee? The marks are being studied.

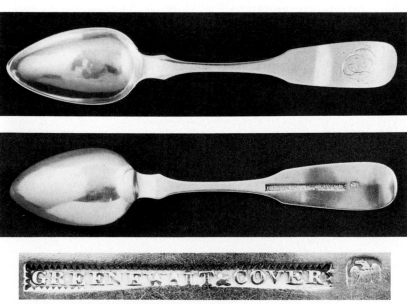

This teaspoon 6 inches long in a private collection has the mark GREENE-WALT & COVER in a serrated rectangle with an eagle on the right. Was this the mark of William Greenawalt, the Halifax silversmith? Did Greenawalt sometimes spell his name with an *e*? Who was Cover?

This serving spoon 8¼ inches long has the mark HILLIARD in a rectangle. Whether or not this was a mark used by George or William Hilliard has not been determined. The spoon is in an early style with a spatulate, down-curved handle and no engraving; the bowl is oval (almost elliptical) with drop.

Two portraits in the Huntington family have been studied assiduously and discussed by William Johnston Hogan in his *Huntington Silversmiths*. Executed by an unidentified artist, the portraits were taken from Hillsborough, North Carolina, to Alabama by the family in 1833. Although William and Frances Howze Huntington were reputed to be the subjects, family members and art critics in recent years have questioned the validity of that identification. Evidence indicates that these quite possibly are portraits of Roswell and Mary Palmer Huntington. Portraits photographed and used by permission of William Johnston Hogan.

HUNC LAPIDEM.

Honorariis Curatoribus hujus Academiæ,

nec non

FRATRIBUS MASONICIS HILLSBORIA *abundique*

RITE *presentibus,*

GULIELMUS R DAVIE, *equestris præfectus,*

Carolinaque Septentrionalis ARCHI-ARCHITECTUS,

Anno Lucis 5793°. *Salutis* 1793°.

AMERICANÆ LIBERTATIS 18.

Y 12° *die Octobris,*

MULTO CUM ORDINE

LOCAVIT.

SIT ÆRE PEREN'NIUS.

Teaspoons with the mark RH and a leaf have come to light in at least two instances. The six shown above are in a private collection (provenance, Hillsborough). They are fiddleback with pointed shoulders and an *M* engraved in a style comparable in details with engraving done by William Huntington. The RH mark on the spoons is not, however, comparable with the RH mark on the reverse of the brass plate originally affixed to the Old East cornerstone.

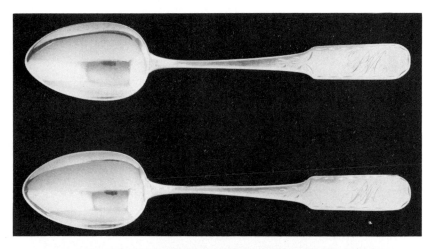

Only a very skilled craftsman could have made such handsome spoons as these tablespoons 9½ inches long with pointed oval bowls, drop, no shoulders, and decorated by bright-cut on the handle and the feathered script engraving *PM*. Who was the LOCHWARD who carefully marked his work?

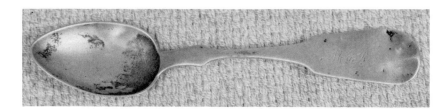

The incused mark RAMSEY is found on this spoon and others in North Carolina. The teaspoon is 6 inches long and has a broad handle with a short midrib, oval pointed bowl, and pointed shoulders.

Still being investigated is the possibility that this mark on a mustard spoon in a private collection is that of J. Y. Savage and his son William M. Savage, who worked independently for some time in Columbus, Ohio. See Belden, *Marks of American Silversmiths,* 373.

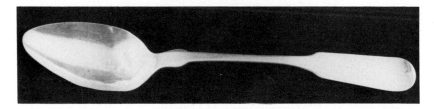

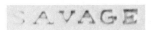
Still another unsolved problem concerning Savage is the incused mark on this tablespoon from a private collection. The spoon is a fiddleback, 8½ inches long, with tipped handle engraved *MLE* in script.

Who was Wm. H. Thompson? Was he a craftsman or a retailer? Unanswered are the questions about this intriguing pair of teaspoons, one 5⅝ inches long, the other a bit longer (5⅞ inches) and wider. Both are engraved *DRU*, and the smaller spoon has *Clara* engraved on the back. (From a private collection.)

Appendix B
Miscellaneous Silver
of Historical Importance

In the course of seeking out silver made in North Carolina before 1860, it was expected that many pieces would be found that were not of local origin but are of historical significance to the state. A few examples of such pieces have been selected for inclusion in this volume.

A cream pitcher believed to have belonged to Dr. Thomas Burke (ca. 1744-1783), governor of North Carolina, 1781-1782, is an item of genuine interest. Mrs. George Burke Johnston provided the following information about the pitcher in a letter of August 18, 1974, to Mary Reynolds Peacock:

My husband's grandfather was George Doherty Johnston of Alabama, who was Miss Mary Williams Burke's nephew and ward. You will see from the photograph of the bottom of the pitcher that it is marked T^{B}M. There are no marks that might be clues to the maker. Probably it was made in Virginia prior to Thomas Burke's move to North Carolina. The grandfather's clock [not pictured] has a bill of sale from Thos. Emons, May 31, 1816, and we assume belonged to George Mulholland Johnston, father of George Doherty Johnston, who moved to Alabama from Hillsborough in 1834. He died the same year and it was after his death that Governor Burke's daughter was made guardian of his infant son.

Mary (Polly) Williams Burke was the only child of Dr. Thomas Burke and Mary Freeman, a native of Norfolk, Virginia. After Thomas Burke's death in 1783 his widow married Major George Doherty, by whom she had two daughters, half sisters of Mary Burke. Valuable genealogical information about the families who moved to Alabama from Hillsborough is contained in William Johnston Hogan's *Huntington Silversmiths*; see also "Burke, Mary ('Polly') Williams," in William S. Powell (ed.), *Dictionary of North Carolina Biography* (Chapel Hill: University of North Carolina Press [projected multivolume series], 1979, I, 279-280.

A shoe-shaped snuffbox believed to have been made by an unidentified Irish silversmith ca. 1750 and to have belonged to Governor Thomas Burke is now owned by the North Carolina Museum of History. The box has the general shape of a modified klomp, with two thirds of the top opening up on a hinge. There are overall floral and scroll designs, with the figure of a cherub used on the top, a pair of figures on the back and right side, and a single male figure on the left side. This item was purchased in 1974 by the museum. The previous owner had found inside the box a calling card with "Miss Burke" printed on one side and a handwritten notation on the other: "The snuff box of Doctor Thomas A. Burke Governor of North Carolina 1781—Elizabeth B. Burke." The identity of Elizabeth B. Burke has not been determined. Governor Burke's wife was Mary Freeman, and his daughter, Mary Williams Burke, never married. Governor Burke had a younger brother, and it is possible that Elizabeth B. Burke might have been a member of the brother's family. The dimensions of the snuffbox are: 70 mm. from toe to heel, 33 mm. at the highest point, and 24 mm. at the widest point.

Abigail Sugars (Sugan) Jones, wife of Edward Jones of Warren County, was the original owner of this small silver tobacco pipe. According to family tradition, Mrs. Jones was one of the first white women to settle in Warren County, arriving there ca. 1732. The pipe was given to her by her grandson-in-law, Bishop John Early. There is no discernible maker's mark, and the style was one not uncommon ca. 1770-1840. The bowl is seamed down the side and has a rolled rim soldered around the upper edge. On the right side is the engraved name *A. Jones*. The shank is of rolled silver, seamed on the right side and tapered down to the heel, where it was soldered around the draft hole. A hollow reed, perhaps 4½ inches long, would have been used as a stem. The bowl is 23 mm. high, 19 mm. in diameter; the shank

is 29 mm. long. The pipe was a gift to the North Carolina
Museum of History from Mr. William Duke Jones and Mr. Bignall Speed Jones.

A chalice and plate in St. Paul's Episcopal Church, Edenton, bear the mark
AK, believed to have been that of silversmith Alexander Kerr of Williamsburg,
Virginia. Photograph by Colonial Williamsburg from George Blake Holmes
(comp.), *History of St. Paul's Episcopal Church in Edenton, North Carolina*
(N.p.: Privately printed, 1964); used by permission of the Reverend Mr. Holmes.

The acquisition of communion silver was most important to
congregations of the early churches, and a few pieces of such
silver have survived in North Carolina. St. Paul's Episcopal
Church in Edenton, founded in 1701, has two chalices, two
dishes, and a tankard. One chalice, made in England ca. 1700,
was the gift of the Reverend John Garvia, who came to North
Carolina in 1742 and died in 1744. The second chalice and one
of the dishes have a much more complicated history. In 1703
Virginia's governor, Francis Nicholson, gave to each of the

three North Carolina parishes an "incentive grant" of £10 to be used for having church silver made. In 1704 the vestry ordered the money sent to Boston to purchase a chalice. In 1714 Edward Mosely wrote to Governor Nicholson that the money had been deposited with Jeremiah Dummer in Boston. In 1715-1716 the parish was divided; thereafter, half of the money appropriated for silver belonged to Society Parish. In February, 1728, the silver was in St. Paul's Church, marked as a gift from Moseley rather than from Nicholson. Moseley was a man of affluence, a distinguished lawyer, and a zealous churchman. The silver bears the mark AK, which E. Alfred Jones, in his monumental work *The Old Silver of American Churches*,[1] says was the mark of Am Kay of Boston. Historians now believe there was no such silversmith as Am Kay in Boston or elsewhere; and while the mark remains one of those not positively identified, the probability is that the pieces were made by Alexander Kerr, who died in Williamsburg, Virginia, in 1738 and who was well established in that place some years before his death. He was a proficient smith, undoubtedly capable of making these pieces, and the only one, so far as is known, whose initials and life dates articulate with this situation. Williamsburg, as the center of southern culture at that time, might appropriately have been called upon to produce this silver, and its comparative proximity to Edenton makes this conjectured identification of Kerr plausible. If, as seems probable, these pieces were made by Kerr outside North Carolina, this fact would suggest that there was no one in Edenton in 1725 competent to accomplish this task.

The second dish was made by Hugh Wishard of New York and was donated in 1812 by the ladies of the church. The tankard was made by Charles Wright and carries the London date letter of 1771. It was presented to the church by George II, whose cipher and royal arms are engraved on each piece. The service consists of a chalice with a paten-cover, two flagons, and an alms basin. Each piece has the London date letter of 1752 and was made by Mordecai Fox. In the vestry book, 1701-1776, of St. Paul's Parish is a notation that in 1750 [no day or month shown] "M. Elaland" was paid £1 11s. 0d. for mending the church plate.[2]

The Presbyterian churches of Bluff, Barbacue, and Longstreet, in Cumberland County, were founded in 1758. They have a pair of silver standing cups donated on April 21, 1775, that were made in America, but the maker's mark is indistinct. The Reverend John McLeod, who came to America from Scotland in

1770, was serving these churches when the donation was made. Flora MacDonald, the celebrated Scottish heroine, was a member of the church at Barbacue.[3]

The First Presbyterian Church of Fayetteville has handsome communion silver that was presented to the church in 1824 and 1828 by the Young Ladies' Missionary Society. John Oates tells the story of how the silver was saved from Sherman's Union soldiers during the Civil War:

On the news of the approach of Sherman's army, Mr. George McNeill packed it in trunks containing valuables from his home and store, and took it out in the country near old Longstreet Church, to the home of his friend Mr. George Newton.

But Sherman added insult to injury by not even coming in the direction he was expected. He marched right down by Longstreet Church, and some of his followers called at the home of Mr. Newton.

The contents of the trunks interested them greatly, and a soldier who had taken charge very generously began to distribute the goods. Mrs. Newton said, "I wish you would give me something, too." "Certainly, Madam," he replied, "Take anything you like." She took the silver communion basket, the only piece of silver yet brought out. He looked somewhat crestfallen, but gallantly allowed her to keep it.

Just then they were called out, and Mrs. Newton quickly moved a bedstead with high headboard, behind which there was a broken place in the plaster. She hastily wrapped the basket, placed it in the crevice, and pushed the bed into place. And so was saved the silver which proves that there was a Young Ladies' Missionary Society in 1824, for the soldiers, fortunately, were called away before any of the other pieces were found in the other trunks.[4]

In one notable instance, a Union soldier left a piece of silver rather than confiscating one. Pictured above is a teaspoon left at Dr. Richard Blackwell's home by General Hugh Judson Kilpatrick following the surrender of General Joseph E. Johnston to General William T. Sherman at Bennett Place in 1865. The spoon is a fiddle-and-thread, but the maker's mark is too worn to identify. Information about the spoon, now in a private collection, was provided by Mrs. James H. Holeman.

Through the generosity of Mr. and Mrs. J. P. Harris, heirs of the late Miss Daisy Green of Raleigh, this unique tea service, with its handsome detail in chasing and repoussé, is presently in the collection of the North Carolina Museum of History. Dr. Cutten believed the teapot and sugar bowl to be the work of Barzillai Gardner of Charlotte. However, more recent research and comparison of the B·GARDINER mark that appears on these pieces with the mark of Baldwin Gardiner pictured in *New York Silversmiths*, 85, show Cutten's identification to be in error. Nothing is known of Barzillai Gardner's activity after

1814; Baldwin Gardiner was in Philadelphia, 1814-1817, and in New York, 1827-1847. No relationship between the two men has been established.

According to family tradition, the cream pitcher was taken by marauding Union soldiers; the soldiers were said to have dropped the matching teapot and sugar bowl, which were retrieved by family servants. C. B. Root, a Raleigh silversmith, was employed to make a second cream pitcher, thereby restoring the set. The cream pitcher has the unmistakable mark of Root on the bottom; it has been pictured and described earlier in the text of this book. The teapot is shown below.

The suffering of many southerners after the Civil War is typi-
fied in the poignant story of the Colonel Charles Courtenay
Tew cup here depicted. Colonel Tew's father, Henry Slade Tew
(d. 1884) tells the story:

My son Col. C. C. Tew commanding 2nd Regt of N.C. State Troops was
reported among the killed at the battle of Sharpsburg Maryland in
1862 but none of his Regt saw his dead body and several years after a
man stopped in Hillsboro, N.C. at the Military Academy of which my
son was the Proprietor and Superintendant [sic] and represented that
he was just released from Fort Jefferson and had left my son there
confined for life for killing the Col. of an Illinois Regt. It was startling
and improbable but the utter absence of all motive for the deception
made upon oath and without demand for compensation induced me to
take the long tedious and expensive voyage from Charleston via Balto
& Key West to the Fort realize its falsity and return cheerless via

Havanna, Key West & Balto to my home. A short time after my son's
widow died and I took my grandchildren home with me—not long after
this we received a letter from "W. Charles Loches of Norwalk Herron
County Ohio" representing that he had the sword of my son obtained
on the battlefield, his name and rank engraved on it but we failed to
get posession [sic] of it and were informed by Loches that it was deposited in the Lodge at Norwalk. We then placed all the papers covering
the correspondence in the hands of W. R. S. Preens then Grand Secty
and since Grand Master of the Grand Lodge of So Car who promised
to use every means official and private to have the relic returned. Mr.
Preems [sic] died and we can learn nothing of the papers. But an incident occured [sic] recently which has given us hope of success.

Some of my friends were fellow passengers from N.Y. with Captain I.
T. Bean of the 18th Regt U.S. Infantry and in the course of conversa-
tion on the events of the War and the uncertainty of the fate of many—
the facts I have stated respecting my son were mentioned when Captain B instantly remarked I can remove all doubt of Col. Tew's death
for I buried him after the battle and have now a silver cup engraved
Col. C. C. Tew 2nd N.C. State Troops which one of my men who had
taken it from his horse also killed put in my hands and I am rejoiced to
have the opportunity of returning to his family. Perhaps the only relic
of his last hours—and to generous kindness and magnanimity of this
gallant opponent on the fatal field it is now in our possession.

The fact has reanimated the hope that the passions incited by the late
deadly strife have passed away and given place to kinder and now
generous appreciation of each other. As truly and admirably remarked
by Captain Bean in returning the cup, "War is between nations or sections not individuals and no truly brave man will ever have any other
sentiment than respect for the valour and patriotism of the men he has
met in deadly strife."[5]

Staff writer Dick Brown is author of a feature article entitled
"An Unknown Artisan," published in the Fayetteville *Observer-
Times* on August 31, 1980. In the article Brown speculated on
the identity of the craftsman who had made a gold medallion
awarded April 23, 1831, to the best marksman in the Fayetteville Light Artillery. As Brown suggests, the medallion could
have been made by any one of several Fayetteville silversmiths—
John Campbell, John Mills, John Selph, perhaps? Or it could
have been made by a skilled craftsman such as John Vogler or,
of course, by someone who lived outside North Carolina. Brown
noted that the twelve-pointed medal was comparable in size to
a silver dollar and that it was in almost pristine condition. He
wrote:

    The occasion was the 12th anniversary of the artillery company, an
occasion probably celebrated like the 4th of July with bands, parade,
and the inevitable rounds of toasting.

Prior notice of the birthday appeared in the weekly Fayetteville Observer, signed by McNair as captain, but no report was published on the festivities.

All that remains today is the medal, a valuable memento that turned up recently in an old Scotland County estate.

The lettering, engraved in elaborate script and design, is contained within a large circle inside the 12 individual points of the sunburst.

One side features the free-hand drawing of a cannon, cannon balls and stacked rifles with the traditional American eagle above. The name J. C. Fenn, Capt., is at the bottom with the words "Fayetteville Light Artillery" enclosed in ribbon across the top.

The reverse reads: "Presented by the Company To Neill McNair for superior Marksmanship on their 12th Anniversary, April 23, 1831."

Without a maker's mark the identity of the silversmith remains a mystery.

Not silver, but pewter, is the goblet (from a private collection) shown on page 260, which measures 5½ inches high and 3¼ inches across the top. Its surface has overall textured ornamentation with beading beneath the upper rim and at the foot. Within a wreath of laurel leaves is engraved

Presented
to the
NL Infantry
Mrs. E. A. Hawley
Charlotte N.C.
May 20th
1859

The Charlotte *Western Democrat* of May 24, 1859, reported that, as part of the annual commemoration of the signing of the

"Mecklenburg Declaration of Independence," a number of de-
tachments of militia from throughout North Carolina had been
invited to attend special ceremonies in Charlotte. There the various militia groups vied with each other and with the Hornet's
Nest Riflemen of Mecklenburg County in target-shooting con-
tests. Apparently the Newbern Light Infantry was awarded a
"Silver Goblet" for its adroitness on the target range. "The
Newbern Light Infantry," the newspaper reported,

... remained here until Monday morning: attending church in com-
pany with the Hornet's Nest Riflemen on the Sabbath.
   In the afternoon of Saturday [May 21] they were presented with a
Silver Goblet by Mrs Hawley and Mrs Windle, through Lieut. L. S.
Williams, whose remarks on the occasion were appropriate and in
good taste.

 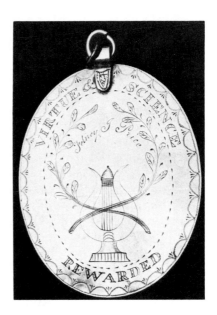

Who made the medals that were so avidly sought by students who attended the boys' academies and girls' schools of the 1800s? This gold medal, awarded to Fetney J. Price in November, 1827, by the Raleigh Academy, is typical of such prizes. It is neatly engraved and precisely decorated with traditional motifs of lyre and laurel wreath. (From a private collection.)

This handsome silver tray, or salver, once belonged to Catherine Ann Devereux (Mrs. Patrick Edmondston [1823-1875]), who had inherited it from her mother, Catherine Ann Johnson (Mrs. Thomas Pollock Devereux [d. 1836]). Mrs. Edmondston kept a diary during the Civil War; the diary has been edited by Beth Gilbert Crabtree and James W. Patton and published as

"Journal of a Secesh Lady": The Diary of Catherine Ann Deve-reux Edmondston, 1860-1866 (Raleigh: Division of Archives and History, 1979). In an entry of July 21, 1863, Mrs. Edmondston wrote of measures she was taking to save her silver from Union soldiers. The tray did survive and was passed on to Mrs. Edmondston's niece, Katherine Johnson Devereux, in 1875. (The name is not correct on the tray.) It has been successively passed on to other Catherines, or Katherines, in the family.

This is a round tray that measures 13⅞ inches in diameter, with a raised rim 1⅜ inches high at the highest point. It has a shell and scroll motif. Made in London, it can be dated at 1757-1758; but the maker's mark has not been traced. It evidently was a partnership, since there are four letters arranged around a middle period within a cloverleaf $w_P^R P$ (see Wyler, *The Book of Old Silver*, 161).

The North Carolina exhibit at the Jamestown Ter-Centennial Exposition, held April 1-December 1, 1907, at Norfolk, Virginia, included silver historically important to the state. These photographs of the Flora MacDonald silver, the Wood silver service from Hayes plantation, and the Cameron silver, as well as a list of the silver on display, were included in Mary Hilliard Hinton's *The North Carolina Historical Exhibit at the Jamestown Ter-Centennial Exposition* (Raleigh: Edwards and Broughton Printing Co., 1916), published by the North Carolina Historical Commission. Mrs. Hinton's listing of North Carolina silver exhibited at the exposition is reproduced below.

Communion service (American) from St. Paul's Church, Edenton, N.C. It consists of paten and chalice and was the gift of Colonel Edward Mosely in 1725. Loaned by the vestry.

Coffee pot and cream pitcher, 1715, owned by Governor Charles Eden, bearing the Eden crest. Loaned by Miss Eliza Harwood Drane, Edenton, N.C.

Service consisting of five pieces, owned by Governor Samuel Johnston, of "Hayes," which were: one tea pot, loaned by Mrs. W. D. Pruden; tea pot and cream pitcher, loaned by Mr. Julien Wood; sugar bowl, loaned by Mr. Hal. Wood.

Dessertspoon, owned by Governor Samuel Johnston, bearing the Johnston crest. Loaned by Mrs. W. D. Pruden, Edenton, N.C.

Cruets, about 1760, belonged to the Paget family and bearing their crest. Loaned by Miss Eliza Harwood Drane, Edenton, N.C.

The Cameron service (American, Johnson and Treat), consisting of coffee pot, sugar dish, cream pitcher, cup (gold-lined) and one tea pot (Sheffield plate), owned by Mr. Richard Bennehan, of "Stagville," member of the Committee of Safety during the Revolution. His daughter, Rebecca Bennehan, was pouring tea from this pot when she met

her future husband, Judge Duncan Cameron. Each piece bears the Cameron arms, having been inherited by Mrs. Duncan Cameron. Loaned by Colonel Benneham Cameron, of "Stagville."

Two tablespoons, owned by Mr. Richard Bennehan, of "Stagville." Became the property of Rebecca Bennehan, who married Judge Duncan Cameron. Loaned by Colonel Cameron.

Two coffeespoons, owned by Mr. Richard Bennehan. Loaned by Colonel Bennehan Cameron, of "Stagville."

Bouquet holder, owned by a very old lady in Macon, Georgia, used to hold bridal bouquets. A gift to Mrs. Graham from a friend. Loaned by Mrs. Paul Cameron Graham, Durham, N.C.

Toast rack. Loaned by Mrs. George P. Collins, Hillsboro, N.C.

Portion of the service presented to Flora MacDonald by Prince Charles Edward Stuart. It consists of waiter, bowl, ladle and cream pitcher. Loaned by Mrs. E. J. Justice, Greensboro, N.C.

Five tablespoons, owned by Louis Poisson, a native of France, and brought during the French Revolution to San Domingo. During the uprisings there they were taken to North Carolina. Loaned by Mrs. E. J. Justice, Greensboro, N.C.

Tankard (English), owned by Mr. Thomas Barker, of Edenton, N.C. Won by an American horse at Pembroke, England, 1754.

Ladle (English), 1754, owned by Mr. Thomas Barker. Loaned by Mrs. James Warren, Edenton, N.C.

Teaspoon, one of a set owned by William Hooper, one of the three North Carolina signers of the National Declaration of Independence. The silver was in the possession of James Hooper, the youngest son, but having no children, his widow gave them to his grandniece. It bears the Hooper crest. Loaned by Mrs. Helen DeBerniere Hooper Wills, Raleigh, N.C.

Sugar tongs, owned by General Frederick Hargett. Loaned by Mrs. George Green.

Candle snuffers and tray (Sheffield plate), owned by General Frederick Hargett, of the Revolution. Loaned by Mrs. George Green.

Ladle (American), bearing the Green crest. Loaned by Mrs. George Green, New Bern, N.C.

Ladle, wedding silver of Gabriel DuBrutz and Deborah Montgomery, March, 1791. Loaned by Mrs. E. J. Justice, Greensboro, N.C.

Goblet, presented to William Hooper, LL.D., by a class of young ladies. Mr. Hooper was a grandson of William Hooper, who signed the Declaration of Independence. Loaned by Mr. B. F. Beasley, Fayetteville, N.C.

Cake basket (Sheffield plate), originally owned by John Appleton, of Ipswich, Massachusetts, 1699. It bears the arms of Great Britain. Brought with the founder of the Appleton family to America, whose ancestors were John Appleton, of Waldingfield, Magna, Suffolk, England, and John ap Ulton, of Wales. Arms granted to him by Henry IV., 1412, and name changed in England to Appleton. Loaned by M. Dawes Appleton Staples, Greensboro, N.C.

Spoon, belonged to Andrew Miller, Rutherfordton, N. C. He was captured by the British and threatened with death unless he gave information concerning the American Army. So steadfastly did he refuse that it commanded the admiration of Colonel Ferguson, who released him and gave him his own knee buckles, from which this spoon was made. Loaned by Mr. R. B. Miller, Shelby, N.C.

One knee buckle, owned by John Lewis, of Virginia. Loaned by Mrs. S. R. Fowle, Washington, N.C.

Cuff buttons, owned by Captain Gilbraith Falls. Loaned by Mesdames Amanda Jameson and S. M. Furr, Mooresville, N.C.

Belt buckle, slide and badge, owned by General Morgan, of the Revolution. Loaned by Mrs. F. A. Jenkins, Nashville, N.C.

Spoon (Colonial), loaned by Mrs. J. R. Thomas, Waynesville, N.C.

Punch ladle, with Harvey crest, owned by President John Harvey, of the Council. Loaned by Misses Harvey, Hertford, N.C.

Basket (Sheffield plate), brought from Scotland, 1782, owned by Mrs. Jane Moore Gray. Loaned by Mrs. Ernest Deans, Wilson, N.C.

---

[1]E. Alfred Jones, *The Old Silver of American Churches* (Lechworth, England: Privately printed for the National Society of Colonial Dames of America at the Arden Press, 1913), 166, 293, 511, hereinafter cited as Jones, *The Old Silver of American Churches.*

[2]Information from the files of MESDA.

[3]Jones, *The Old Silver of American Churches,* 166, 293, 511.

[4]John Oates, *The Story of Fayetteville* (Fayetteville[?]: n.p., 1950), 490-491.

[5]Information, pictures, and typescript copy of the manuscript were provided by Mr. and Mrs. E. D. Sloan, Jr. Mrs. Sloan is a descendant of Colonel Tew.

Appendix C
North Carolina Documents Referring to Silver

Documents frequently provide valuable information about people and social customs because they refer to tangible property such as silver items. Two examples of such documents are a bill of sale from Thomas Pollock and extant items from the files of Thomas Agnis.

Thomas Pollock (d. 1722), deputy of Lord Carteret and agent for Carteret and Beaufort, owned extensive tracts of land on the Roanoke, Chowan, and Trent rivers. As president of the governor's council, Pollock twice acted as governor of North Carolina— the first time, 1712-1714, after the death of Governor Edward Hyde and the second, 1722, after the death of Governor Charles Eden. The original document reproduced below is from the Council Journal, 1712-1728, Governor's Office Records, State Archives.

[138] North Carolina ss.

Know all men by those presents That I Thomas Pollock of Chowan precint in the Province abovesaid Merchant for a valuable Consideration in hand Received and Secured to be received have Bargained and Sold and doe hereby firmly Give Grant Bargain Sell and make over to Captain David Henderson of the same Precint Merchant his Executors Administrators and Assignes all the Negro Men Women and Children I had by my now Wife Esther being Twenty in Number videlicet a Negro Woman called Cutto and her Children Negro Dower his Wife Phillis and their Children Negro Mingo and Nanny his Wife and Their Children Negro Joe and Jenny his wife Negroes Jack Tom and Deborah Also all the Plate in the Dwelling house at Sandy Point where I now live not marked with my name Videlicet one Large broad Brim'd Bason one Lesser without Brims Three Silver Tankards four Cupps three porringers one Tumbler one Spice box one Salt Sellar a Duzen and halfe of Silver Spoones also Eight bedds now in the aforesaid Dwelling house with the Bed cloaths belonging to [139] them will all the Tables and Chaires of all Sorts one Case of Drawers all the Pewter Kettles Potts Broken Glasses panns Tongs Shovells and Spits of all Sorts and all other household Goods properly belonging to the said House Excepting the Clock my Books and all Chests also Stills and Tubbs allso all the Stock of Cattle hoggs horses Mares Colts and Sheep belonging to the Said Plantation being those that I had with my Aforesaid Wife unto him the said David Henderson and his forever with Warrenty Against any Person or Persons that can pretend any

Lawfull Title or claim to any of the above mentioned Negroes Stocks and household Goods In Witnesse wereof I have hereunto Set my hand and Seale this 12th day of Jany. 1707/8.

Tho. Pollock

Sign'd Seal'd and Delivered

in presence of us
John Stuart
Thos. West

Know all men by these presents that I David Henderson of Chowan Precint Doe assigne over all my Right Title and Interest of the within mentioned Negroes Plate hoggs horses and Cattle with the household Stuff or whatsoever else is within mentioned in the Sale from me my Executors Administrators or Assignes to Collonell Thos. Pollock Merchant of Chowan aforesaid his Heires of Assignes for ever As Witnesse my hand and Seale This 16th day of January 1707/8.

David Henderson

John Stuart
Tho. West

Mr. Thomas West made Oath on the Holy Evangelists that on the day of the Date of the within Deed he did See Collonell Thos. Pollock Sign Seale and Execute the Same and at the Same Time did See a Negro man deliver'd for and in the name of the Whole and did also see Captain Henderson Signe Seale and Deliver the above Assignment on the day of the date hereof.

Sworn before me Tobias Knight

Several items from Thomas Agnis's account books for 1761 and 1762 and two personal letters afford insight into the life of the silversmith and his business operation. Little is known about this early Edenton silversmith, and no extant pieces made by him have been identified. This unfortunate paucity of information makes his records especially significant; they are from Jeweler—Thomas Agnis, 1761-1762, Chowan County Miscellaneous Records, State Archives. Mr. W. M. Biggers was generous in sharing his research on Thomas Agnis with the editor.

Thomas Agnis

Sir
If the Knee Buckles, & Sleeve Buttons I gave you to mend are done please send them by Mr. Rainey also the Shoe Buckles I spoke to you

for, with the charge of the whole, which if agreeable to you will place to your credit in acct. with Wm. Campbell, if they are not done please doe them as soon as convenient, will oblige Sir

Your Hum: Serv:
Alex Wood (?)
Ford (?)

S[illegible] Hill, Dec. 22, 1761
Mr Thomas Agnis

1761 M^r. Thos. Agnis, ^{do}/ To Joh^n Rombough

May 18
% small brass Hinges   £ 1

July
% Turning 2 Doz. & half   ..6
  File Handles

16 Making a Stool --- ..1
Aug^t. %Making a Safe ---
Nov. %Ballance Left unpaid for Work Done on the Shop   ..17..

1762
  March 3 % Making [100?] bricks .... £-2..6..
  May 10th. 1762 Received of Thomas Agnis the Sum of two Pound ten
             Shillings in full of This Bill
             to me   John Rombough

[Note: on back of this bill is this addition]

% 2 Gallons of Rum	1..18..0
% Proc. rcvd. for AV	0..11..0
% Mak^e Silver S B [stock buckle?]	0.. 5..0
% Knee Buckles	0..
	£ 1..18..0
Thos. Skinner's order	12..1
	2..10..1

April 27 1762 Received of Thomas Agnis the
                Sum of one Pound thirteen
                Shillings in Part of the Within
                Account by me
                    Geo. Ramsay

[On the other side is this account]

Edenton Decr. 1761 M^r. Agnis to Geo: Ramsay	%

Edenton Decr. 1761 M^r. Agnis to Geo: Ramsay   %
    % 6½ yds. Spotted flannel 6/s   2: 3:1
    % 2½ yds. Shalloon . . . 2/s   : 6:8
17   % 1 pr. shoes   :10:8
    %2 pr. stock^s.   :17:6
    Rec. of the above by Silver Buck^s.   3: 8:2
     1:10:8
     ———
     1:17:6

    %   M^r. Thomas Agnis in acco. with Robert Hardy

1761
Date	Item		£	s	d
Feb^r. 16th	% prod. lent you		£ 6		
May 13th	% 19 yd. gablo Lace	7/	6	16	3
June 13th	% 1 loaf sugar 11½ ^{lb}.	20		19	2
June 17	% 1 D° 10½ ^{lb}.	21	1	1	
July 18th	% 1 gall. Rum			8	8
Aug. 6th	% 1 gall. D°			5	
12	% 1 gall. D°			10	
Oct. 9th	% 1 Loaf Sugar 10¾ lb.	21	1	1	6
			£ 17	1	7

Cr.

1761
Date	Item	£	s	d
Apr. 8th	By Prod. Lz. Virg. Sur.	£ 3	18	
	By D°	1	18	4
		5	16	4
	By Ballance Due	11	5	3
	By 6 Tea Spoons	1	15	0
	By Proc. Due to R^t. Hardy	9	10	3
	Excepted by R. Hardy	17	1	7
	Due to Robt Hardy	5	10	3

Edenton—May 28th 1762 Rec^d. of
M^r. Thos. Agnis five pounds ten shillings
& four pence proc, money in full of the
     above Acct.   Robt. Hardy

M^r. Thos. Agniss

1762	% Benj. Allison	%
July 31st	% 12 Nests Crucibles @ 2/7	1..11..6
	2 p^r. Jewellers Tongs @ 1/	0..14..0
	2 p^r. Hand Vice 5/3	0..10..6
		£ 2..16..0

Rec^d. Aug^st. 3 The above contents in full
Wm. Allison

M^r. Thomas Agniss   %

1761 Sep^t.	% Cask...................10/9...................£	..14..4
Oct.	% 1 button viz.25	5.. 5..
	%10 casks D°	44..13..
Dec^r.	% old silver../22/6	1..10..
	6 Silver Tea Spoonsset	1..15..
Decr. By Cash Blaine		16..10
	26 windows [?]	1..
	[illegible]	5.. 5..
	[illegible]	2.. 2..
	By 16 bushels oysters	8..25..8
		£ 28.. 9..4
	By my order for M^r. Jo^s. Blount	£ 12
	By 2 thimbles	8..12..8
		£ 16.. 1..4
1762 June 2 By my order in [?] M^r. Jn°.		5..14..6
		£ 10.. 6..10
	To cash for M^r. Blount	3.. 6..
		13..16..10
	Cr. by Cash	12.. ..
		1..16..10

[On the reverse side of this bill is this note:]

June 1st 1762—Rec^d. of M^r. Thomas Agnis Five Shillings in full of this and all Acct^s.

       Peter Copeland

Address:
  To
  M^r. Thos. Agnis   Jeweler
  in Edinton   North Carolina

___

London   Dec 6 1761

Dear Thomey i have Received all your Letters you sent by your
friends particular Captain Scott & Captain Jones Delivered them into
my own hands i had y^e pleasure of Dineing with M^r. Ewes [?] at my
own house about y^e 20 of august i have Sent all y^e things you sent for
by Captain Scot your Cousin William Cutbird & Thomas Ludman is
much in ye same way as you left them but not better as for little Phillis
Cutbird she is at our house & delivers her duty to you your Cousin
Ludman has got a fine promising boy about 12 years old But it is not
[in] his power to clothe at present   Therefore if you think well of haveing him over Reason well with yourself and order what Captain the
think proper to Bring him over for i think it will Be a Deed of Charrity
my Dear you writ to me concerning altering your condition i advise
you to do it if anything offer to your advantage   But Rem^b you have a
sister in London when i am Dead & gone That has no Friend Left
witch is now oblige to go to service for her daily Bread it not being in
my power to keep her i being no better myselfe

there is no [illegible]   So no more at Present
   to be held   From your loveing mother & Sister
                                       Phillis & Mary Cutbird

Address on outside:
  To
  M^r. Agness

___

June	M^r. Agness c/o John Cumming	£	s	
29	% Supper and Club at the Lodge		3	8
July				
15	% Club at Crickets	0	1	8
17	% Club at Ditto	0	2	0
	% 8 pounds of butter at 1£	0	8	0
			15	4

Sr I [torn] the favour that you may send me the above
Ballance as I have no butter in the house now. in fact
no money   both my wife and I are Very Sick and
Hope you will not take it amiss
   and am
       Yours D^r. Brother
         John Cumming

Oc^t. ye 16 1761

Thos. Agnes Esqr. to W^m.Flury Esq.   %

% a ball^c. at Settlement	0..7..8½
% 13½ lb. of Beef @ 12½	2..7½
% 1 quar^t. of porke	5..3
ye31 % 1 pigg	4..0
% 25 lb. of Beef	5..2½
% 1 line of mutton	2
	1..6..9½

[Note on outside]
    Rec^d. the within contents
    But remains Dec. 1 Line of Beef &
      2 halves 8 Sheap [?]
      % M Flury

London   Dec. 6—1761

Dear Thomey
i hope you will receive theese Letters and Things i have sent you By
Captain Scot i have had a great [deal] of Troubel to Get these Things
Sent to you for i could get no intelligence at Mr Bacon   Mr Sharpe call
upon me to take any things that i pleased to send you but then i had
seen ye Captain & [he had] promised he [would] see you   Should I
have them safe   Therefore i thought there was no need to troubel
every Body   The 2 gentlewoman call upon me ye 5 of november   i had
ye pleasure allways of entertaining all your freind in the Dineing
Room though i am but a servant in my own house my Dear i shall
allways Be Ready to send any thing you send for But i hope you will
be so kind as to send the money for it is not in my power For i have
nothing to Live upon but a Littel place about 12 £ a year and some of
the same work as i Did when you went away   Mrs Griffis give her
Love to you & There is none left But Mrs Black & herselfe the Rest
Being all Dead a year ago as to your uncle Stanley her as [he has?]
Been out in the Windsor Man of War for 4 year and has never ret^n
[returned?] in England nor Sent any thing to his wife & he is well your
aunt kinchily has been stone Blind this 3 Years Dear Brother   My 2
brothers would have wrote to you Themselfe But they are in a great
Deal of Troubel & cant   Dear Thomey i have seen the jeweller in
Smockally & he is glad To heare you are well & hope you wont Forget
him when in your power

So no more From your
Loveing Mother & Sister
Phillis and Mary Cutbird

Address:
M^r. Thos. Agnis   Jeweler
in Edinton   North Carolina

M^r. Thomas Agnes   %
William Jackson
1761
March % 2 Sheepskins
6 % Sundrys from Philadelphia
£ 7..13..10 @ 33 1/3 advance   10..5..1
" % a sheepskin   3
" % a/^c. Leather for y^e
wine [illegible]   8
                                              ‾‾‾‾‾‾‾
                                         11.. ..1

Supra
March By [illegible]   £ 3..10..
"   By Proc.   1..10..
"   " D°   1.. 5
May 27 By D°   0..6
                                           ‾‾‾‾‾‾‾
                                         9..13..6
                                         1.. 9..1

Excepted
Wm. Jackson

‾‾‾‾‾‾‾‾‾‾‾‾‾‾‾‾‾‾‾‾‾‾‾‾‾‾‾‾‾‾‾‾‾‾‾‾‾‾‾

[On the reverse side of this account]

Ballance Bro^t. over   £ .. 9..7
% 7 bus. lime   7..6
                                        ‾‾‾‾‾‾‾
                                        1..17..1
% a skin   2
By 1 doz. button   5/   1..19..1
By mending [illegible]   3/8   .. 8..8
                                        ‾‾‾‾‾‾‾
                                     £ 1..10..5

Rc^d. December 19th 1761 the contents in full for Co. & Self
Wm Jackson

July 21, 1761
Sir
I Rec^d yrs yesterday by y^r boy Joe Baker a Bagg & 35 Dollars in it,
&% Bill   I have sent all ye things ye mentioned except ye cutting ply-
ers which I could not get here. There is some expected soon when they
come I shall bring you a pr, ye sent but for 2 salts & I never sell fewer

than four here whis [?] is a salt I sent glasses & shovels for them as they all ways come in from England to me so, ye may think them Dear but I Assure sir I have very little profit on them, I believe I have about 20/ our money by them which I dare say ye will think little a nough they are very neat well made salt [torn] them to ye much cheaper than I should to a customer I made inquiry at same on March to have what is ye most that is given for Dollars & they say 6/3 is ye most which I will allow, & if I can get more ye may Depend on haveing it returned, I am sorrow ye should blame me for not writing   I must own I deserve it, for I really do hate writing as much as ever man did I believe, I am very glad to hear ye are coming to Virginia this fall, I shall [be] very glad to assure ye to see ye & tho: I dont like much to write, I like much to speak & I hope we shall fall on scheme to serve one a nother   I have many things [I] want ye to see them I dare say they mold [them?] in Carolina. I had no Diamond spark that would [suit?] for that ring I put in a very good filestone spark. I have no [illegible] that comes to 5 Dollars   They are other dearer and cheaper so I will not send any, as y^e are to be hear y^{r}self soon then ye will know better what will please I hope ye will not fail to come to Virginia ye expence wont be so much as ye think & I hope ye will think it wth y^r while I had no past for rings [illegible] ever half so well as crystal.

Sir   I remain y^r friend & hum serv^t.

James Craig

P.S.   I have sent by y^r, boy Joe Baker ye articles below

M^r. Thos. Agnis to James Craig	%
1761 July	
% 4 sets silver salt glasses & shovels	7.. ..
% 1 pr silk mittons, which I [m^d.?]	.. 7..
% 2 doz. ring crystals @ 6/ per doz.	[12?]
% 6 garnets cost [torn] each	.. ..
% 4 stock buckles	1..14.. ..
% 1 doz watch crystals	.. 7..6
for garden seeds	.. 2..
% 6 nests best crucibles @ 1/3 per nest, which I m^d.	.. 7..6
% 1 pr. best watch flat plyers	.. 3..9
% 1 paper snuff Box	.. 5..
% Cash % the boy to [illegible] 7/6	£ 12.. 1..3
	7..6
	12.. 8..9
By 35 Dollars and 6/3	10..18..9
By 20/0 Bill	1.. ..3
Ball Due to me	..10..

[Address on outside]

To
Mr Thos Agnis Jeweller
     in
          Edenton

John Beasley

January	M^r. Agnes to Robt. Gibson	D^o
the 21st 1761		£
to a juto of close making		1--15--0
to a paire of knee garters		0-- 2--4
to Linin for 2 paire of breeches		0-- 7--0
	Paid	2--21--4

[On outside of account]

M^r. Agnes
   Acc^t. 1 & 4

Blackstone Studios. Courtesy Colgate University Archives.

Colgate University Archives.

GEORGE BARTON CUTTEN

George Barton Cutten (1874-1962) was a versatile scholar, churchman, and educator. Born in Amherst, Nova Scotia, he attended several universities and was awarded numerous degrees. This impressive list includes a B.A. from Acadia University, 1896; an M.A. from Acadia, 1897; a B.A. from Yale, 1897; a Ph.D. from Yale, 1902; a B.D. from Yale, 1903; a D.D. from Colgate, 1911; a D.D. from McMaster, 1920; an LL.D. from Acadia, 1914; a Ph.D. from New York State College for Teachers, 1932; an L.H.D. from Muhlenberg College, 1935; and a D.Sc. from Alfred University, 1942.

Dr. Cutten was an ordained Baptist minister who held several pastorates before he was made president of Acadia University in Wolfville, Nova Scotia, in 1910. During the course of his illustrious career as a college administrator, Dr. Cutten served as president of Colgate University from 1922 to 1942. After retirement from his post at Colgate, Dr. and Mrs. Cutten, née Minnie Warren Brown, resided in Chapel Hill, North Carolina. For the remainder of their lives, Dr. Cutten and his able partner in research devoted much of their time to the related hobbies of collecting early American silver and ferreting out information about the men who made it. Dr. Cutten wrote more than a dozen invaluable books and articles about silver and silversmiths; among these are *The Silversmiths of Utica*; *Silversmiths, Watchmakers, and Jewelers of the State of New York outside of New York City*; *The Silversmiths of North Carolina*; and *The Silversmiths of Virginia*.

Because he was such a thorough and meticulous researcher, George B. Cutten made an inestimable contribution to the history of American silversmithing. His works have become collectors' items in their own right.

Representative pieces of early American silver collected by Dr. Cutten were purchased by the state of North Carolina in 1956; they are now on display at the North Carolina Museum of History in Raleigh.

Mary Reynolds Peacock. Photograph by Walton Haywood.

MARY REYNOLDS PEACOCK

Mary R. B. Peacock of Raleigh is a former historical publications editor in the Historical Publications Section, Division of Archives and History, North Carolina Department of Cultural Resources. Born in Isle of Wight County, Virginia, she has lived in North Carolina for most of her life and was educated in schools of the state. Mrs. Peacock received a B.A. degree at the University of North Carolina at Greensboro and taught for several years in the Johnston County and Wilson city schools.

After an interim period devoted to homemaking and community activities, Mrs. Peacock earned a master's degree at North Carolina State University, Raleigh, in 1970. From June of that year until her retirement in December, 1981, she worked primarily with documentary volumes and pamphlets. She is a member of Phi Beta Kappa and Phi Kappa Phi.

Mrs. Peacock was married to the late Lucian Allen Peacock and has three children and seven grandchildren.

INDEX

Hyams, _____: briefly identified, 83
Hyde, Edward: 266
Hyde County: 67

I

"Interesting History Surrounds Silversmith," by Lucille Johnson: 155
Iredell, James: 73, 105
Iredell County: 99
Ireland: 111
Irving, Thomas P.: 84
Irwin, Robert: 4
Izlar, Mildred Hill: 158

J

J. W. Paxton & Son: mark of, 123; silver of, depicted, 123
J. Y. Savage & Son: mark of, discussed, 248
Jack (slave): 266
Jackson, Andrew: 21, 166, 199
Jackson, Mal.: 156
Jackson, Thomas J. (Stonewall): 21
Jackson, William: 273
Jackson (Tenn.): 131
Jamaica: 164
Jameson, Amanda: 265
Jeffers, Simon: 177
Jefferson, Thomas: 84
Jefferson County (Tenn.): 52
Jenkins, Mrs. F. A.: 265
Jennings, Jonathan: 74
Jenny (slave): 266
Jessup, Catherine (second wife of John [Tyng] Peabody): 126
Joe (slave): 266
Johnson, Elisha: sketch of, 83
Johnson, Frances Iredell: 105
Johnson, John: 63
Johnson, Lucille: her "Interesting History Surrounds Silversmith," quoted, 155
Johnston, Mrs. George Burke: quoted, 249
Johnston, George Doherty: 249
Johnston, George Mulholland: 249
Johnston (Johnson), John: brief sketch of, 83
Johnston, Joseph E.: 255
Johnston, Samuel: 135, 262
Johnston, William: mentioned, 86, 166; sketch of, 83-85

Jolliff, Latimer: 177
Jones, _____: 89
Jones, Abigail Sugars (Sugan): 251
Jones, Bignall Speed: 252
Jones, Captain: 271
Jones, Edward: 251
Jones, Frederick: 159
Jones, Horatia (Horatio?): 72
Jones, Thomas: 36, 37
Jones, William: 144
Jones, William Duke: 252
Jones, Willie: 63, 142
Jonesboro (Tenn.): 8
Jones County: 159
Jugnot, Charles: 16
Justice, Mrs. E.: 264
Justus, Meridy D.: sketch of, 85

K

Kalmar, John: 139
Kay, Burl C.: 91
Kean, Edward: 84
Kearny, William Kincher: 147
Kearny, Mrs. William Kincher (Maria Alston): 147
Kellam, Ida B.: her *Wilmington Town Book*, cited, 17
Kelly, John: 59
Kelly, Patrick: sketch of, 85-86
Kenansville: 56
Kendall, Mrs. Henry: 123
Kerr, Alexander: 253
Killingsworth, John: brief sketch of, 86
Kilpatrick, Hugh Judson: 255
Kinchily, Aunt (aunt of Thomas Agnis): 272
King, Solomon: 189
Kinsay, Thomas: 188
Kinston: 18
Kirkland, John: sketch of, 86
Kirkwood, Anne Jeane: 86
Kirkwood, John: 86
Kirkwood, Mrs. John (Margaret): 86
Kirkwood, Mary: 86
Kirkwood, Robert Alexander: 86
Knight, Tobias: 267
Knox, John: 177
Kramer, Fanny (Mrs. Henry Mahler): 107
Kunsman, Henry: sketch of, 87. *See also* Savage & Kunsman
Kunzel, Anna Maria (Mrs. George Michael Vogler): 178

L

LaGrange: 134
Lake Placid (N.Y.): 107
Lambertoz, Dain (Desiré?): sketch of, 87-88
Lane, William [I]: 88
Lane, Mrs. William [I] (Eliza): 88
Lane, William [II]: sketch of, 88-89
Lane, Mrs. William [II] (Martha Pool): 88
Lange, Maria Theresia (Mrs. Traugott Leinbach): 93
Langworthy, Elisha Perkins: 11
Lankford, Elisha: 63
LaPlace, Charles: sketch of, 89
Latta, Nancy Cabe (Mrs. Robert Donnell): 79
Laubinger, George: 34
Lauer, Anna Barbara (Mrs. Ludwig Leinbach): 89
Lawing, Biddy: 89
Lawing, Samuel: sketch of, 89. See also Lawing & Brewer
Lawing, Mrs. Samuel (Susan Means): 89
Lawing & Brewer (Samuel Lawing and N. Alexander F. Brewer): mentioned, 18; sketch of, 89
Lawrence, Jas.: 7
Lawrence, Mrs. Jas. (Catherine Sneed): 7
Lawrence, William: 198
Lawson, John: 110
Lebanon (Conn.): xxii, 160
Lebanon Baptist Church: 11
Lee, Joseph: brief sketch of, 89
Lee, Walter Hatch: 117
Lee, Mrs. Walter Hatch: 117
Legare, Solomon: xxi
Leinbach, Felix: 93
Leinbach, Heinrich: 93
Leinbach, Ludwig: 89
Leinbach, Mrs. Ludwig (Anna Barbara Lauer): 89
Leinbach, Nathaniel Augustine: 93
Leinbach, Traugott: marks of, 93; retailing activities of, discussed, xxviii; silver of, depicted, 90, 91, 92; sketch of, 89-93
Leinbach, Mrs. Traugott (Maria Theresia Lange): 93
Leming, John: briefly identified, 93
Leming, Joseph: 190
Lennon, Donald: his Wilmington Town Book, cited, 17
Lewis, Alexander: 40

Lewis, John: 65
Lewis, John (of Va.): 265
Lexon, Thomas: 34
Lincolnton: 8, 17, 114, 190
Lindeman, Dirk: 133. See also W. J. Ramsey & Company
Litchfield County (Conn.): 28
Litchford, James O.: 157
Little Rest (R.I.): 11
Lloyd, John: 129
Loches, W. Charles: 257
Lochward: mark of, discussed, 247
Locke, Susan A. (Mrs. James Brandon Hampton): 68
Locust Hill (Caswell County): 188
Logan, John M.: 172
London (England): 2, 6, 39, 57, 111, 155, 197, 271
Long, Mary (Mrs. Barzillai Gardner II): 59
Longmeadow (Mass.): 205
Longstreet Presbyterian Church (Cumberland County): 253
Lord, _____: 93. See also Lord & Gale
Lord & Gale (_____ Lord and Joseph? Gale): brief sketch of, 93; mentioned, 59
Louisburg (Lewisburg): 62, 63
Lovick, Penelope: 40
Lowthrop, Francis: 84
Ludman, Thomas: 271
Lukeman, John A.: briefly identified, 94
Luten, William: 34
Lutterloh, Mrs. H. McR.: 70
Lynch, L. George: 95
Lynch, Lemuel: marks of, 95; mentioned, 77; silver of, depicted, 94; sketch of, 94-95. See also Huntington & Lynch
Lynch, Mrs. Lemuel (Margaret W. Palmer): 94, 95
Lynch, Moses: 94
Lynch, Mrs. Moses (Susan Dickey): 94
Lynch, Seabourn: 95
Lynch, Thomas: mark of, 96; mentioned, 95; silver of, depicted, 96; sketch of, 95-96
Lynchburg (Va.): 116
Lyon (Lyons), George: sketch of, 96

Mc

McAdoo & Scott (_____ McAdoo and David Scott): 52, 143

Thomson, William (N.Y.): 165
Thomson & Beckwith (William Thomson and Robert W. Beckwith): mark of, 166; mentioned, 164; silver of, depicted, 165; sketch of, 165
Tignor, Elizabeth (first wife of John Gill): 64
Tinley, John: 166
Tisdale, Elizabeth: 170
Tisdale, Nathan: mentioned, 84, 169; sketch of, 166-167
Tisdale, Mrs. Nathan (the first, Mary Bryan): 166
Tisdale, Mrs. Nathan (the second, Polly Wade): 166
Tisdale, William, I: xxii; marks of, 167; mentioned, 166; silver attributed to, 167; sketch of, 167-169
Tisdale, William, II: marks of, 169, 170; mentioned, 64; silver of, depicted, 169, 170; sketch of, 169-170. See also Selph & Tisdale
Todd, Joseph: 11
Tom (slave): 266
Tomes, Nathaniel (Nathaniell, Nathanill): sketch of, 170-171
Tompkins, _____: 109
Toone, James: 198
Torrence, Alexander: 29
Townsley, James: mentioned, 11; sketch of, 171
Townsley, James, II: 171
Trammell, Mrs. L. N.: quoted, 155
Travis, John: 68
Trenton (N.J.): 161
Trippe, William: his tailor shop, 32
Trotter, James: 189
Trotter, Pinckney: sketch of, 171
Trotter, Thomas: marks of, 175; mentioned, 3; silver of, depicted, 172, 173, 174; sketch of, 172-175. See also Trotter & Alexander and Trotter & Huntington
Trotter, Mrs. Thomas (the first, Margaret Graham): 172
Trotter, Mrs. Thomas (the second, Jane Elizabeth Brown): 113
Trotter, Thomas, & Co. See Thomas Trotter & Co.
Trotter, Thomas, & Son. See Thomas Trotter & Son
Trotter & Alexander (Thomas Trotter and Samuel Parks Alexander): mentioned, 3, 172, 173; sketch of, 175
Trotter & Huntington (Thomas Trotter and John Huntington): mark of, 176; mentioned, 172; silver of, depicted, 176; sketch of, 175

Troxler, John: 140
Truewhitt, Levi: 110
Tryon, William: 198
Tucker, James M.: 7
Tucker, Mrs. James M. (Frances Sneed): 7
Tull, J. G.: 56
Turner, Franklin: sketch of, 176. See also Clark & Turner
Turrentine, Samuel: 75
Tuscaloosa (Ala.): 74
Twigg, Cynthia (Mrs. John Bryant Mills): 111
Tyson, Betty: 57

U

"Uncle Johnny." See Palmer, John C.
"Unknown Artisan, An," by Dick Brown: quoted, 258
Utzmann, Christina (Mrs. Johann George Vogler): 187

V

Vail, Bond: 168
Valentine, John: 190
Vance, Robert: 116
Van Hook, John, Jr.: 82
Van Norden (town): 71
Van Wyck: 101
Vaughn, Thomas: 35
Veale (Veal), John: 177
[Veale], Patience: 177
Veale, Richard: sketch of, 176-177
Veale (Veal), William Bridges: 177
Virginia: xx, xxi, 17, 54
Vogler, Christoph: 51
Vogler, Elias Alexander: mark of, 178; silver of, depicted, 178; sketch of, 177-178
Vogler, Mrs. Elias Alexander (Emma Antoinette Reich): 177
Vogler, George Michael: 178
Vogler, Mrs. George Michael (Anna Maria Kunzel): 178
Vogler, Johann George: 187
Vogler, Mrs. Johann George (Christina Utzmann): 187
Vogler, John: his house, noted, 182; marks of, 187; mentioned, 2, 51, 57, 89, 177, 258; silver of, depicted, 179, 180, 181, 182, 183, 184, 185, 186, 187; sketch of, 178-181
Vogler, Mrs. John (Christina Spach): 177, 180, 185

Vogler, John Utzmann: mark of, 188; silver of, depicted, 188; sketch of, 187-188
Vogler, Mrs. John Utzmann (Maria Louise Reich): 187

W

W. J. Ramsay & Company (Walter J. Ramsay and Dirk Lindeman): marks of, 134; mentioned, 132; silver of, depicted, 133; sketch of, 133
Waddell, Rebecca: 94
Wade, Catherine (fourth wife of G. W. Hilliard): 70
Wade, Polly (second wife of Nathan Tisdale): 166
Wadesboro: 33, 176
Waite, William: 11
Wake County: 55
Walker, A. J.: briefly identified, 188
Walker, Nathan B.: sketch of, 188
Wallace, James, Jr.: sketch of, 188-189
Wallace, Mrs. James, Jr. (Elizabeth Slaughter): 188
Wallace, James, Sr.: 188
Wallace, Robert: 189
Walnut Grove (Burke County): 53
Ward, Benjamin: 51
Ward, Thomas: 51
Warren, Mrs. James: 264
Warren County: 63, 72, 147, 251
Warren Prior & Son: 128
Warrenton: 112
Washburn, Fanny [or Frances] (Mrs. John Selph): 148, 151
Washington (N.C.): 15, 71, 126, 128, 131, 140, 170, 198
Washington, George: xxvi; mentioned, 72, 83; Sully portrait of, saved, 49
Washington Hotel: 40
Watkins, Constance (Mrs. Obadiah Woodson): 205
Watson, Josiah: 142
Way, James: sketch of, 189-191
Weathers, Lee B.: 69
Wellwood, Moses: apprenticeship paper of, depicted, 34; mentioned, 33
Welsh (Welch), David: sketch of, 190
Welsh, Mrs. David (Rose Wesson): 190
West, Thomas: 267
Whedbee, Joseph: sketch of, 190-191
Whedbee, Mrs. Joseph (Thomazen Garrett): 190
Wheeler & Carpenter: briefly identified, 191

Whipple, David: mark attributed to, 192; silver attributed to, depicted, 192; sketch of, 191
White, James: 36
White, Mrs. Philo: 116
White, Thomas: 177
White, William: 48
White, Mrs. William (Mary J.): 48
"White Rock Plantation": 159
Whitehouse, John: 6
Whitehurst, Maria Forbes Gooding: 170
Whitford, H.: 201
Widdefield (Widdifield), William, Jr.: mentioned, 33, 151; sketch of, 192
Widdefield, Mrs. William, Jr. (Mary Campbell): 192
Wilcox, Alvan: marks of, 195; mentioned, 124; silver of, depicted, 193, 194, 195; sketch of, 192-194
Wilcox, Mrs. Alvan (Rachel Porter): 192
Wilcox, Cyprian: 194
Wilcox, Jacob: 192
Wilcox, Wallace: 194
Wiley family: 154
Wilkings (Wilkins), William: sketch of, 195-196
Wilkins, Rebeckah (Mrs. John Cleland): 33
Wilkinson, Curtis: brief sketch of, 196; mentioned, 143
Wilkinson, J. G., & Co.: mentioned, 171, 174, 196; retailer's mark, 196; sketch of, 196
Williams, Anderson B.: 109
Williams, Benj. [Benjamin]: 84
Williams, George Burns: 130
Williams, John: 126
Williams, L. S.: 260
Williams, Mary Burke: 249
Williams, Nathan: 72
Williams, Richard: 71
Williamsburg (Va.): 61, 62
Williamson, George: 123
Williamson, Theodorick L.: 7
Williamson, Mrs. Theodorick L. (Mary Sneed): 7
Wills, Helen DeBerniere Hooper (Mrs. James Hooper): 264
Wilmington: 6, 9, 17, 19, 21, 29, 38, 40, 57, 73, 86, 88, 89, 96, 111, 124, 126, 140, 195; early smiths in, xxii
Wilson, David Vaner: 4
Wilson, Elizabeth (Mrs. John Griffen): 67
Wilson, James: 190